NATURE, DESIGN, AND SCIENCE

SUNY Series in Philosophy and Biology
David Edward Shaner, editor

NATURE, DESIGN AND SCIENCE

The Status of Design in Natural Science

Del Ratzsch

State University of New York Press

Published by
State University of New York Press, Albany

© 2001 State University of New York

All rights reserved

Printed in the United States of America

For information, address State University of New York Press
90 State Street, Suite 700, Albany, New York 12207

Production by Dana Foote
Marketing by Fran Keneston

Library of Congress Cataloging-in-Publication Data

Ratzsch, Delvin Lee, 1945–
Nature, design, and science : the status of design in natural science / Del Ratzsch.
p. cm. — (SUNY series in philosophy and biology)
Includes bibliographical references and index.
ISBN 0-7914-4893-2 (alk. paper) — ISBN 0-7914-4894-0 (pbk. : alk. paper)
1. Religion and science. 2. God—Proof, Ontological. I. Title. II. Series.
BL240.2 .R335 2001
215—dc21
00–049647

10 9 8 7 6 5 4 3 2 1

Contents

IV
THE PERMISSIBILITY QUESTION

PREFACE

Still waters may run deep, as the old addage has it, but the reverse is not always true. Issues and emotions surrounding the relationship of science and religion run deep indeed, but obviously the interactions involved have not always been particularly placid. That is not at all to say that the deliberately polemical "warfare" metaphor is either historically or philosophically accurate. But it certainly cannot be denied that there has been what might be described as a dynamic ferment in the interaction— one which has historically been surprisingly frequently fruitful.

The current ruffling of the waters involves Intelligent Design Theory. Advocates claim that there are a variety of familiar, everyday empirical criteria for identifying deliberately constructed products of intelligent agent activity, that those criteria are in principle applicable to nature itself and to specific phenomena in nature, and that some phenomena in nature in fact meet the relevant criteria and are thus empirically confirmable as products of intelligent design. Advocates contend further that incorporating such criteria and the resulting descriptions and explanations into natural science proper is rationally, philosophically, and scientifically legitimate, and moreover that doing so can be scientifically fruitful, giving science the means to move beyond looming theoretical and explanatory dead ends. Some critics in their turn argue that design theories are empirically empty, conceptually sterile, scientifically illegitimate, already historically refuted, and ultimately perhaps no more than cynically disguised religion.

As I became involved in the growing design debate, it became clear to me that almost none of the foundational philosophical work essential for such debate to make real progress had been or was being done. The present book is thus not a piece of advocacy either for or against such claims. It is a philosophical attempt to clarify some of the conceptual landscape which productive pursuit of broader design debates must negotiate.

In pursuing this project, I have acquired quite a catalogue of debts. I wish to thank David Van Baak, John Suppe, and William Lane Craig for comments and suggestions on the entire project. I am also indebted to series editor David Shaner, and to Jane Bunker, Katy Leonard, Dana Foote, and Kay Bolton of SUNY Press. Special thanks are due to Donna Kruithof for her usual clerical heroics, to Dorcas Chung for important bibliographical help, and to the Pew Foundation and Calvin College for generous support making possible a year of unbroken work.

I am especially grateful for the surrounding context of love, affirmation, support, and patience provided by my wife Betsy, and for the dynamic ferment brought into our lives by our sons, Dylan and Philip. It is to Dylan and Philip that this work is, in appreciation, dedicated.

INTRODUCTION

The beliefs that nature displays evidences of supernatural design is perhaps as old as the human race itself. Historically, such beliefs found enthusiastic and articulate advocates among educational and scientific elites. In the present century, however, the concept of intelligent, supernatural design has been less well received. Appeals to the idea of supernatural design as actually *explaining* anything in nature are frequently taken as not only empty, but as betraying a failure to grasp that science by very definition must exclude all reference to anything supernatural. Alternatively, such appeal is taken as a now-indefensible holdover from past centuries when given the undeveloped state of science, such attempts to explain nature's mysteries might have been reasonable.

Recently, however, there are some signs that barriers against design theories are eroding just a bit. A few legitimate scientists are experiencing a bothersome suspicion that the *apparent* fine tuning for life exhibited by the cosmos is just a little *too* exquisite to attribute to blind coincidence. A number of philosophers of science now suspect that the conceptions of science underlying prohibitions on supernatural design are conceptually inadequate, and that making such prohibitions stand up may require work which no one at present knows how to do. And a very few professional scientists have even begun developing ideas concerning specific phenomena for which legitimately empirical cases for supernatural design can, they believe, be made.

Surprisingly, virtually none of the foundational work essential to exploration (pro or con) of key issues has been done. Such foundational work is the focus of this book.

Section I. Design Basics

Despite its long history (centuries of prominence in philosophical "arguments from design," for instance), there have been virtually no attempts to formally analyze the concept of *design*. Section I (chapters 1 and 2) is devoted to investigation of the concept of design as related to activities and productions of nonsupernatural beings (*finite design*). Primary topics include the character of design, the nature of evidences for design, principles of design recognition, and the relationship between the concept of finite design and relevant scientific endeavors (e.g., anthropology, Search for ExtraTerrestrial Intelligence [SETI]).

Section II. Supernatural Design

Although supernatural design has some significant core similarities to finite design, it exhibits a number of extremely important differences as well. Those are related to the special character, capabilities, and alternatives open to supernatural beings. Those differences have substantive consequences both for the scope of design explanations and for principles and prospects of recognition of supernatural design. Such issues are explored in chapters 3 through 6.

Section III. Boundaries of Scientific Legitimacy

Whether or not the concept of supernatural design falls outside the bounds of scientific legitimacy depends both upon features of that concept and upon exactly where the boundaries of scientific legitimacy lie. That latter issue is addressed in chapters 7 through 9. A general picture of the conceptual structure of science is sketched, and a legitimacy criterion is developed within that context.

Section IV. The Permissibility Question—Conceptual and Pragmatic Issues

The relevant pieces being in place, the overall issue comes down to whether or not relevant design concepts (Section II) are ever capable of meeting the legitimacy criterion (Section III). The answer, as it turns out, is that some types of supernatural design can, under some circumstances, meet the relevant conditions. The main thrust of chapters 10 and 11 consists of arguments that the standard objections to design theories do not demonstrate what they are intended to, that a case for the in-principle permissibility of supernatural design considerations within even the "hard" sciences can indeed be made, and that such considerations even offer some potential scientific payoffs.

Assessment of specific cases for or against design in nature demand clarity on a number of foundational concepts and issues. Unfortunately, clarity is not prominantly evident in current discussions of the issue, and as the discussion heats up positions seem to be becoming increasingly entrenched. The usual consequences of entrenchment preceeding clarity are evident in most discussions in this area. The present work is an attempt to step back and survey in systematic fashion the conceptual landscape on which the growing dispute is being and will be fought. Entrenchment can come later—it seems never to be too late for that.

I
DESIGN BASICS

1

Design Preliminaries

Initial Characterizations

Formal definitions of design are almost completely absent from the literature. Although it is evidently assumed that the concept is too simple and familiar to need explication, the term is in fact employed in widely divergent ways. One can find *design* used interchangeably with among other things *order, plan, function,* and *artificiality.*

My own usage will be as follows:

i. a *pattern* is an abstract structure which correlates in special ways to mind, or is *mind correlative.*
ii. a *design* is a deliberately intended or produced pattern
iii. to be *designed* is to exemplify a design

Pattern here is much broader than, say, geometric figure, repeated sequence, and so on. Historically, laws and other formal uniformities, as well as even such things as the adaptation of means to ends, certain types of isomorphisms, and significant sequences of events were considered to constitute patterns.

A key question concerning the above characterization, obviously, is: What is it for a structure to be mind correlative? I will have more to say about this concept later, but for the moment I will merely informally point to intuitions. Some abstract structures attract our notice, they grab our attention, they seem in varying degrees to somehow *fit* human processes of cognition, to be sense making, to bear intelligibility.[1] Some deep correlation of this kind was linked to the Greek conception of reality as *rational,* and other thinkers on up to the present have seen a presumption of such patternedness in nature as underlying the structure and prospects not only of science, but of any rational thought about the world at all.[2] This correlation to mind can be linked to other concepts crucial to our general picture of science, and some of those connections will be sketched later.

As defined, pattern will not imply the existence of any agent or cognizer, of any intent or purpose, or of any agent activity. However, design will typically suggest all those things—designer, intention, and (possibly extremely indirect) agent activity.[3] While design refers to the intention-generated pattern, designed refers to the phenomenon (object, sequence, event, etc.)—embodying that design.[4]

There are, those who employ the term *design* in scientific contexts while refusing any commitment to (or even while denying the existence of) any designing agent. It is telling that some of the more prominant among this group are unable to dispense entirely with the *concept* of agency. Richard Dawkins, for instance, says:

> We may say that a living body or organ is well designed if it has attributes that an intelligent and knowledgeable engineer might have built into it in order to achieve some sensible purpose.[5]

I take such counterfactual references to intelligent designers to be a tacit means of capturing what I have called "mind-correlative" in the definition of pattern.

But what Dawkins intends here by "design" and what others would prefer to call "apparent design," I am calling "pattern." Other concepts in the area can now be located. *Order* I take to be a synonym of pattern. *Plan* is ambiguous between pattern and design, depending upon context and usage. In these terms, most traditional arguments from design actually argue from pattern *to* design, the specific patterns being chosen on grounds that they exemplify special characteristics—adaptation, complexity, fine turning, improbability, evident purpose, analogy to human artifacts, and so on—which are thought to support such inferences.

Counterflow

With respect to humans and aliens (or other finite beings), *designed* is roughly (although not exactly) synonymous with *artificial,* and contrasts with *natural.* Of course, natural is ambiguous, depending upon whether it is being contrasted with supernatural or with artificial. Human and alien intelligence and activity is typically classified as natural as distinguished from the supernatural (and is thus generally taken to be perfectly legitimate in science—e.g. SETI). But we would not classify, say, the Eiffel Tower as natural in the other sense, given our intuitive conviction that unaided by deliberate, intentional activity, nature would not (probably could not) produce any such entity.

Fully explicating this latter sense of 'natural' is not straightforward. In this sense, we normally classify as natural things which nature unaided by agency if given a free hand, would do or produce, and as artificial things which nature, unaided by agency, would not do or produce (or would not do via the specific means in question). But some things fall between those two categories—things that, were nature given a free hand, she *might* do or produce. The "might" here is not mere logical or physical possibility. Suppose that you come into a room and find someone splattered flat on the ceiling. According to quantum mechanics, there is a nonzero chance of the molecules in that person's body suddenly all spontaneously heading straight up, resulting in the splattering. But although that is both logically and physically possible, we'd never believe that that was the proper explanation. Before buying that, we'd accept the *Weekly World News* explanation involving space aliens and malfunctioning tractor beams.

Or take a less spectacular case. No law of nature would be violated were the seedlings in some forest to end up precisely evenly spaced in straight rows. It could happen, both logically and nomically. But despite that possibility, despite no laws being violated, we'd never believe that it was natural. The pattern is simply too artificial, too mind correlative for us to think otherwise without extremely pursuasive reason.

On the other hand, consider the particular spacing of seedlings found in some undisturbed forest. Although nature did produce that spacing, nature might have or could have produced some slightly different spacing than she actually did (or, had the forest been disturbed, than she *would* have had it not been disturbed), but which would still have been perfectly natural.

In the splattering and the uniformly spaced seedling cases, we think that although nature could have, she wouldn't, and we thus look for other sorts of explanations. In the case in the previous paragraph, we think that although nature didn't, she could have and might have and the "might" seems powerful enough to keep such cases in the "natural" category.[6] I'll have more to say on this matter later.

Next, I will use the term *counterflow* as follows:

iv. *counterflow* refers to things running contrary to what, in the relevant sense, *would* (or *might*) have resulted or occurred *had* nature operated freely.[7]

Obviously, things or events nature could not produce will involve counterflow.

Finite creatures (humans, aliens) operate within natural boundaries. Thus, when we redirect, restrain, or constrain nature, we leave marks—counterflow marks. Shortly, I will argue that indications of counterflow typically underlie our evidences that something has resulted from finite agent design. Our judgment that counterflow is exhibited rests in turn on our conception of what the natural flow might or could be—in short, upon our scientific and commonsense pictures of the world.

Counterflow, Agency, and Nomic Discontinuity

If indications of counterflow constitute evidence that something occurred which nature on her own would not have generated, that points to causal activity of some other agency—human, alien, or whatever. A number of matters here will depend upon our views of finite agents. On a thoroughly deterministic view, even if finite design might be a legitimate explanatory concept, it will ultimately be shorthand for some longer but completely nomically defined account. On the other hand, any conception of the relevant agent activity as genuinely free will mean that in general, instances of counterflow (and thus, instances of either artifactuality or design) will involve a *nomic discontinuity* at exactly the point of agent activity—that is, at the point of counterflow introduction, whether that be in initial conditions, processes, or wherever.[8] That does not, of course, mean that there will be violations of law, but that there will be causal components of genuine design which any science restricted to law-bound explanations will simply be inadequate to.

There are, inevitably, complexities here.[9] But although some important qualifications will become necessary later, as a first approximation working picture, *design* (by finite agents—or *finite design*) will be taken to involve either directly or indirectly, free, deliberate, intentional agent activity, aimed at generating some phenomenon typically embodying a mind-correlative pattern, which, if left to itself, nature would not (normally) produce.[10]

Artifactuality

One more definition:

    v. an *artifact* is anything embodying counterflow.

Humans (and perhaps other finite beings) sometimes generate counterflow with no relevant mindful or occurrant intention. Someone idly whittling on a stick may produce something which nature never would, but the person may even be unaware of what he or she is doing. In a case like this, there may be no pattern produced (in the sense defined) and thus there need be no design involved. But the product might still be a recognizable artifact, exhibiting clear indications of counterflow.[11]

So, pattern entails neither finite design, intention, counterflow, agency, nor artifactuality. With respect specifically to the finite realm, design does entail pattern, counterflow, intention, agency, and artifactuality. Artifact entails counterflow and agency, but not necessarily either intention or pattern (although it is obviously consistent with both). Counterflow entails artifactuality and agency, but neither pattern, design, nor intention.

Defining the scope of artifactuality is not completely straightforward. If one finite agent produces one small artifact, then it is true that the cosmos itself is not as it would have been had there been no agent activity. It seems obvious, however, that we should not merely on that ground alone classify the entire cosmos as an artifact.[12] On the other end of the scale, we do not want to automatically consider all constituents of actual artifacts to be artifacts themselves. For instance, a rope woven of vines is clearly an artifact, but the vines that constitute it are not, although in this case their arrangement, relationships, configurations, and location probably would be. The same would apply to, say, the constituent atoms making up a diesel bulldozer—the bulldozer is clearly an artifact, but the atoms themselves likely are not, although their arrangement, location, and so on would be. Thus, the boundaries of artifactuality must be restricted to some intuitive but hard-to-formalize minimum so that it does not engulf too much in either direction—either the entire cosmos containing some artifact or each microconstituent an artifact contains.

The following roughly captures what I take to be the core intuition concerning the boundaries of finite artifactuality for an entity *S*. (There are some technical niceties that would require further articulation, but I will not specify them here.) Let *A* be any entity, and *S* be a subpart/constituent of *A* (*S* may or may not be a proper subpart/constituent):

S constitutes the *outer bound* of artifactuality (if any) for *A* when

    a. removing *S* removes completely all the counterflow *c* which *A* embodies (if any)

and

    b. there is no proper subpart *d* of *S* such that removing *d* would remove completely all the counterflow *c* which *A* embodies (if any).[13]

S constitutes an *inner bound* of artifactuality for *A* when

    a. complete removal of all counterflow *c* embodied in *A* (if any) would not *materially* alter *S*[14]

Locating Counterflow

Production of nearly anything—natural or artificial—typically involves three components. A system is in some *initial state*, it then moves through some (usually causally driven) *process*, and generates some *result*. Our evidences that something involves deliberate design, or that it is not purely natural, generally involve recognition of some active injection of counterflow into one or more of those three areas.

Result

If, in crossing a heath, we should stumble across a watch, we would immediately recognize it as artifact. We would recognize that, even if we had no idea how it was produced, who had produced it, what it was for, how it got there, or how long it had lain there. An object having the observable characteristics of a watch simply will not be natural. Merely observing some of its more obvious characteristics, we identify it as not only an artifact but as designed. (*How* we do that will be discussed a bit later.) Direct or nearly direct recognition of counterflow typically underpins our most common cases of design identification.

Process

Suppose that aliens plopped a molecularly exact duplicate of the Matterhorn where Cleveland had previously been. Obviously, natural process can produce Matterhorns, so examination of the new mountain itself would reveal no properties out of the ordinary. But we would suspect something rather unusual about the processes by which the new one had in fact been produced.

Or examination of a molecule of some familiar protein might yield no indication of whether the molecule was purely natural or had been synthesized at great cost and effort in a high-tech lab and was thus produced by intelligent intent. Here the result bears no direct clues. Thus, the fact that an object is a product of deliberate intent and activity does not entail that the object itself bears counterflow marks. But the processes giving rise to a particular artificially synthesized molecule would bristle with counterflow indications—buildings, computers, intricate instruments, lab smocks, coffee pots, grant applications, and other artificial devices for constraining nature and steering it into paths it would basically never otherwise follow.

Initial Conditions

Even in cases where the result exhibits no direct, obvious indications of counterflow, and where the production processes likewise exhibit no evident counterflow indications, the initial conditions out of which the relevant processes produced that result might be ones that nature, left to itself, would never generate. For instance, suppose that after thirty thousand years of investigation it looks as though life can indeed begin spontaneously, but only under one set of circumstances. There must be ten thousand and three gallons of six specific chemically pure substances, no molecule of which has ever been chemically bonded with any other, combined in proportions determined down to the molecule, the mixture must be sealed into a ten thousand and three gallon Tupperware container, into which one sterile Beatles record is introduced. Do all that, set up those initial conditions, and with no intervention in the subsequent process at all, life spontaneously generates and subsequently replicates by ordinary means. Spontaneous development of life within those conditions would thus be a wholly natural process.

Again, examining the result—life, the organisms generated—might reveal nothing outside the ordinary bounds of natural law. And the generation process once begun requires no further input or intervention—producing life is simply what nature, under those circumstances, by itself does. But we would likely begin to suspect that the origin of life had not just happened, given the character of the required initial conditions. Those conditions involve circumventing the natural flow with a vengeance.[15]

So we typically recognize artifactuality—and get our first clues to designedness—through recognizing indications of counterflow in results, processes, or initial conditions, and we recognize such counterflow against the background of and in contrast with our understanding of the normal flows of nature. That is essentially our method whether applied to watches, TVs, houses, marbles, stands of pine trees growing in evenly spaces rows, shocks of wheat tied up with strands of twisted straw—or signals from outer space.

Identifying Counterflow

When we immediately recognize a watch or a giant Tupperware vat as artifact, or when we recognize some form of counterflow as counterflow, what exactly are the tip-offs? What properties constitute our clues? In discussions of design, whether of the traditional design arguments or of more recent cases, proposed signs of design almost invariably consist of complicated development, complex structure, coordination of components, interlocking functions, vanishingly small probabililties, adjustment of means to ends, purposelike behaviors, and the like. Those do play important roles in some situations, and will be investigated later. But the initial clues are often much simpler and far more prosaic. Surprisingly often, the clues involve geometric properties exhibited at a roughly human scale. In houses, screens, fans, Stonehenge, cars, watches, gardens, and soccer balls, we see straight edges, uniform curves, repetitions, regularities, uniform spacing, symmetries, plane surfaces, and the like. And the clues often involve regularities of other sorts also—uniformity of material (purified metal, glass, etc.), uniformity of color, uniformity of pattern (sometimes immaterial, as in algorithms), uniformity of sorting. I am not claiming any logical or invariable connection—only that these are often our de facto clues.[16]

Although nature does also produce geometric features and broad regularities, they are often on a very different scale (molecular, cosmic) than the human scale, and what nature produces on the human scale typically does not have the sharpness, angularity, and rigidity of human design.[17] Trees are not as symmetrical as cars, rivers are not as straight as fences, patches of daisies are not as uniform as wallpaper, mountains do not have the sharp boundaries of lasagne noodles, lakes do not have the regular spacing of parking meters. Indeed, over the years, manufacturers of artificial flowers have learned to make their products look more *natural* by introducing asymmetries, irregularities of color, and so forth.

It is at the very least ironic that the same geometricity recognition of which, in nature, was essential to the rise of modern science should so often be a basic key to our recognition of artifactuality. I do not, however, think that that is entirely coincidental. Early scientific investigators believed themselves to be exploring an artifact—a creation—and (as Kepler put it) to be thinking God's thoughts after Him. Even contemporary scientists are sometimes struck with similar impressions.[18]

In any case, we typically recognize artifactuality through recognizing indications of counterflow in results, processes, or initial conditions, and we recognize such counterflow against the background of and in contrast with our understanding of the normal flow of nature. That recognition of counterflow is frequently by the immediate means of middle-level geometric characteristics that are recognized (perhaps only intuitively) to be extremely reliable indicators of counterflow and finite agent activity. As will become clear, we usually recognize design only derivatively. It is counterflow and artifactuality that we often identify more immediately.

Some Counterflow Characteristics

Counterflow comes in a variety of forms. Let us begin with an example. Suppose that you found yourself playing poker with a stranger in a saloon in the Old West. The stranger is an innocent-appearing sort, seemingly all thumbs when it comes to dealing. You spot nothing outrageous or suspicious in any given deal, but you begin to notice over time that the stranger never loses when he deals. You correctly conclude that you have tangled with a shark who is somehow managing to skew the odds in his favor somewhere, that you are being made a victim of some subtle counterflow.

But this counterflow situation exhibits a number of special characteristics. Among the more important ones are the following.

Parts vs. Systems

Given the slickness with which you are being taken, there is no readily evident counterflow (of the type you are increasingly concerned about) in any individual deal or hand. But something about the overall collection of events is clearly being deliberately manipulated. We can distinguish here between counterflow evidences in *parts* and in entire *systems or ensembles.*

Surface vs. Deep

But in exactly what does this *systemic* counterflow consist? It is nothing so simple as the familiar properties that tip us off to the artifactuality of a diesel bulldozer. It is something more complicated and less flagrant—in this case involving, among other things, medium-run sequence probabilities. We can thus distinguish surface counterflow from deep counterflow.

Direct vs. Indirect

Surface counterflow recognition is almost immediate. For instance, recognition of artifactuality of a diesel bulldozer would be very nearly a matter of direct perception—any inferences involved would be virtually automatic. But the cardshark case is not quite like that. Recognition is more inferential, even more gradual. We can thus distinguish virtually direct identifiability of counterflow from more inferential indirect identifiability.

Synchronic vs. Diachronic

A further distinction involves temporality. With a diesel bulldozer, the properties required for recognizing counterflow are present and evident in a bulldozer at any given moment. We could detect its counterflow from a photograph. With card-shark counterflow, the counterflow is only evident over time, and the relevant indications need not be wholly present in any given time slice. Thus, some counterflow is exhibited at given moments—synchronically—whereas some counterflow is exemplified only within stretches of time—diachronically. Identification here would require a video—not a photograph.

Hard vs. Soft

In cases like a diesel bulldozer or an Eiffel Tower, all we need in order to identify the counterflow is some familiarity with nature's normal operation. Nothing else. But in some card-shark cases, something additional is required. Compare two cases—one in which a dealer gets two straight identical losing hands consisting of 7 and 2 of clubs, 4 of hearts, 10 of diamonds, and 5 of spades, and one in which a dealer gets two straight identical royal flushes in spades. In the former case there would be some surprise (if it was even noticed). In the latter case the dealer would be buried in a shallow grave behind the saloon.

The raw mathematical probabilities and other relevant "natural" features of the two types of hands are similar or identical. But the denizens of the saloon would distinguish the cases because there is a significant assigned value to the latter hand but not to the former. And that value is an important tip-off to the presence of special counterflow in the latter instance. In this sort of case, then, identifying the presence of counterflow requires more than mere familiarity with nature (e.g., probabilities, laws, etc.) It would require acquaintance with the relevant valuations. We can thus distinguish cases where recognizing counterflow requires (in principle) only the requisite familiarity with nature—hard counterflow—from cases requiring information beyond that—soft counterflow.

Card-shark counterflow, then, is systemic, deep, indirect, diachronic, and soft, generated by finite nomic agency. Diesel-bulldozer counterflow differs most prominantly in being surface, direct, synchronic, hard, and not merely systemic—even its screws exhibit surface, direct, synchronic, hard counterflow.

Some Counterflow Correlations

There is one other distinction that is both important and harder to explicate. The above types of counterflow are nearly invariably associated with finite-agent activity and designedness—that is why they are such reliable clues. They constitute primary marks of agent activity (and can by implication be marks of artifactuality, counterflow, and design). But there are other, qualitatively different characteristics that frequently accompany agent activity, and so on, and which (as mentioned earlier) are typically appealed to in traditional design arguments—complicated development, complex structures, coordination of components, adjustment of means to ends, interlocking functions, extreme improbability, purposelike behaviors, and so forth. Characteristics of this sort constitute what I'll call "secondary" marks.

Phenomena that exhibit primary marks frequently also exhibit secondary marks (e.g., diesel bulldozers exhibit surface, direct, hard, etc., counterflow *and* they are complex, exhibit adaptation of means to ends, and the probability of nature producing one is essentially zero). But the association is by no means invariable. For instance, suppose that we found a hundred-meter perfect cube of pure, isotopically uniform titanium on Mars. Such a cube would carry obvious primary marks (and would be an obvious artifact), but would exhibit virtually no complexity of any sort. And an idly whittled stick bears primary marks, but may have no teleological end whatever, much less constitute or exemplify means adjusted to that end.

On the other hand, secondary marks can occur in the complete absence of primary marks—indeed, in the absence of any finite agent activity (or counterflow, artifactuality or design). For instance, consider a particular silicon atom formed in a particular supernova. The improbability of that particular silicon atom being in a particular grain of sand stuck to a particular spot on your left front tire which contains a particular carbon atom formed in some other specified supernova, is overwhelming. But it happens. Nature on its own frequently does the very improbable. We feel no inclination to interpret the above improbability, enormous as it is, in terms of counterflow, agent activity, or design.

Nor is complexity necessarily an indication of counterflow, agent activity, or design. For instance, at one point in the deep past in Oklo in what is now Gabon, a number of very precise conditions came together in just the right way and the right order to generate a small, sustained nuclear reaction in some concentrated river sediments. Generating small, sustained nuclear reactions is a highly demanding affair—our best science and technology were not equal to the complexity of the task until historically very recently. Yet, nature did it, and (given the complete absence of counterflow at Oklo) no one takes there to have been any agent activity involved. Thus, although complexity is frequently associated with agent activity and designedness, nature obviously can and does produce instances of extreme complexity quite naturally.[19]

Finite Design: Basic Recognition

Recognizing artifactuality is conceptually relatively straightforward—it requires only identification of counterflow. Of course, the "only" is deceptive. In some cases (to be examined later) such identification is not even in principle scientifically possible. In others, identification requires observation of the actual agent activity—which in some cases cannot be done.[20] But the basic principle of recognizing finite artifactuality is unproblematic.

Recognizing design, however, is potentially more difficult. Design involves deliberate production of pattern, which mere artifactuality does not. Again, an idly, unmindfully whittled stick can be a recognizable artifact, but need not be in any clear sense designed. Or an instance of obvious vandalism might exhibit evidences not only of artifactuality and agent activity but even of deliberateness. But despite the counterflow and the deliberateness of the activity, there need be nothing of designedness exhibited in the result—nothing in the destruction need involve the relevant correlation to mind. So although counterflow is in many instances obvious, making recognition of artifactuality and agent activity often trivially easy, that artifactuality does not quite establish actual designedness.[21]

Design essentially involves pattern (as defined earlier), so recognizing designedness requires recognition of that patternedness—of that essential correlation to mind. How exactly is that gap bridged? In many cases involving human design, recognition of intended pattern is not difficult for us at all. Not only do we have an inside track—being human agents ourselves—but we have a lifetime of experience with human agent activity, cognition, purposes, and designs.[22]

In other cases, the move from recognizing artifactuality to attributing design may be more indirect. This is one place where secondary marks come to the fore. To take that further step beyond mere artifactuality, we have to move from counterflow (involving things *nature wouldn't* do) to design (involving things *minds would* do). And although secondary marks do not provide the close connection to designedness that counterflow does to artifactuality, they frequently do constitute clues.

The clues in question may come in a variety of forms. For instance, in some cases extreme improbability can suggest that production of the artifact requires not only pushing against nature but pushing against nature extremely hard. In such cases, it might be prima facie implausible to think that the required quantity of effort and resources were devoted to such production unmindfully. Or the counterflow nudges required might be of nearly unimaginable delicacy. In such cases, it might be prima facie implausible to think that the required precision in the agent activity had occurred by accident. Some types of complexity are extremely precarious in both their generation and their maintainence. In such cases, it might be prima facie implausible to credit it all to serendipity. So were we, for instance, to come upon some wildly intricate alien artifact on Pluto, that wild intricacy would probably support an inferential move from mere alien artifactuality to alien designedness, even were we utterly unable to figure out what the design was about.

Thus, while primary marks constitute evidence of artifactuality, *in the context of identifiable artifactuality* secondary marks can constitute legitimate (albeit perhaps weaker) evidence for designedness in those artifacts. Secondary marks will become even more crucial when primary marks are either invisible (as they can be even in cases involving finite agents) or completely absent (as they can be in the case of supernatural agent activity, as we will see).

Correlation to Mind

It is time to try to make a bit more explicit what *correlation to mind* might come to. Under certain circumstances, something clicks into place between the shape of our cognition and the focus of our experience. Something fits. There is on some level some kind of match. The match may be simple, or may be between complex structures of cognition and complex structures or sequences in nature. For instance, Whewell, in his Bridgewater Treatise, refers to "correspondencies" in nature between, for example, prior states and final states of an organism or system, or between survival requirements of an organism and means for satisfying such requirements, and he tacitly takes those correspondences themselves as mind correlates.[23] But whatever the details of specific cases, something meshes between mind and phenomenon (whether natural or artificial), and that meshing is the core of the correlating-to-mind of pattern.

As is well known, being very explicit (in useful ways) about the nature of fittings between intensional objects in cognition and the phenomena to which they correlate is not a trivial matter. Such fits may involve direct isomorphism or even identity (on idealist schemes), some looser correspondence (e.g., conceptions of truth involving some symmetry between propositions and reality), or even some much looser relationship. (For instance, a Dickens novel may not contain a single sentence that expresses any true proposition—so the match to reality is very loose. Yet for all that, his fiction often does exemplify important realities—truths—about human nature, society, and history.)[24]

But however exactly the match constituting pattern is to be explicated, it is, I think, the fundamental component in something *making sense* to us. And the fact that something does make sense, that it is appropriately cognizable by us, or is reason-able by (and to) us, is our primary indication that the correlation obtains.

Identification of such sense-constituting correlation—that is, pattern noticing—presents itself to us experientially as a particular feel, a particular seeming, that defines our conviction that something makes sense, that we have gripped the correlation. The presence of this experiential dimension may explain why our talk in this area is so often metaphorically experiential—we "see" it, we "grasp" the matter, and so on. And we cannot get behind or underneath this experience to examine its credentials. Any evaluation of its credentials would have to employ resources and procedures whose justification would ultimately track back at least in part to that experiential dimension itself—the support for those credentials would have to strike us as themselves making sense. As with our other faculties of cognition, at some point and in some circumstances it must simply become, at least from our own perspective, a brute given of the process. This general point was behind the remark of the physicist Sir Denys Haigh Wilkinson that even on purely scientific questions, after having done all the science we can do, finally we "cannot do more than say 'this makes me feel good; this it how it has to be.'"[25]

The phenomenological presentations of sense making generated by this pattern-noting faculty play pivital roles in several foundational facets of science. Among the key tasks of the scientific enterprise, perhaps none is more fundamental than that of generating understanding. That concept is difficult to explicate precisely, but understanding involves coming to see an answer to a particular sort of "why?" question.[26]

Similar connections can be found in what are sometimes referred to as "plausibility structures." We find the same thing in evaluations of explanatory satisfactoriness. In all these cases, what is ultimately being expressed is one's having (at least temporarily) come to rest at some stable, human-mind-appropriate standing place. And such places, such correlates to mind, are what I take to be definitive of pattern.

What patterns we choose to bring about will often (perhaps nearly always) involve considerations not only of the patterns themselves, but of perceived value and other axiological factors. Thus, in at least some instances, identification of artifactuality and of pattern will not yet constitute identification of specific intent.[27] But in many cases, especially cases where basic axiological matters are not in reasonable doubt, it will be enough. This issue will be discussed in more detail later.

Design: Preliminary Picture

So design is to be understood in terms of deliberate agent activity intentionally aimed at generating particular patterns. Pattern, in turn, is to be understood in terms of structures that have special affinities to cognition—which correlate to mind. The agent activity involved produces artifacts that are defined via counterflow and that frequently exhibit familiar primary marks of agent activity and counterflow by which that activity and artifactuality can be identified. And where the correlation to mind is sufficiently powerful, further conclusions of designedness or even of the specifics of the design and intent themselves, can be warranted.

2

SCIENCE AND FINITE DESIGN

We are now in better position to address a number of basic questions. Is the very concept of design, as understood above, somehow inherently illegitimate in scientific descriptions and explanatory theories? In this chapter, issues involving finite design and science will be discussed. Issues of supernatural design and science will be explored later.

Science and Human Design

Design and related concepts are commonly employed in everyday explanations of everyday events. Of course, descriptive and explanatory use of such concepts is not confined just to everyday discourse. Social sciences could not fruitfully function without such concepts. More to the present point, some "harder" disciplines require those concepts as well. Archeology and anthropology, for example, deal extensively in design concepts, and designedness is often clearly evident even in cases where precise usage, intended function, and so forth are completely unknown (e.g., Stonehenge a century or so back).

Such use of the concept of human design in broadly "scientific" explanations and descriptions is clearly not only legitimate but essential. Any description of Stonehenge (let alone a VCR or a linear accelerator) that made no reference to artifactuality and designedness would be seriously inadequate. Any proposed explanation that made no reference to designedness (or at least artifactuality and agent activity) would be woefully off the mark indeed. And any view according to which a proper "scientific" description and explanation of Stonehenge and VCRs could not use such concepts as design would surely be seriously inadequate.

In cases like those above, we have a substantial fund of experiential familiarity with human purposes, and capabilities, and an equally substantial familiarity with products of human design, so our references to human design in connection with Stonehenge and VCRs are relatively well grounded.

Of course, the legitimacy thus provided to the use of design concepts in the human case by that experiential familiarity might be lacking in attempts to extend such explanations beyond the human realm (to sprites, aliens, and the like), where such familiarity may be lacking or unrecognized. That point does, I think, provide a cautionary note. But it is only that—it would not generate any prohibition on such extensions, especially if we had rational grounds for thinking that the principles of recognition generated from experiences with human design could be legitimately extended.

Science and Alien Design

It is evident that at least some of the products of some types of aliens (if any) would be readily recognizable as such. Recalling an earlier example, if we discovered on Mars a perfect hundred-meter cube of isotopically uniform titanium, and knew that no human technology had that capability, identification of that cube as both artifact and alien would be relatively trivial. We might be able to go even farther. Suppose that on Mars we discover an abandoned alien artifact, produced in some inexplicable fashion from some alloy we couldn't duplicate, containing mystifying intricate mechanisms the purpose of which we couldn't even guess at. Recognition not only of its artifactuality but of its designedness would be unproblematic. Certain sorts of complexity do not arise by accident out of finite agent counterflow activity. Perhaps such complexity can arise out of *natural* processes by either law or chance, but *artifacts* of relevant degrees and types of complexity typically do not arise without intent. Given that the Martian object is an artifact (a counterflow product of agent activity) and given its intricacy and other secondary marks, and given the consequent tight controls and difficulty of manufacture and thus the apparent care involved in that manufacture, then deliberate intent in its production—and designedness—will be reasonable conclusions.

It is worth noting that some within the scientific community have committed substantial resources to projects that explicitly assume that at least some alien artifacts would be straightforwardly recognizable. Most prominent of these is the Search for ExtraTerrestrial Intelligence (SETI). The underlying idea is that intelligent alien cultures might deliberately or inadvertently produce electromagnetic signatures that would be distinguishable from anything generated by purely natural processes, and that by identifying such signatures for what they are, we could verify the existence of such aliens.[1] The fundamental presumption is that some things that aliens might produce, we humans could correctly identify, describe, and explain in terms of activities—and possibly intentions and designs—of aliens.[2]

Inability to sort out purpose, intent, and function need have no serious impact upon our ability to recognize designedness. Indeed, that situation arises even with some human artifacts. The Smithsonian reportedly has a number of obviously human, recognizably designed artifacts, the purposes of which have been entirely forgotten. (And I remember as a kid, during a clandestine investigation of my sister's room, puzzling over the purpose of an object which I nonetheless had no difficulty identifying as deliberately designed. It was, I learned later, an eyelash curler.) In the appropriate type of alien case, *design* would be a legitimate and straightforwardly "scientific" explanatory concept.

It is worth noting that SETI discussions typically involve de facto distinction between artifactuality and designedness. For instance, without aliens intending or even being aware of it, alien manufacturing, communications, or other processes might spill microwave radiation into space—energy whose signature would indentify it as artificially generated and thus as artifact.[3] On the other hand, aliens might deliberately broadcast sequences of prime numbers in binary. The standard SETI position is that those broadcasts would be identifiable not only as artifactual, but as intentionally designed.[4] The underlying presupposition seems to be that any energy artifact carrying information of that degree of mind correlativeness must be deliberately produced to do so. The *carrying of information* of a particular sort is thus a strong secondary mark.

In cases involving aliens, we might be utterly unable to figure out much concerning the aliens themselves. Inferences from artifacts to agent characteristics involve presuppositions concerning the cognition, needs, desires, aims, technology, capabilities, behavior, and so forth of those agents. We have reasonably good ideas concerning those things with respect to humans, but might have very little clue as to such things with respect to the aliens in question.[5]

Of course, objects might also be discovered concerning which it was simply unclear whether they were alien artifacts or products of as yet unknown natural processes.[6] In an actual case of a different sort, the first researchers to detect pulsars wondered initially if they were picking up alien signals, there being at that time no known natural process capable of producing such signals.[7] But such possibilities pose no problem in principle for employing the concepts of finite artifactuality and design in descriptions and explanations of other alien objects.

Alien Design Explanations: Scope and Character

The potential scope of application of the idea of nonhuman design is enormous. A few well-known scientists have suggested, for instance, that life on earth is a result of deliberate seeding—that given the available time and reigning conditions, life could never have emerged by purely natural means.[8] Were the claimed impossibilities scientifically established, scientists might come to believe that something like alien seeding was the best available explanation of life on earth. Such a view would be no more inherently unscientific than would the belief that the traces found on Mars in the preceeding examples were the result of alien activity, or the view that the life now flourishing in a quarantined, previously sterile nutrient solution must have been inadvertantly introduced by one of the scientists in the lab.

In fact, were biochemists to discover some new fundamental biological law which precluded transitions across the major taxonomic boundaries, scientists might (probably grudgingly) accept the view that aliens had successively seeded the planet numerous times with, for example, different phyla. Frantic attention would then likely turn to attempts to identify where the aliens might have come from, what sort of creatures they were, at what intervals they had apparently returned, what their intentions might be, and what their diet might include (e.g., us?).

That is not, of course, where science presently is, and it may never be. But if such were to happen, there would be nothing scientifically suspicious about it. It is simply not an a priori principle of science that we on this earth had to have resulted from natural processes all of which began and progressed "naturally" wholly upon this earth, unaffected by the activity of any other being or beings. In fact, *even from the standpoint of philosophical naturalism,* it does not follow that terrestrial life had to begin on this planet, and that all aspects of its development and diversification had to be driven wholly by agent-free natural processes. To suppose that it did would be to risk exactly the same sort of mistake some far future Martian scientist would be making were he or she (or whatever) to insist on entertaining only theories according to which life arose spontaneously on Mars, when in fact life had gotten its start there via microbes on a human Mars lander. If philosophical naturalism is true, then that Martian scientist would be right that life had begun naturally, but the specific Martiocentric requirement that it have happened on Mars might guarantee that Martian science hobbled itself to theories that were in fact ultimately biologically impossible. For instance, if because of specific local conditions, Mars was incapable of generating the biologically necessary originating conditions, then any theory required to conform to the demand that it explain how life had in fact originated spontaneously on Mars would of necessity be scientifically confused.

What the foregoing reveals is this. Even granting the appropriateness of prohibitions against science entertaining theories referring to supernatural activity or design, still, the views that some aspects of life on earth are artifacts or are designed, and that there are or can be evidences of that artifactuality or designedness exhibited by certain aspects of terrestrial life, are in principle legitimately scientific. Specific proposed instances of such identifications might, of course, be horribly confused. But that is a very different matter.

Many (both philosophical naturalists and others) would insist that the existence and characteristics of any other beings involved in the origin of terrestrial life would have to ultimately be accounted for by natural processes, so that any problems of origin and development of life would be transplanted to some other venue—that is, to wherever the aliens had arisen (or perhaps to wherever who or what had seeded them originated). That demand may or may not stand up to scrutiny, but even if it does it is irrelevant to the present point, which is that not only is there nothing scientifically suspect about explanatory use of the general concept of finite design, but that there is nothing inherently unscientific in claims that life and the diversification of life as we know it could not biologically have arisen naturally on this planet, that life on Earth shows evidences of design, or that ascriptions of designedness provide parts of legitimate explanations of the life on Earth and its diversity. Such views would be as scientifically legitimate in principle as would be the identification of any (other) artifact found on Earth as being of intelligent extraterrestrial origin. There might at present be no evidence whatever for that, and such an explanation might not even in the imagined circumstances be the first choice of most scientists, but those are different matters.[9]

Design Explanations

One more matter needs brief attention before we turn to deeper issues, and that is: in what sense can design function as an *explanation?* Exactly what might it explain and how, and what constraints might it place on explanation? With respect to the design activity of finite creatures (humans, aliens), the answer to the latter is straightforward. Identification of some puzzling phenomenon on Mars as an alien artifact or design would among other things indicate that completely "natural" explanations would be inadequate, that counterflow introduction lay somewhere in the causal history of the object, and that any complete story of the object would have to contain reference to agent causation

In fact, given the essential link between finite designedness and counterflow, in the absence of design activity the design characteristics or possibly even the phenomenon itself would not have existed. Should we find an alien bulldozer on Mars, it will be perfectly safe to say that without alien design and activity that object simply would not have been there. Design is thus explanatorily implicated not only in some of the specific characteristics of a designed entity, but sometimes in its very existence.

That means that on some definitions of "cause," design can constitute a cause. David Lewis, for instance, develops a counterfactual analysis of "causal dependence" where b is causally dependent on a *iff* (in Hume's words)

if the first object had not been, the second never had existed[10]

Given the essential involvement of counterflow activity in finite designedness, design meets the criterion on the right of the above formula in any ordinary case of finite designedness and thus, if this analysis is correct, constitutes at least part of the causal explanation of the designed phenomenon. The explanation provided by human or alien design thus appears to be a particularly robust one. In any case, given the implication of agent counterflow activity attaching to finite design cases, the core of the counterflow causation will be agent activity, and any adequate theory of agent causation will provide the causal, explanatory substance of (finite) design explanations.

Human/Alien Design and Nature

Finally, can the idea of finite designedness be properly employed in explanations or descriptions of phenomena in nature? I think not (although one peculiar sort of possible case will arise later). Given the virtual entailment of counterflow from finite design (and artifactuality), finitely designed phenomena will nearly by definition fail to be natural in the relevant sense. (They might still be natural in the sense of not being supernatural, but that is not the issue here.) Were we to come to believe that human (or perhaps more likely, alien) design or activity was a factor in something we had previously thought of as part of nature, our inclination, it seems clear, would be to simply change our opinion about what was or wasn't part of nature.[11] As we will see, however, the situation with respect to supernatural design and activity is significantly different.

Further Links: Pattern and Science

Historically, the concept of pattern in nature has figured prominently in the metaphysics underlying science itself. As mentioned briefly earlier, the presupposition that nature is comprehendable and thus that if we go about the scientific project correctly we will be able to make sense of nature, is scientifically essential.[12] But making sense of nature is possible only if there are mind-correlative, sense-making patterns there to be recognized.

That there evidently are such patterns in nature has been recognized from very early times. According to many Greeks, mind-correlative pattern was a defining characteristic of both the cosmos and the structure of existence itself. The cosmos and reality were thus rational. But despite its familiarity, the presence in nature of mind-correlative pattern has been and is still a source of deep wonder. In our century, Einstein commented on nature's "peculiar accessibility to the human mind." de Grasse Tyson expresses amazement that "mathematics, which is a pure construction of the human mind, . . . actual works" when applied to the real cosmos. Wigner remarks on the "miracle . . . of the human mind's capacity to divine [natural law]." Davies refers to the "rationality mystery."[13] They are all in various ways expressing wonder about pattern—that what does and can go on in human cognition, and what is, are in some deep way correlated. And the scientists just quoted are far from alone in those sentiments.

Pattern Origins

If there are patterns associated with nature that are indeed mind correlative, how are they to be accounted for? What is their source and basis? There are a variety of options, among them:

a. something mindlike (but not personal, living, etc.) *informs* nature (one Greek position)
b. nature is a deliberately designed artifact, a creation of (personal, but not finite) mind (the Western religious picture)
c. our minds are products of nature, generated by processes that structured our cognition along lines already bound into nature (some Darwinians accept this view)
d. mind is flexible enough to find pattern (whether it's *really* there or not) in virtually any sort of cosmos there might be
e. our mind imposes its own structure on what is "out there" (some Kantians, Kuhnians, and some other idealists)

Western science initially carried a strong commitment to (b), which operated not only in the area of philosophical foundations and justifications, but even internal to theorizing.[14] Mainstream science has, of course, moved away from any overt commitment to (b), many scientists rejecting (b) outright, and many even among those who accept it seeing it as having no relevance to or legitimacy in any purely scientific context.[15]

The implications and proposed justifications of such rejections will be well worth exploring. After all, were we to learn that some object on Mars was a result of alien design activity, that recognition would certainly have significant implications for our theories about the origins, character, and behavior of that object. By parity, one might expect that were nature a result of supernatural design activity, that would likewise have enormous implications for adequate theories about its origins and operations. Yet, most hold that allowing supernatural design theories into science is impermissible—*even should it be true* that the cosmos is a product of supernatural design.[16] That raises a number of questions. Exactly what is the difference between the alien design and the supernatural design cases? And exactly why would that difference be scientifically relevant? And on exactly what basis should scientific prohibitions rest? Those questions will be taken up in the next several chapters.

Conclusion

There is more to be said here, but it seems clear that the concept of finite design—of deliberate, intentional, (finite) agent activity moving objects, processes, or events into channels along which nature left to herself would not direct them, toward patterns they otherwise would not exemplify—is scientifically legitimate and often descriptively and explanatorily essential.

That conclusion should not outrage most sensibilities. Most people would admit that in the sorts of cases cited, human or even alien intelligent design could function as a properly scientific explanatory concept. But theories of intelligent supernatural design are widely considered to be a can of worms of an entirely different color. Thus, for instance, Eugenie Scott:

> To be dealt with scientifically, 'intelligence' must also be natural, because *all* science is natural. [A]ppeal to . . . SETI is fallacious. SETI is indeed a scientific project; it seeks *natural* intelligence. Any theory with a supernatural foundation is not scientific.[17]

So the theory that aliens did it (initiated life on this planet, say), even if wrong, is still in principle scientific. But on the view just quoted, the theory that God did exactly the same thing (initiated life on this planet), based on exactly the same evidence is, even if true, inherently not science (not merely bad science, but not science at all).[18] A bit later we will have to investigate the intuition underlying such prohibitions.

II

SUPERNATURAL DESIGN

3

SUPERNATURAL DESIGN: PRELIMINARY BASICS

In the previous chapters, *finite* design was characterized generally as involving delibe-rate, intentional, agent activity moving objects, properties, processes, or events into channels along which nature left to herself would not direct them, toward patterns that otherwise would not be exemplified. *Supernatural* design, while exhibiting some important similarities, can also exhibit significant differences. Several are relatively obvious. For instance, a supernatural being might be able to contravene, suspend, or even change the natural laws in terms of which counterflow is defined. Furthermore, even within the boundaries of reigning natural law, a supernatural being might have much greater knowledge of and capability of employing those natural laws. And a supernatural being who created the cosmos could presumably build intended patterns and structures into the primordial, ultimate, initial conditions of the cosmos, or into the very laws and constants of the cosmos. And a supernatural being could simply decree the existence of things exhibiting intended patterns.

For present purposes, I will divide supernatural pattern-producing activity into four broad categories. The first category, which I shall call *nomic agency*, involves design activity which at least in principle could be performed by (perhaps very special) finite agents. The second, *supernatural nomic agency*, will consist of super-natural pattern-producing activity structurally identical to nomic agency in ways which will be specified, but which involves unique supernatural agent characteristics not even in principle available to finite agents. The third, *supernatural contranomic agency*, involves pattern-producing procedures that employ suspension of, or breaking of, the normal laws of nature. The fourth, *supernatural creative agency*, will consist of supernatural pattern-producing activity involving initial setting of the parameters definitive of nature's normal structures and operations. Following is a brief character-ization of each category.

Nomic Agency

Production of design by finite agents (whether human, alien, or whatever) consists of intentional generating of some patterned result. The standard structure involves agent initiation of some specific initial state which, via relevant natural laws, generates (or itself transmutes into) the target state. So simple a project as boiling water begins with the setting up of an initial state—cold water in a pan on an operating stove—which, by perfectly ordinary nomic processes of heat flow, energy increases, phase changes, and the like, and with no further activity required of the agent, eventually results in the system achieving the target state—boiling water.

Within that general structure, many specific factors are relative to the agents involved. Agents differ in basic capabilities, affecting what starting conditions they can initiate. Agents differ in what patterns they do (or even can) recognize, and in which patterns they can intend to actualize. They differ in what natural laws and processes they are aware of, and in what laws they are able to employ in their producings. But despite such differences, the underlying structure of pattern production by different finite agents is constant.

It seems perfectly evident that a supernatural agent could employ exactly this structure of pattern production. Furthermore, there is no reason to think that a supernatural agent could not, if so minded, initiate counterflow conditions identical to those available to finite agents, then allow the relevant natural processes to run their courses, thus producing (counterflow) results—artifacts—identical to any produceable by finite agents.[1]

Supernatural Nomic Agency

Let us begin with an alien case. Imagine some aliens who, although finite, are vastly—perhaps unimaginably—different from human beings. Such aliens might have vastly greater scientific capabilities than humans, vastly greater knowledge than humans, and utterly incomprehensible psychologies—truly alien intentions, and cognitive structures incommensurable with ours. Design by such aliens might involve activity that we could not even recognize as activity, aimed at producing patterns that we might neither grasp or even recognize as patterns, employing means that utterly escaped us, relying on natural processes whose existence was neither understandable nor suspected by us, for purposes that would totally baffle us, resulting in phenomena even the artifactuality of which we had no means of discovering.

Despite all that, such cases would fit the basic structure of the *nomic agency* category. In addition, all components involved—initial conditions, processes, and results—would be consistent with natural law. Of course, nature alone, without the involvement of agent causation, would not and perhaps could not produce the given results by the route employed.[2] Such cases would be unusual only in the employment of higher-level (though finite) capabilities, knowledge, and so forth—not in their basic structure. In an exactly similar manner, a supernatural agent might engage in design activity that still fit the basic nomic agency structure, but which involved employment of capabilities which, although still consistent with natural law, were not merely beyond *us*, but in principle beyond any (even alien) finite agents. For instance, the scope of agent causation available to a supernatural being (especially if omnipotent) even within the context of existing law might extend vastly beyond that of any (and all) finite agents. The character and resources of a supernatural agent's cognition (especially if omniscient) might well extend beyond that of any finite agent's. The nature and content of the intentions of a supernatural agent might extend into domains not graspable (nor intendable) by finite agents. And, of course, were a supernatural agent to employ existent natural laws in the realization of some intentions, that agent (especially if omniscient) would likely know of employable laws and natural processes of which finite agents were (perhaps even essentially) utterly unaware. While within the context of reigning law, this type of supernatural pattern producing might involve activity that finite agents could not recognize as such, employing laws that finite agents could not grasp, to produce patterns that could not be mind correlative for any possible finite agent.

So a supernatural agent engaged in pattern-producing activity even within the conceptual boundaries of nomic agency could perhaps produce artifacts or designed phenomena beyond the capabilites of any finite agency

Nomic and Supernatural Nomic Agency—Some Implications

Both of the above types of agency involve the initiation and production of counterflow, and in both cases counterflow will be located either in results, processes, or initial conditions. Furthermore, both types involve nomic discontinuity—not only will there be something different than there would have been had nature operated undisturbed, but description of the causal history of that difference will be incomplete without some reference to agent causation. Neither case, however, will involve any breaking of any natural law. The discontinuities are results only of nomic incompletelness, not of nomic violation.

Although counterflow would be present somewhere in any instance in either category, we might have difficulty recognizing it in specific cases. It might be of a sort we were incapable of grasping as counterflow, or it might involve some law the existence of which we did not (or could not) suspect, or it might be so subtle as to be beyond our capacity even to notice. But there is no requirement that either the counterflow or the artifactuality in question be unrecognizable by humans or other finite beings. Consider again the Martian titanium cube discussed earlier. If aliens could produce one, so could a supernatural being. A supernatural agent might even employ means available to those aliens in producing it. Or a supernatural agent might employ special means available only to a supernatural agent (but still within the bounds of natural law) to produce a cube identical to that which finite aliens could make (although only by other means).[3]

But regardless of the fact that a supernatural agent had produced it, and regardless of how that supernatural agent might have produced it, the primary counterflow indications exhibited by that titanium cube would be instantly recognizable. In fact, whether or not we had the slightest clue as to who had produced it, how it had been produced, or what the intent and purpose (if any) were, we would not have the slightest trouble recognizing the cube's artifactuality. And even given all that ignorance, the rational legitimacy of recognizing that artifactuality is unproblematic. Indeed, if the first human explorers on Neptune discovered, say, an apparently abandoned automated factory still turning out what are obviously oscilloscopes, refusal to admit the factory's artifactuality until we determined the identity and character of the agent(s) who built it would be flatly irrational.[4]

At this point we can see three important things. First, supernatural activity in either of the initial two categories can produce recognizable counterflow, recognizable artifactuality, and even recognizable design. Second, even within the scientific context, acknowledgment of such counterflow, artifactuality, and design is perfectly legitimate—even if the (perhaps unknown) fact of the matter is that the producing agent is supernatural. And third, that legitimacy would remain even if it turns out that the structure and operation of science make attributing the phenomena to supernatural agency scientifically impermissible. This latter issue will be explored later.

Contranomic Supernatural Agency

Within the nomic and supernatural nomic categories, design activity operates within the stream of natural law and process,[5] but laws are neither suspended nor broken. However, by most definitions a supernatural agent is able to do that if so minded. Such *contranomic* activity, while not a possibility for finite agents, could factor into supernatural design activity.[6]

As noted, there are three locations within cosmic history where counterflow (and the generally associated nomic discontinuity) can be injected into the otherwise normal flow of nature—results, processes, and initial conditions.[7] Supernatural contranomic activity could, obviously, inject counterflow at any of those locations as well. For instance, a supernatural agent could simply decree the existence of some result bearing counterflow marks—by the miraculous, ex nihilo bringing into existence of a Roman coin, for instance. Such a coin would bear all the marks of counterflow and design of any other Roman coin—there just wouldn't be any usual history behind it. Or an omnipotent supernatural being might bring into existence some material object which itself violates natural law (e.g., a perpetual motion device or something which accelerates and decelerates across the light velocity boundary).[8] Or supernatural activity might involve processes clearly distinguishable as contranomic. A withered arm straightening out and becoming normal over the course of a few seconds would obviously involve processes different from those by which normal arms are naturally produced—processes that normal laws might forbid. Or if the beginning of life on Earth required very special initial conditions which nature herself not only could not generate but positively forbade (such as some nomically forbidden variant of the earlier Tupperware origin scenario), a supernatural agent could perhaps set up those nomically forbidden conditions out of which life would then purely naturally arise.

There is, in each of these cases, supernatural intervention into the flow of nature's history. In fact, in contranomic cases, the counterflow is usually of a particularly strong character. Not only does the intervention and normally associated nomic discontinuity generate things nature *would* not do on her own, but given the contranomic nature of the cases, they typically generate (or at least involve) things nature *could* not do on her own.[9]

It is, of course, perfectly possible that contranomic activity might result in marks that we recognize as counterflow. However, the situation is far from simple. As before, there is no *guarantee* that we could recognize any of the resultant counterflow or artifactuality. For any of a number of reasons the indications might be beyond our noticing or recognizing. But there are deeper complications, and the qualifications above ("usually," "normally." and "typically") are not just pro forma. For example, it might be that certain kinds of contranomic activity could suppress the indications of counterflow, so that while normally operating law would dictate the production of counterflow marks, their contranomic absence is one of the very effects brought about.

Quantum Intervention

Even more complications emerge with respect to quantum phenomena. Let us assume that the standard interpretation is correct and that there simply is no causation operating in some quantum events—there are merely certain probabilities (e.g., of decay or not) and that that is as far down as causation goes. A supernatural agent might be able to simply decree the decay (or not) of specific particles at specific times. Suppose that a supernatural agent foreknew that some particle, left to itself, would not decay at some specific time. Assume further that the agent wishes it to decay, and decrees that it do so—which it consequently does.[10] There is obviously counterflow in this case, since had the interventive decree not been made, nature would have done something different—the particle would not have decayed.

The sense in which this agency is contranomic is a bit peculiar. If the fundamental governing quantum laws are purely probabilistic, then either event—decay or nondecay—falls within the boundary of the relevant laws. There is thus nothing contranomic in the sense of some quantum event that nature forbids. Nor is there a nomic discontinuity in the sense of a gap which otherwise nature would have in some way filled. (There is a causal gap, but one nature would have left unfilled. That is the nature of quantum events.) But on the other hand, there was causation (agent causation) where quantum theory as usually construed claims there is no causation at all. Thus, this quantum intervention is at the very least contratheoretic.

There are further complications, of course. Suppose, for instance, that the decay event normally happens in 90 percent of the relevant instances, and that a supernatural agent wishes the decay to occur on this occasion. (Perhaps that agent is overseeing the evolution of human beings, and this specific decay event is essential to the emergence of a key mutation.) But being omniscient, the agent foresees that this will be one of the 10 percent of cases where decay will not occur.[11] If that agent supernaturally, contranomically intervenes and brings about the decay, then although contrary to what nature would have in fact done, that intervention will bring about what nature would have been expected to do it with 90 percent likelihood. That specific case of counterflow (and it is) will have a slightly peculiar flavor.

There is one further complication connected with design in this case.[12] Consider again a supernatural agent overseeing the evolution of human beings. The intention is that eventually there be beings of our general sort, natural processes being employed to the extent possible. Suppose that mutations are fundamental to the evolutionary development, and that often they occur at useful times. But although essential mutations frequently arise naturally, they do not always do so, and when they fail to occur the supernatural agent intervenes (perhaps on the quantum level as in the previous case) to generate them. At some point, the next needed mutation is a real long shot (the quantum-based probabilities are a quillion to one against), and the agent has already adopted the policy stance of readiness: that were the mutation otherwise not going to occur naturally, then the agent would intervene to generate it. But the long shot, as it turns out, will in fact occur after all, so no intervention will be necessary.

What exactly ought we to say in this case? There is no agent activity, no actual counterflow, no intervention, no nomic discontinuities of any agent-relevant sort. Yet, the deliberate adoption by the agent of a (counterfactual) readiness to act had things *been* going to go differently seems relevant. And it seems intuitively plausible to associate the new mutational development with intent, even though no actual agent activity or causation was involved. In any case, I will classify these cases of counterfactual intent as exemplifying genuine artifactuality or design.[13]

It is obvious that many of these sorts of quantum interventions might be in principle scientifically undetectable. That would seem to be especially true of cases where even though intervention in the specific instance was necessary, the probability of the event occuring naturally had been significantly larger than zero. But that is not to say that detection and recognition are always impossible. If we had evidence that a long string of wildly improbable quantum events produced a solar flare spelling out a message in English, we'd likely get suspicious concerning those quantum events, and rightly so.

Supernatural Contranomic Agency—Preliminary Conclusion

It is clear that a supernatural agent having the ability to act contranomically could produce instances and evidences of design by such means. And, as with the previous categories of supernatural agency, while nothing guarantees that we would be able to recognize either the resultant designedness or the artifactuality or even the counterflow (if any), there is nothing forbidding such recognizability either. For instance, that the legendary Martian titanium cube might have been produced contranomically—even miraculously—would not have the slightest implications for its recognizability as artifact.[14]

There are three other points to note here. First, the fact that nature could produce something (e.g., if all the quantum events went a specific way) does not conclusively establish that nature on her own did produce it. After all, those events might have been going to go some other way if left to themselves. If so, given the relevant subjunctives concerning directions nature left alone would have taken, it might be that intervention was absolutely essential for bringing about the result in question. Second, in the case of contranomic supernatural activity, the invisibility or complete absence of evident counterflow marks closes the case neither on design, nor even on design as a result of direct agent activity.[15] And finally, any evidence that something is in fact genuinely contranomic is simultaneously evidence that the agency involved is supernatural. Arguments of this sort fall into the ill-thought-of "God of the gaps" category, which will be discussed later. But such arguments—that if neither nature nor any possible finite beings can even in principle produce some existing phenomenon, then some other being not bound by nature must have—do have one great virtue. They are formally logically valid.

Supernatural Creative Agency

All the foregoing cases (whether of finite or supernatural agency) take place within the confines of cosmic history. The context of nature is already in place and operating, and those agent activities and results (however produced) become part of the ongoing stream. Furthermore, each of the above three categories is defined relative to natural law. Finite agency of any sort falls into the nomic category, and nomic agency of any variety operates within the bounds of natural law, achieving its aims in part by virtue of those already-operative laws. By contrast, contranomic agency is not bound by natural law in that same sense. (That indeed is why contranomic agency is available only to supernatural agents.) But while laws do not bind the contranomic, their existence is presupposed in the very concept *contranomic*, which is defined in contrast to the background of those laws. So effects generated by contranomic activity are interjected into (or involve diversion of) already-flowing causal streams and become a part of cosmic history (although parts whose explanation lies partially outside of that history).

But there is one additional arena of possible activity uniquely available to supernatural agents and that is the protohistorical, involving the establishment of nature itself.[16] The structure of nature is defined by its governing laws and natural constants, and the specific shape that the cosmos and its history exemplify both at any moment and across time is shaped by the ultimate primordial initial boundary conditions of the cosmos. A supernatural (omnipotent) *creating* agent in bringing a cosmos into existence would decree the laws and constants by which the new cosmos would subsequently operate, and would set up the primordial boundary conditions— quantity, character, and distribution of matter and energy, for instance—upon which operation of the mandated laws would commence.[17]

It seems obvious that a supernatural creating agent (especially if omnipotent and omniscient) could infuse design into the cosmos or its components by deliberate, calculated selection of laws, constants, and primordial boundary conditions. Such an agent could set in motion a system designed to exhibit specified characteristics, exhibit specified patterns, or generate specified phenomena, without any further intervention by the agent. Those desiderata might be exhibited throughout the entire history of the created system, or might be designed to emerge at certain points, in certain orders, at preselected moments of that unfolding history. In fact, if there are specific empirical characteristics that constitute good evidence of designedness, it seems at least prima facie possible that laws, constants, and primordial boundary conditions could be chosen in such a way that those design-evidencing characteristics would be exemplified by or within the resultant system.

Creation Locations

As before, there are three areas into which design could be structured—(i) natural laws and constants, (ii) primordial boundary conditions, and (iii) results of their combined workings. Following is a brief look at each.

Laws and Constants

Given the logical contingency of natural law, there are unlimitedly many law structures by which the cosmos could have been ordered (or disordered). Although it is only through their operation on matter that we come to know the shape and content of those laws, it is possible that a supernatural creating agent might deliberately weave design into the very law structure of a cosmos, irrespective of any consequences those laws might produce. For instance, in constructing a cosmos, a supernatural being might enact a set of laws simply because of some inherent appeal their structure held. Many major physicists both past and present have been struck by an aesthetic dimension in nature. Nature's laws have often been cited for their symmetry, their elegance, their order, their unity, their exquisite meshing, and for the harmonies sung by their mathematical structure. All of those have been taken as constituting part of their *beauty*.[18] This aesthetic dimension is perceived as so fundamentally infused into the structure of law that many physicists take beauty to be a pointer toward truth. For instance, the physicist John Polkinghorne:

> There is a deep feeling among those who practise fundamental science—a feeling that has so far proved reliable—that the way to true understanding is the one that satisfies the canons of economy and elegance; the way which, in a word, is mathematically beautiful.[19]

Similar remarks have been made by, for example, Einstein, Weinberg, Dirac, Wigner, and others.[20]

Of course, aesthetic properties represent correlations to mind, and are thus possible aspects of pattern. Those properties seem to be dimensions of the deep match between cognition and the cosmos (and are part of the intuitive "rationality" of the cosmos), and aspects of that match often prompt comparisons to human design. For instance, Ghyka: "There are then such things as 'the Mathematics of Life' and 'the Mathematics of Art,' and the two coincide."[21]

Comments here are sometimes tinged with just a bit of wonder. Weinberg, for instance, remarks on "the rather spooky fact that something as personal and subjective as our sense of beauty helps us not only to invent physical theories but even to judge the validity of theories."[22]

It seems evident that a supernatural creative agency could intentionally build mind-correlative patterns into the law structure of a cosmos in the process of creation. It is of course possible that finite beings might be unable to recognize those patterns. But as in previous cases, there is nothing logically preventing laws being constructed according to patterns accessible to humans or other finite beings.

Primordial Initial Conditions

The distinction between the creation of natural laws and the initiating of primordial boundary conditions, and the recognition that each presents separate possibilities for injecting design into a cosmos, was already familiar to early-nineteenth-century natural theologians.[23] In fact, boundary conditions were seen by some as much stronger evidences of design than the structure of laws, especially since the laws alone were thought to be adequate only for sustaining life—not for initiating it.[24]

It seems evident that a supernatural agent creating a cosmos could deliberately shape primordial initial conditions to exemplify specific patterns. But there are a number of ways that could go. In the steady-state cosmos of the early nineteenth century, patterns manifested in the present cosmos had to have been built in from the beginning. Thus, the "target" patterns would themselves have been directly created as initial (and thus also subsequent) conditions. With more contemporary pictures of present cosmic states evolving over time from primordial conditions, the tendency is much stronger to think that any characteristics deliberately structured into primordial conditions would have been chosen not for any pattern or design characteristics inherent in those conditions themselves, but rather, merely as instrumental for generating later states in joint operation with set natural laws. Thus, the key patterns exemplified by primordial initial conditions would have to do with the aptness of those conditions in conjunction with natural law to give rise to the intended ultimate results. Those two types of patterns may have very different characteristics, and require very different recognition procedures.[25]

Generated Results

One possible option open to a supernatural agent creating a cosmos would be to coordinate selection of laws and primordial conditions in such a way that under the operation of those laws, the conditions would naturally evolve into (or produce) intended target states or objects or patterns—for example, life, diversity of species, human beings. (Even were the laws in some sense necessary with no choice possible, a supernatural creating agent could still structure primordial boundary conditions in precise ways required to generate a range of desired results under the given laws.)

There might, however, be limits as to what could be achieved by such means. Suppose, for instance, that a supernatural agent creating a cosmos did so under the self-imposed condition that the cosmos be one in which moral virtues were possible, or in which evil could not grow beyond a certain limit, and suppose that such conditions had consequences for permissible structures of natural law.[26] Given those constraints, it might be that there simply were no possible primordial conditions which under those laws would by natural means and without further agent activity, eventually generate a factory which automatically produced vacuum-tube oscilloscopes with machined, cast aluminum cases held together by sheet-metal screws. Those sorts of objects might under the specified constraints only be produceable in ways involving direct agent activity.

It might even be that the conditions for life were so tight, so rigorous, that (given other relevant constraints) there was no acceptable way of constructing any combination of laws and primordial conditions that would result in the "natural" emergence of life from nonlife. It might be, in other words, that under any acceptable set of laws, the constraints upon conditions would be so demanding that the only possible ultimate source of earthly biological life was direct creation of biological life itself.[27]

But whatever constraints and limits there might be, it seems evident that a supernatural being having the capability both of determining what set of laws would define nature and of instituting the primordial boundary conditions upon which those laws would operate, could employ such capabilities to bring about specific results. Those results, being intended outcomes of deliberate choice and activity aimed at producing specific cognizable states and phenomena, would clearly be products of design.[28]

Some Significant Consequences

If all relevant designs either of or within the cosmos were introduced into the cosmos protohistorically—whether via the structure of laws, primordial conditions, or both—then there would obviously be no necessity for supernatural agent intervention (either nomic or contranomic) into the historical course of the cosmos in order for those designs to be achieved. Any relevant pattern exhibited within nature would be a purely natural result of the laws that defined nature operating upon previously existing conditions, all the way back to the very beginning of the cosmos itself. All such results would be expectable, predictable, in accord with all reigning natural principles and processes, and *causally explainable in terms of those laws and conditions.*[29]

But in any situation driven solely by natural processes and in which there is no supernatural agent intervention there will obviously be no relevant nomic discontinuities either. Thus, in a cosmos where supernatural agent activity of the relevant sort occurs only in the initial defining of the structure and operation of nature within that cosmos, there will be no causal or explanatory gaps in nature or nature's history that require filling by supernatural agent activity. Equally obviously, if there are no interventions or relevant nomic gaps in the natural world, there will be nothing contranomic either. More generally, if everything in nature results from natural law acting upon prior conditions, then there will be no counterflow exhibited. Those implications attach not only to nature itself, but to each individual phenomenon in nature—life, the eye, bacterial rotary electric flagella motors, and so on.[30]

But remember that we are considering possible cases where results intended by a supernatural creating agent are obtained by deliberate selective choice of law and primordial boundary conditions. Deliberately intended products of deliberate (protohistorical) agent activity would surely qualify as designed.[31] But if so, then in distinction from earlier types of cases, these instances of design exhibit no counterflow, no nomic discontinuity (much less anything contranomic), and involve no relevant agent activity within cosmic history. Even more generally, there is nothing artifactual here—life, eyes, and bacterial motors are perfectly natural. Any cases for supernatural design within this category will obviously *not* be of the "God of the gaps" type.[32]

Some Complicating Implications

The above points bear upon present concerns in a variety of ways. For one thing, it cannot be claimed that the mere fact that something is natural implies that it is not a result of deliberate design. And again, it cannot be claimed that design invariably involves counterflow, nomic discontinuity, or artificiality in any straightforward sense of those terms. And that generates complications because in recognizing design, we typically rely on our capacity for recognizing artifactuality (or associated agent causation), and recognition of that typically rests in turn on our capacity for recognizing counterflow—usually via primary marks. We recognize counterflow (and allied matters—artifactuality, contranomicity) *against the background of nature.* We recognize those things in terms of what nature if left undisturbed would or would not have done.

But in the present case, the design in question would be produced by uninterrupted natural processes, and relevant agent activity must be tracked back to the founding of nature itself. That creative activity, of course, involves supernatural specification of what nature will be, what nature will normally do, what will or will not be natural. Prior to such creation, there simply is no nature against the background of which counterflow, artificiality, and contranomic activity can even be defined. So either those concepts can play no role in recognition of this type of design in nature, or else they are going to have to be redefined in some entirely new manner.[33] That will have an immediate and significant consequence. As I argued earlier, our recognition of finite designedness rests at least implicitly upon recognition of artifactuality. Within the context of artifactuality, secondary marks are extremely reliable indicators of designedness. Indeed, artifactuality conjoined with secondary marks very nearly entails designedness. But is it clear that secondary marks alone, outside the context of artifactuality—as the present case would be—support that same identification? Furthermore, as we will see later, reliable recognizability is one crucial issue in the question of the scientific legitimacy of any concept. But the implication under discussion may suggest that recognition of supernatural creative designedness would have to be by some means different from the counterflow-linked basis on which we normally identify finite designedness.

That latter point will itself have one further significant consequence. It is generally held that traditional arguments concerning supernatural design are analogical—that is, that they rest upon inferential moves from recognizable characteristics of finite (human) design, to characteristics of and recognition of supernatural design. That is the way Paley is popularly read, for instance.[34] If that general view is correct, then those arguments face serious difficulties, because key contextual components of recognizing finite design—counterflow, artifactuality, agent activity in historical causal paths—are precisely what are systematically missing in the type of supernatural cases at issue.

4

IDENTIFYING SUPERNATURAL DESIGN:
PRIMARY MARKS

Design activity of finite agents always leaves counterflow marks. Such marks can range from evident to subtle beyond what we may be capable of recognizing, but they are always produced. Supernatural design activity would in some instances also generate counterflow marks, in some cases recognizable and in some cases utterly invisible to finite observers. However, supernatural *creative* agency as defined in chapter 3 could include deliberate design activity that did not involve counterflow at all. For present purposes, supernatural design activity will be divided into two broad categories—that involving evident counterflow, and that involving invisible or non-existent counterflow. Since those two broad categories require very different treatments, the first will be discussed in this chapter, and the second will be explored in the next.

Supernatural Agency, Counterflow, and Artifactuality

We begin with a very brief look at the first three categories which are open to supernatural agent activity—nomic agency, supernatural nomic agency, and contranomic agency.[1]

Nomic Agency, Evident Counterflow, and Recognizing Artifactuality

A supernatural (and omnipotent) being could produce virtually anything of which finite beings were capable, and could do so employing only those means of which finite agents were capable. Any such result, even though in fact produced by activity of a supernatural agent, would bear exactly the same counterflow indications (whether direct, indirect, hard, soft, surface, deep, etc.) as that produced by finite beings. If artifactuality were recognizable by those counterflow marks in the one case, it would be equally recognizable as such in the other case as well. A vacuum tube radio is trivially recognizable as the production of an agent—and not nature—regardless of who the agent was (finite or supernatural), regardless of the motivation, regardless of means of production, and even regardless of whether or not the truth of any of those matters was accessible to us.[2] It follows immediately that it is possible for a supernatural agent to produce phenomena readily identifiable as artifactual, whether or not it is either possible or scientifically permissible to attribute the agent activity to a supernatural agent.

Supernatural Nomic Agency, Evident Counterflow, and Artifact Recognition

Supernatural nomic agency, recall, encompasses production that does not involve violation of any natural laws but that employs resources and capabilities available only to a supernatural agent. Although the means would be unique, there is nothing preventing the produced results from being directly recognizable as artifacts. Such recognition could even be via familiar hard, surface, counterflow marks, the difference being merely that such marks were generated in ways not available to finite agents. For instance, there might be some natural, lawful process which could only be triggered by agent activity on a scale not possible even in principle for finite agents, and a supernatural agent might choose to employ that particular process as part of the means of producing a robotic factory on Neptune.[3] The artifactuality of such a factory (and associated counterflow indications) would be readily evident, even though actual production of the factory had been accomplished not only by a supernatural agent, but via means which (although within the boundaries of natural law) were not employable by any finite agent.

So here again, specific instances of artifactuality which were in fact produced by a supernatural agent might be trivially recognizable as artifactual via ordinary counterflow means, and that would be unaffected even should it turn out that attribution of such design activity to a supernatural being were neither scientifically warranted nor even rationally legitimate.

Contranomic Agency

It is in the contranomic category that one of the more frequently noted characteristics of the supernatural comes into play—the ability to transcend, suspend, or break the laws of nature. It is evident that contranomic intervention could produce counterflow not only involving things that nature *would* not do, but by definition also a stronger form involving things that nature *could* not do. Either form could in specific cases be straightforwardly recognizable by finite agents, that recognition being by ordinary, primary counterflow means.

Again, such recognizability would be unaffected even by prohibitions upon *admitting to* either supernatural agency or contranomicity within science.

Counterflow Invisibility

Although in all three of the above categories it is possible that recognizable counterflow be involved, there is no guarantee of that in specific cases. Counterflow would typically be involved, but for any of a number of reasons it might be completely invisible to us. For instance, given our incomplete knowledge of nature, it is perfectly possible for us to mistakenly take as normal something nature not only would not do, but even could not do.[4] Or the produced indications might be too subtle for human notice or in various ways beyond human capacity to recognize. Counterflow in such cases might be invisible to us for practical reasons, but in others it might be invisible to humans even in principle. It is possible that the aspect of nature that some phenomenon runs counter to is not even thinkable or cognizable by human beings (although perhaps unproblematic for other finite beings). Or a supernatural agent might directly override the laws governing the production of humanly observable counterflow marks.

Some counterflow might be in principle invisible to any finite beings. For instance, although many physicists hope that the ultimate theory of everything may be compact enough to be statable on a single sheet of paper, that hope might be spectacularly wrong.[5] Perhaps the real ultimate explanatory theory is so wildly complex that understanding it requires an infinite mind and expressing it would take infinitely many characters. And the immediate activity of a supernatural agent working in quantum gaps in the causal structure of nature could be invisible even to a complete science.

In cases where counterflow is invisible, recognition of designedness must take a different route than the usual one involving recognized artifactuality. That issue is the focus of the next chapter.

From Artifactuality to Design

In the above cases where counterflow and artifactuality are unproblematically recognizable, there still remains the step from recognizing artifactuality to recognizing designedness. As discussed previously, *once artifactuality has been established,* the move to designedness is often straightforward. Complexity of suitable degrees, difficulty and demandingness of production conditions and procedures, interlocking functions, adjustment of means to ends, assignable value—all of those things make conclusions of deliberate intent, purpose, and designedness perfectly plausible. Given the direct link between counterflow and artifactuality, that means that *in the presence of primary marks the above secondary marks very nearly close the case in favor of design.*

We often legitimately conclude that some human artifact is designed, sometimes without knowing the purpose, production process, identity of the designer, and so forth. (I knew that my sister's mysterious eyelash curler was designed—not merely that it was an artifact.) We draw such conclusions quite legitimately on the basis of properties exhibited by the artifact. We could in some instances do something similar even in the case of alien artifacts, despite having no knowledge of their technology, psychologies, or purposes—although we might not do it quite so well.

But if we are sometimes able to identify designedness on the basis of observable characteristics of artifacts (such as primary and secondary counterflow marks),[6] then at least in some cases there should be no difficulty with that same identification even if in fact the design agent is supernatural. It would be perfectly legitimate to identify the robotic oscilloscope factory on Neptune as designed—and not just as artifactual— regardless of the identity and nature of the agent involved. And that recognition of designedness remains legitimate even should it turn out that identifying the agent as supernatural is neither possible nor legitimate within science.

Keep in mind that this is within the context of recognized artifactuality— artifactuality recognized via counterflow. The situation concerning natural objects— objects not exhibiting counterflow at all—is one of the foci of the next chapter. The present point is that if a supernatural agent produced an artifactual phenomenon, identifiable as such by evident primary marks, there would be no rational reason why we could not at least in some specific instances recognize that phenomenon itself as designed, on a basis identical to that by which we sometimes recognize designedness in finite artifacts. Perhaps we could not establish that the agent was in fact super- natural, but that is a different matter—a matter to which we now turn.

Recognizing Artifact Design as Supernatural

In the above instances, recognition of counterflow, artifactuality, and agency would be unproblematic. The direct, surface, hard counterflow marks of the titanium cube on Mars or the robotic factory on Neptune would leave little doubt on any of those counts. But establishing on such bases that the agent involved was actually super- natural might not be as straightforward. Would it in fact be possible to do so?

In any instance of design recognizable via counterflow where generating of that counterflow could not be done by finite agents, the answer would obviously be yes. Following are three potential schemas.

Contranomic

Any finite agent would by definition have to act within boundaries set by the laws of nature. Thus if the existence of genuine contranomic agent activity were established, the conclusion that the agent in question was supernatural would follow easily.

Prebiotic Initial Conditions

Recall the earlier example of the Tupperware theory of the origin of life. In that story, after forty thousand or so years of research, science finally concludes that life can indeed emerge spontaneously from nonliving chemicals, but only under one specific set of conditions involving a huge, light green Tupperware vat and a particular vinyl record. None of that would violate any known laws of nature.[7] But given the highly artificial character of the necessary initial conditions, it is equally obvious that beginning biological life in that way requires prior agent activity.[8] Since such activity must be prior to the beginning of natural biological life and hence prior to natural biological agents, the conclusion that the agent responsible for the relevant activity (constructing Tupperware vats) is not a nature-produced agent is certainly reasonable.

Infinite Properties

Nature contains a number of laws which only become "operative" under extreme circumstances. Some nuclear processes we can trigger only via detonation of nuclear explosives. Some quantum processes which operated in the initial split second of the Big Bang have not operated since then because there has nowhere in the cosmos been sufficiently concentrated energy to initiate them. If there were processes which were only activated by energy beyond what any finite agency could generate—for example, infinite energy—such processes would thus constitute evidence that supernatural agency was involved.

Establishing Relevant Law

Each of the above cases depends crucially upon certain unusual scientific results. For instance, the contranomic case requires both that a law and a violation of that law be established—otherwise, either it isn't really a violation or else what is violated is not really a law. The Tupperware theory provides a genuine example only if the Tupperware vat is the only really viable means. And in the third case, the conclusion depends essentially on the claim that initiating the relevant process requires infinite energy. There are, of course, those who would argue that such cases (even if correct) could never be scientifically established.

But it may not be quite that simple. Since all three of the above cases are formally similar, I will discuss only the first. Considerations concerning that case can be adapted to the other two. One additional consideration concerning the third will emerge later.

Establishing Contranomicity

A *definitely established, genuine violation* of a real natural law would indeed support a conclusion of supernatural agency. But could any such thing actually be established?

Wouldn't the rational path be to take the data constituting the evidence for "violation" of some law as actually constituting evidence refuting the alleged law? Aren't natural laws by definition inviolable—if they are violated, they aren't laws.

But the presupposition that natural laws cannot be violated entails the claim that there cannot be agents who are above the laws of the purely material realm. That rather substantial (not to mention empirically problematic) *metaphysical* pronouncement may constitute a perfectly legitimate position. But it is certainly not a rationally obligatory position. In fact, that laws are inviolable may not even be a scientifically obligatory position. It is at least in principle possible that some specific theory (or putative law) might be so deeply entrenched within our scientific picture of reality (or even within the broader "scientific worldview," or even within our inbuilt structures of cognition) that abandoning it would come at simply too high a price, and that our science itself could more easily survive admission that that law had in fact been violated (with the implication of supernatural contranomic intervention) than it could abandonment either of the theory (or putative law) at issue or the specific data.[9] At least in principle, acceptance of contranomicity may be permissible in the right sort of circumstances.

How might such a circumstance go? Suppose that we had an apparently ordinary chunk of uranium ore. Suppose further that it began triggering clicks on our decay detectors that contained messages in Morse code—and perhaps even engaged in Morse conversations with us.[10] We would, naturally, immediately suspect the nearest graduate assistant of having tampered with the detector (meaning, of course, that we recognized prima facie evidences of design in this case).[11] But suppose that the best efforts of the best experts on Earth established not only that the ore was otherwise perfectly ordinary but that the detector was in perfect working order. We would likely be forced at least to the conclusion that agent causal activity—causal activity of a sort forbidden by most current theory—was involved. Given the belief common among physicists that quantum mechanics is the best scientific theory ever developed (and the consequent perfectly natural reluctance to junk it), we might eventually conclude that the communicating agent involved had overridden natural law to generate the communication.[12] Ruling that option out on, for example, definitional grounds would (ironically) be to insist on giving up our best *empirical* science—quantum mechanics—in order to protect a favored *philosophical* view of the character of natural law

I am not arguing that anyone is rationally forced to concede anything contranomic in this case. Protecting a favored philosophical conception of natural law by abandoning our best science and speculating that the (unknown) agent is harnessing some (unknown) process by some (unknown) means in order to communicate is at least potentially defensible.[13] But abandoning our best science and denying contranomicity would hardly be logically obligatory, much less a scientifically established obligation.

Gaps

In each of the above cases, identification of the agency as supernatural depends upon the implicit claim that neither nature alone nor finite agent activity is causally or explanatorily adequate for the phenomenon in question. Those conditions constitute the defining characteristics of God-of-the-gaps explanations—explanations that appeal to supernatural activity, on grounds of allegedly otherwise unbridgeable explanatory gaps in broadly scientific accounts of relevant phenomena. As noted earlier, such arguments have no formal logical problems. After all, if neither nature nor finite agency can produce some phenomenon inarguably before us, then supernatural agency is about the only option left. But despite that, such explanations are generally seen as so obviously illegitimate that merely labeling an explanation as "God of the gaps" is often taken to constitute an unanswerable refutation of it.

Rational Legitimacy

But *illegitimate* is a relative term. Suppose it is granted for the moment that appeal to supernatural agency is scientifically impermissible. That does not imply that such supernatural explanations are incorrect. It does not even imply that such explanations are rationally illegitimate unless one holds the positivist philosophical position that *rational* and *scientific* are coextensive. But no defense of that philosophical position ever given has withstood critical scrutiny. And the fact that in demanding scientific justification for everything rational this philosophical edict is self-defeating is among the lesser of its defects.

In fact, it is fairly evident that the concepts *rational* and *scientific* cannot be coextensive. If there are boundaries of scientific legitimacy, those boundaries are philosophically—not scientifically—defined. Thus, if it is rational to accept some specific position concerning boundaries of scientifical legitimacy, then of necessity the realm of the rational extends beyond the realm of the scientific. So, if it is rationally legitimate to claim that supernatural explanations are not scientifically legitimate, then *rational* and *scientific* cannot be coextensive.

Thus, even should it turn out that explanations in the general category of "God of the gaps" are scientifically illegitimate, and even should it turn out that recognition of supernatural activity or design always involves a God-of-the-gaps appeal in some guise, that by itself is not automatically problematic for the mere rational recognizability of supernatural design.[14]

Scientific Legitimacy

What of the scientific context? The first general point to note is that there is nothing inherently unscientific in the idea of gaps in nature—of things that nature cannot do.

Science, in fact, is littered with impossibility claims. Perpetual motion is impossible, acceleration across the light-speed barrier is impossible, simultaneous determination of energy and position of certain particles to arbitrary degrees of precision is impossible. Every conservation principle is a claim that permanent unbalanced changes in specified parameters are impossible. In fact, every statement of a natural law is logically equivalent to a claim that nature cannot produce certain (contranomic) phenomena. Thus, scientific justification for the claim that nature does not or cannot produce some specific phenomenon turns out to be a routine, unproblematic aspect of scientific activity.

There are, of course, gaps in nature's capabilities that human agents can bridge. Most cases of counterflow and artifactuality are just such cases. There is a gap between nature's capabilities and a diesel bulldozer that human agents can bridge, although nature cannot. Generally, any identification of a phenomenon as artifactual on the basis of counterflow involves an implicit gap argument that since this (counterflow) is something nature would not do, an agent must have had a hand in it. Thus, the basic structure of (finite) gap arguments is suspect only if our recognition of artifactuality is generally illegitimate—which it manifestly is not. It must be recognized, of course, that it is quite possible that there are gaps that nature cannot bridge, and that humans cannot bridge, although other finite agents—for example, aliens—might be able to. In fact, the special case of alien signal recognition in SETI programs differs from everyday earthly gap cases only in depending upon identifying actual signals that neither nature nor we produce, but that other finite agents could.[15] Such cases are, of course, scientifically unproblematic.

Supernatural gap arguments would have an identical logical structure, with merely the added condition that aliens couldn't produce the relevant phenomenon either. In specific cases, we could have scientific justification for thinking that neither nature nor humans could produce the phenomenon in question, and there is no compelling reason for thinking that we could not also have scientific justification for thinking that no alien could produce some given phenomenon either.

Some, of course, would push the normative claim that occurrence of such a phenomenon *ought* to be taken as indicating that science was simply wrong about nature (or us or aliens) being unable to produce that phenomenon, rather than as providing evidence for supernatural activity. And historically, that has indeed often turned out to be the rational path. The discovery of pulsars, initially suspected by some astronomers as alien signal sources, ultimately resulted in changes in our scientific conception of what nature could and couldn't do. But that type of response is, again, not rationally obligatory for every possible case.

So if God-of-the-gaps explanations are *scientifically* illegitimate, it will have to be solely due to their reference to the supernatural—not because their logical structure violates any other canon of science or rationality. Whether or not and why such reference might be properly forbidden within science will be taken up later.

Conclusion

Whether employing resources consistent with or in contravention of natural law, a supernatural agent clearly has the capability of producing phenomena exhibiting properties that permit unproblematic recognition of those phenomena as both artifactual and designed (e.g., the factory on Neptune). In some of those cases, identification of the agent involved as supernatural may not be possible. But there can in principle be instances where identifying the agent involved as supernatural is at least rationally defensible, whether or not that identification can be legitimately acknowledged within science itself.

5

IDENTIFYING SUPERNATURAL DESIGN: SECONDARY MARKS

The conclusion of the previous chapter is that a supernatural agent could produce phenomena which themselves exhibited recognizable indications of both counterflow and designedness, and that acknowledging such designedness would be rationally legitimate. However, the most difficult cases still remain—cases *in nature* where key familiar means of identification fail because relevant agent activity and counterflow are either invisible or completely absent.

Invisible Activity

With either finite or supernatural activity, so long as the produced phenomena themselves carry primary marks, any hiddenness of the actual agent activity has no consequences for recognition either of designedness or of the fact that there *is* agent activity. The situation is very different, however, in cases where not only is there no visible agent activity, but where the results themselves exhibit no primary clues to either artifactuality or designedness. That is typically the situation we face regarding phenomena of nature. Natural phenomena typically do not exhibit diesel bulldozer type counterflow marks, and if there is direct supernatural activity within the processes and phenomena of nature, it may thus not appear to be directly visible. There are two relevant basic possibilities here. It may be that while there is supernatural agent activity—and counterflow—within nature, the activity is unobservable and produces no primary marks. Or it may be that there is no supernatural activity *within* nature and thus no counterflow and no counterflow marks, primary or otherwise.[1]

One further preliminary distinction is necessary here. Suppose that life on earth began with the supernatural de novo creation of the first cell. Life and living organisms would thus not be products of unaided nature. But we would still consider life (and descendant living things) to be parts of nature—to be natural in a sense in which the Eiffel Tower is not—and biology would still be classified as a natural science. Phenomena that are in this sense intuitively part of nature, but that have a component of (supernatural) agent intervention within the existing flow of history and are thus not products of unaided nature, I will call "natural artifacts" or "natrifacts." This is, I think, the category Newton was suggesting in the following:

> Also the *first* contrivance of those very *artificial* parts of animals, the eyes, ears, brain, muscle, heart, lungs, midriff, glands, larynx, hands, wings, swimming bladders, *natural* spectacles, and other organs of sense and motion . . . can be the effects of nothing else than the wisdom and skill of a powerful ever-living Agent [my emphasis].[2]

Note that Newton places natural lenses on the list of artificial parts, due to the direct creation of their first instances. All those things, viewed as being parts of nature which are nonetheless the descendants of progenitors directly created by supernatural agent activity, would be natrifacts.

Invisible Agent Activity, Counterflow, but No Primary Marks

Supernatural or finite agent activity can produce results which do not in themselves exhibit any primary marks at all. For instance, human genetic engineering activity might produce organisms whose partially artifactual character would be completely undetectable to scientists far in the future when all identifiable traces of human activity in this century were gone. Those organisms might be things nature could have and (in the right circumstances) very well might have produced (such as the recently engineered bioluminescent tobacco plant). The agent activity would be (temporally) invisible, and the results—the descendant organisms—would bear no tip-offs to their engineered origin. In any such case there would indeed be counterflow in originating conditions or productive processes but that fact would be completely unrecoverable. Similar situations could result from supernatural agency constructing the first cell or the first generation of some "natural" phylum.

As noted earlier, there are two categories of agent activity uniquely available to a supernatural agent—contranomic agency and supernatural creative agency. Each of these categories has special potential for generating deliberately produced design lacking all primary marks. In the first case, such marks might be missing because the primary marks that would otherwise have been produced are contranomically hidden or prevented. That absence would itself constitute counterflow—albeit of a nonprimary and (perhaps recursively) hidden type.[3]

Invisible Agent Activity, No Counterflow, No Primary Marks

The other category of supernatural agent activity is of more significant interest. It is evident that a supernatural agent in creating a cosmos de novo could deliberately select law structures, physical constants, and primordial initial conditions (quantity, character, and distribution of matter and energy, for instance) with the specific intent that the natural, unaided development of that system eventually produce some specified phenomenon, system or structure. (The combination of laws, constants, and primordial initial conditions I will refer to as the *initial structure* or the *initiating structure* of nature.)

Some qualifications are of course necessary. For instance, a supernatural agent might not necessarily have a completely free hand in the precosmic selection. Principles of logic might preclude some selections. Axiological or moral principles might preclude others. Or a supernatural being might work within the background of some "hyperphysics" that constrained choices defining any physical cosmos.[4] For instance, a prevailing hyperphysics might render impossible an initiating structure which, if left to operate on its own independently of any further agent activity (finite or supernatural), would in due time produce an exact duplicate of the CERN particle accelerator.[5] But still, the possible scope of realizable results would be huge. For instance, if evolutionary theory is correct there was some selectable initial structure from which it was possible for human beings to result.[6]

But the crucial implication for present concerns is that any normal, deliberately designed phenomenon intentionally produced by means of primordial, creational choices, would have in its postprimordial history no agent activity, no supernatural agent intervention into history or nature, and no nomic discontinuities. It would be completely natural—and not just natrifactual—in the sense of being produced solely by purely natural historical processes. (We might term such a phenomenon whose natural antecedents track back to primordial structures, *pronatural*.) The first significant consequence is that since counterflow is defined *against* the background context of nature, any such deliberately intended, designed, pronatural phenomenon would neither exhibit nor involve any counterflow at all, either primary or otherwise, either in itself or within its cosmic ancestry.

So being pronatural (produced unaided by nature) does not preclude something also being a deliberately intended result of deliberately undertaken activity (primordial creative activity). Conversely, that something is a product of deliberate supernatural design does not imply nomic discontinuity or gaps in nature, nor does it imply intervention (much less evidence of intervention) within nature. The only relevant agent activity might be the creative activity that defined nature to begin with. And if the cosmos itself being deliberately designed to produce specific results is a possibility, there is no obvious justification for a priori stipulations that empirical evidence of such designedness is either impossible or rationally illegitimate. (Any such evidence will not involve counterflow, but that is a different matter.)

The reason there is no counterflow in the pronatural case is, of course, because counterflow is defined against the context of nature, and in the precosmic context there would as yet be no nature for counterflow to be defined against. Still, there might be initiating structures which, although obviously not contrary to what nature would do (there being yet no nature at all), might nonetheless be of a sort which would not become the foundation of subsequent nature were it not for agent activity. It is at least possible that we might extrapolate back to the initiating structures of the cosmos, and discover them to be in some sense "artificial." So it might be that although prior to the instituting of nature it would be false that:

> pre-nature if undisturbed would establish initial structure S as the foundation of nature

thus precluding any counterflow in the establishing of S, it might nonetheless be true that

> initial structure S would not plausibly end up as the foundation of nature except through the action of an intelligent agent

An initial structure that met this latter condition we might define as exhibiting *quasi counterflow* and to be *quasi natrifactual.*[7] That the initiating structure of the cosmos is quasi natrifactual is in effect the underlying intuition of some interpretations of cosmological anthropic principles.

Brief Comparisons

The previous two categories—the natrifactual and the pronatural—will have some important characteristics in common, but will differ in significant ways as well. They will be similar in that both types can be instances of designedness. If designed, both will have characteristics that track back to supernatural agent activity somewhere. Both will typically lack primary marks of agent activity, and thus any evidence of designedness or agent activity will typically consist of something other than primary marks.

But the two will differ in key ways. Although both will have characteristics that track back to supernatural agent activity, in the first case that activity will be within history, and in the second the activity will be primordial. In the first case, the activity will involve (invisible) postprimordial intervention, in the second the activity will involve selection of initiating structures. The natrifactual will always involve (often unidentifiable) counterflow, the pronatural will have no counterflow, invisible or otherwise. In the natrifactual case, it is possible that secondary marks may be results of the intervention, and they thus may constitute counterflow evidences (even if not always recognizable as such). It is in that case at least possible that secondary marks constitute visible counterflow, even in the absence of primary marks. With the pronatural, secondary marks cannot be evidences of or results of counterflow, since there is no counterflow in those cases.

Some Implications

There is a widely held, vague supposition that the discovery that a phenomenon is purely natural removes any prospect of its being designed. That something is a product of unaided nature (pronatural) does entail that its history does not involve any intervention into the historical course of the cosmos (i.e., that it is neither artifact nor natrifact). But since both the pronatural and the natrifactual can be intended results of agent activity deliberately aimed at producing the manifested patterns, the distinction between them is not one of presence or absence of designedness. Discovering a wholly natural process for producing some phenomenon in nature entails only that *if* it is designed, the relevant agent activity is primordial.

This distinction between design resulting from intervention and design produced by the unaided outworking of initiating structures has an extremely long history. Bacon, for instance:

> God . . . doth accomplish and fulfil his divine will [by ways] not immediate and direct, but by compass; not violating Nature, which is his own law upon the creation.[8]

And in Whewell one finds explicit recognition of some of the implications—for example, that discovering purely natural processes for producing phenomena does not entail absence of design, but would involve a shift in the location of agent activity:

> We have shown, we trust, that the notion of design and end is transferred by the researches of science, not from the domain of our knowledge to that of our ignorance, but merely from the region of facts to that of laws.[9]

It is worth noting that both of the above quotes predate 1859. Contrary to common myth, this move was not simply an ad hoc attempt at salvaging some bit of design while in forced retreat from Darwin.[10]

Recognizing Design Without Primary Marks

In the absence of any primary marks, there are relatively few means by which designedness could be identified. One of the possibilities is agent-initiated communication. Since design nearly always entails agent activity somewhere, it might be open to the agent in question simply to reveal to us the fact that some particular phenomenon was designed by that agent.[11] It cannot plausibly be maintained that a supernatural agent *couldn't* tell us that life, for example, was a deliberately designed phenomenon.[12] Another possibility is that we might have the ability to directly perceive designedness in some natural phenomena. (Whewell, Reid, and others held this position.)[13] Although there are important features of interest in both those views, I will not pursue them further at the moment.

Bridge properties—From Artifactuality to Designedness

As argued earlier, recognition of finite design nearly invariably begins with (often implicit) recognition of artifactuality, which depends in turn upon (often intuitive) counterflow identification made typically on the basis of primary marks. Counterflow and artifact recognition provide the context for identification of designedness—an identification that follows so closely on the heels of recognition of artifactuality that we typically do not explicitly distinguish the two.[14]

But they are distinct. Compare an idly, inattentively whittled stick with a stick carved in detailed resemblance of the main tower of the Rouen Cathedral. Both sticks are recognizable artifacts, and both obviously have properties necessary for recognition of artifactuality. But we would make a further judgment of intentional designedness in the second case. Evidently, some special properties underlie that identification of designedness—properties absent in the first case.

What are the properties that can support the shift in recognition from mere artifactuality to designedness? In general, they seem to be the secondary marks—complexity, functionality, adjustment of means to ends, or beauty, elegance, simplicity, and the like. But why those particular properties? What is it about complexity that generates confidence that we are seeing not merely artifactuality but deliberate designedness in an artifact which is complex and intricate (even if we have no idea what any purpose, function, or intention might be)? What is it about elegance that underlies our suspicion that an elegant artifact is not just an artifact, but is deliberately designed?

Properties that can support a shift in recognition from mere artifactuality (or natrifactuality) to designedness obviously supply something that closes the gap between the two. Since the basic difference between artifactuality and designedness is that the agent activity involved in artifactuality must be intentionally aimed at producing (mind-correlative) pattern, these *bridge properties* must provide evidence of intentionality and mind correlativeness in the artifact.

Secondary marks provide that necessary additional evidence because they represent properties that would virtually never result accidently from casual, unmindful, agent activity. A daydreaming whittler may produce something recognizably artifactual, but will never make the astonished discovery that while paying no attention whatever he or she has inadvertently whittled a detailed model of the main tower of the Rouen Cathedral. Anyone doing that had their mind on their business.

In the context of recognizable finite agent activity, then, secondary marks carry design implications. The same holds true in the context of supernatural agent activity.

For example, suppose that it was discovered that eyes could not have developed by natural processes and that supernatural agent activity was thus involved in their origin. On the basis of their complexity, functionality, intricacy, and other such properties, we would reasonably conclude that the supernatural agent activity that had originated them was not just casual and accidental, but that eyes were products not only of agent activity but of design.[15]

Design evidences can be extremely sensitive to agent activity contexts. The degree of sensitivity is at least suggested by the following case involving finite agent artifacts. Beyond some level of primitiveness, genuine stone hand axes are difficult to distinguish from stones shaped and chipped by natural processes—rockslides, freezing, wildfires, and the like. But when an ambiguous stone is found, if some group of hominids believed to have had hand axe capabilities was known to have operated in the area during the right prehistoric period, the plausibility of tentatively identifying the particular stone as a hand axe is increased, even in the complete absence of any really definitive marks. Thus, even the reasonable possibility of agent activity affects the epistemic potential of otherwise ambiguous marks.

Design Relevance

In the above cases, secondary marks exhibited their evidential force for designedness within the context of recognized artifactuality. But it is surely, in principle, possible for there to be properties that constitute evidence of design independently of any such context—properties that are evidentially relevant to questions of design even outside the context of artifactuality. I wish to contend that any property which *by its mere addition to a context of artifactuality* comes to constitute evidence of deliberate design, is *design-relevant simpliciter* in the sense of itself constituting some evidence for design even outside that context. In short, I take the following *Principle of Design Relevance* (PDR) to be true:

> *PDR:* any bridge property is design-relevant simpliciter

The following considerations may heighten the plausibility of PDR. Suppose that we are given a full description of the physical means and mechanisms by which the parts of a watch are formed and arranged. Still, there is something further about the watch ensemble that requires explanation. Explaining how the parts were produced and united leaves something—the obvious designedness of the watch—unaccounted for.[16] The explanation would be clearly incomplete. (We would of course normally fill that incompleteness with agent activity and intent.) Suppose now that the explanation for the formation and arrangement of the parts tracked (uninterrupted by any direct agent activity) back to the Big Bang. Why would that render the explanation of the formation and arrangement of the parts a now complete explanation? There seems no reason whatever to think that where an explanation of *a*, *b* and *c* does not constitute a complete explanation for *A*, that some alternative explanation for exactly the same *a*, *b*, and *c* *would* somehow constitute a complete explanation of *A*.[17]

Now consider a bridge property. Bridge properties in the context of artifactuality are best accounted for by design. Assume that phenomenon *A* is an artifact, has physical characteristics *a*, *b*, and *c*, plus bridge property *d*, and that *a*, *b*, and *c* are the properties indicating artifactuality. *A* being an artifact means roughly that it has a history essentially involving agent activity somewhere, and that history plus *d* implies that any explanation not including design is incomplete, *d* being a bridge property. Suppose now that we give *A* an alternative history in which production of *a*, *b*, *c*, and *d* do not involve agent activity and *a*, *b*, and *c* no longer signal artifactuality. None of the basic, physical, structural properties of *A* are any different than before, when the presence of *d* constituted evidence for designedness, and when any explanation for *A* that omitted design would have been an incomplete explanation. Why, given *A*'s *indistinguishability* from before, should its altered *past* change the evidential status of *d*? But if it does not, then PDR stands.[18]

It is important to note that the principle says nothing whatever concerning the strength of the evidential support for designedness provided by a bridge property outside the agent activity context.[19] Something constituting powerful evidence in the context of agent activity might be quite weak beyond that context. All that PDR claims is that the property would still have some evidential content.[20] For instance, if we knew that eyes were produced by agent activity, we would never place them in the "idly whittled stick" category. According to PDR, the characteristics of eyes that would make it reasonable to believe them to be deliberately designed, were they known to be direct creations of a supernatural agent, would be at least relevant to the question of their designedness even if we had a completely natural account of their origin and character.[21] In slightly different terms, if it were reasonable on the evidence to accept eyes as deliberately designed (and not merely natifacts), were they known to be results of supernatural intervention, it would also be reasonable on the evidence to accept that they might be results of deliberately designed initiating structures. (Again, PDR does not suggest that the reasonable degree of acceptance would be the same in both cases.)[22]

Judging from popular discussions concerning the effect of Darwin's work on design cases in general, it is apparently often believed that the evidential force for design that a characteristic exhibits as a bridging property is always greater than any evidential force it would exhibit as design relevant simpliciter. Thus, discovery of a relevant natural process would weaken the case for design in nature. But I do not know of any actual attempts to show that, and it is not completely obvious that it is true.[23] Again, such discovery would seem to undercut most design arguments involving supernatural intervention, but that can be taken as ruling out design only if one mistakenly holds that design requires intervention.[24]

Recognizing Design in Nature

Secondary Marks as Counterflow

Design advocates sometimes cite secondary marks as indirect evidence of counterflow. For instance, although the eye does not exhibit the hard counterflow visible in diesel bulldozers, it is sometimes argued that the integrated and operative complexity it does exhibit could not have been produced by unaided nature. Furthermore, secondary marks of this sort often involve extremely mind-correlative characteristics—for example, intricacy and tight means/end constraints, aesthetic properties, apparent purpose, and the like.[25]

Do secondary marks constitute evidence of counterflow? That is equivalent to asking whether or not unaided nature could or would generate the requisite complexity and other secondary marks. That is a scientific question, and I am not sure how it should be answered. Fortunately, whether or not secondary marks are evidences of design does not depend upon whether or not unaided nature could or would produce them. If PDR is correct, then if they would constitute evidence for design if produced by agent intervention—that is, as counterflow—then they will also constitute evidence (of some degree) for design if produced by the outworkings of nature.

The importance of PDR is that with respect to designedness itself, it allows us to bypass the question of exactly what nature's capabilities in relevant respects might be. That is quite fortunate, since scientific theories concerning what nature can or cannot do have been historically unstable. It also allows discussion of issues concerning design to be discussed completely independently of any God-of-the-gaps diversions. Another way of reading PDR is that if something would constitute evidence of design in the context of some presumed gap in nature, then it will also constitute at least some degree of evidence of design even if the gap in question gets closed naturally. So whereas presence or absence of gaps might be relevant to the evidential strength of some characteristic, it has no bearing upon the fundamental status *as evidence* of that characteristic.[26]

Recognizing Pronatural Design

Once outside the context of recognized agent activity, how much epistemic force do secondary marks really have? In a context of recognized artifactuality, secondary marks do not have to provide any part of the case for agent activity—that is already given by the artifactuality. But design entails not only pattern but agent activity directly or indirectly generating that pattern, and if secondary marks are to provide a design case outside an artifactual context, they presumably must bear the entire evidential burden alone. Can they do it?

Initial prospects might not look promising. One intuitive conception of *complexity* involves the precise intermeshing and coordination of multiple causal factors in some phenomenon. Traditional design cases frequently cite that conception as a (even the) key evidence of design in nature.[27] But does complexity in nature in that sense really imply design? Recall the prehistoric natural reactor at Oklo (discussed in chapter 1). That incident exhibited enormous complexity of the indicated type, yet few have any inclination to see it as designed. Another concept of complexity involves the quantity of information required to describe relevant aspects of the relevant phenomenon. Does complexity in nature in that sense imply design? Consider the three-dimensional geometry at a molecular scale of the top six inches of a large natural beach. The complexity there in this information sense is arbitrarily high, but few would have any inclination to see that geometry as designed.[28]

Others have taken extreme improbability as a sign of designedness in nature. But prospects there don't look particularly promising either. The probability of a particular proton formed ten minutes after and thirty kilometers from the epicenter of the Big Bang currently being exactly four meters above the top of the Eiffel Tower is vanishingly small—but its happening would raise no reasonable suspicion of agent activity having brought it about. Much less would that wild improbability raise suspicions of deliberate intent.[29]

Prospects for recognizing designedness through secondary marks indeed look dark. In the context of identifiable artifacts (or natrifacts), that artifactuality by itself automatically establishes some of the crucial conditions for design—the existence of an active agent, for instance. In such a context, design is a reasonable candidate explanation for various observed phenomena. But in a context of purely natural phenomena, the secondary marks do not constitute counterflow. In fact, it is they that are supposed to establish not only the designedness, but the crucial necessary conditions as well.

The question that must be addressed is: Can they bear that weight?

6

DESIGN IN NATURE

There are basically three possible ways secondary marks could be linked to super-natural design. First, as seen earlier, secondary marks in finite agent counterflow (artifactuality) contexts are typically indications of design. That would hold for the supernatural cases as well. In a context of supernatural agent counterflow activity, secondary marks would again typically indicate design. Such cases would involve nomic gaps, and are frequent foci of creationist discussions.[1]

Second, secondary marks in the context of primordial quasi counterflow (or developing out of that context) would also typically constitute rational indications of design. In general, given the character of secondary marks, any evidence that agent activity is crucially involved in their production would constitute rational grounds for suspecting designedness.[2] Even though there is no counterflow involved in primordial selection of initiating structures, any evidence that initiating structures were carefully organized would be at least some grounds for suspecting agent involvement. This is, again, the foundational intuition of many cosmological anthropic and fine-tuning arguments.

Third, secondary marks might on their own constitute some evidence of design even in the absence of any other indications of agent activity. On this view, secondary marks might constitute evidence of design totally independent of the question of how those characteristics were in fact produced. This is the position of some current Intelligent Design advocates.[3] And this position is the focus of the present chapter.

Secondary Marks and Mind Correlativity

As noted at the end of the previous chapter, such secondary marks as complexity, apparent adjustment of means to ends, and extreme improbability do not by them-selves look initially promising as design evidences. Evidence of deliberate design must be evidence of intent to produce *mind-correlative pattern*. Many cases of the most incredible complexity and the wildest improbability stir no intuitions of either intent or mind correlativeness at all. But in other cases, secondary marks do initially appear to have some evidential relevance. We will begin with a few examples, then try to sort out what might distinguish the various cases.

Cases: First Set

Some years ago, the far side of the moon was mapped for the first time. Like the near side, the surface of the far side seemed to be just a random jumble of craters of varying size. The complexity of that jumble of craters was extreme in a number of senses. For instance, the amount of information required to fully describe in fine detail the sizes, shapes, locations, overlaps, wall surface contours, and radial ejecta marks would have been huge. And that information would not have been compressible into one or a few neat equations either.[4] Furthermore, the prior probability of the cosmos producing precisely that array of cratering was virtually zero.

It was noted earlier that in general, secondary marks in the context of agent activity constitute evidence of designedness. But the "in general" qualification is crucial. Despite the improbability, tight constraints, and complexity, the crater jumble would not elicit any strong sense of designedness, even were that jumble known to be the result of agent activity.[5] The jumble, even if produced by an agent, would likely be put into the "inattentively whittled stick" category.

Now, had some agent wished to deliberately produce precisely that array of cratering by choosing appropriate initiating structures and having the array develop naturally over the next few billion years, the constraints on the initial structures would have been almost impossibly tight and adjustment of means to ends would have been phenomenally demanding.[6] Initial constraints had to fit through a vanishingly small window of opportunity. Change one quark one millisecond after the Big Bang, and the exact actual crater jumble perhaps (maybe even probably) wouldn't have occurred. Improbabilities, constraints, adjustments of means to ends just about don't get tighter than that. The feat, if possible at all, would have been utterly stunning.[7]

But despite complexity, despite improbability, despite the demanding means required to the given end, despite the fact that if planned it would have been a magnificent achievement, the moon crater jumble in itself does not seem to nudge us at all toward a design explanation. In fact, the temptation is to say that there is nothing of significance in the crater layout to be explained. That denial is simply an intuitive way of claiming that there is nothing specially mind correlative in the crater distribution. The conjunction of the explanations for each individual crater exhausts the explanatory field. The craters do not constitute a larger ensemble having characteristics which in their turn require an explanation not simply reducing to that conjunction.[8]

However, suppose that the first photos had revealed not a jumble of craters but a pattern of uniformly sized craters exactly at each intersection of a two-dimensional Cartesian grid. We might—just barely—contrive to believe that some natural process had generated that result. Perhaps some large cosmic crystal exploded, the particle at each vertex becoming a gravitational seed in its journey through space, the resultant clumps of matter slamming into the moon and creating the pattern in question.[9] But regardless of whatever the causal history might be, the grid displays markedly more mind correlativeness than the jumble.

Suppose now that the first photographs had revealed a pattern of cratering clearly spelling out "John 3:16." Here, *even if there were a natural explanation for each individual crater,* the craters would constitute an ensemble of a sort for which the conjunction of the individual crater explanations would seem inadequate as an explanation. In this case, although we might not appeal to supernatural activity, we would not seriously doubt the involvement of agents of some sort.[10] Here is intrinsic mind correlativity irrespective of means of production.

What are the differences between these moon crater cases? Objective complexity of crater distribution in the first and third cases might be of comparable degrees. And it is not clear that the probabilities of the precise actual cratering, of the grid, and of the message pattern are significantly different. (Indeed, it is unlikely that we have any reliable clue at all as to what the respective probabilities even are—except slim.) In any case, enormous complexity, wild improbability, and incredibly tight production constraints seem to have no implications for designedness here, since each is essentially identical in all the above cases whether design is obvious or only reasonably plausible or clearly absent.

So what is the intuitive plausibility or implausibility of design tracking? It seems to be tracking a special sort of mind correlativity. And once we see that special correlativity, our conceptions of the cases are driven by that recognition, regardless of improbabilities, causal histories, or anything else.[11] A fundamental match between cognition and nature is necessary for a genuine scientific understanding of any phenomenon, but in the crater grid case and especially in the John 3:16 case, correlativity has deepened. There is a particularly stark mind correlation—a *mind affinity*—in these cases which goes beyond that involved simply in understanding some natural phenomenon or structure. Exactly what is the nature of that affinity?

Mind Affinity

I believe that there are several varieties of mind affinity. Although they are related in various ways, they differ in evidential strength, in degree of design relevance, and in other ways as well. Following are brief descriptions of what I take to be the key varieties, in descending order of evidential strength.

Conceptual Content

The pattern in the John 3:16 case incorporates some specific, particularly evident *conceptual content.* There is something in that pattern, a specifically expressed substance, that the mind grasps in the special fundamental way that minds grasp content. Even if we were able to trace the causal chain back to the Big Bang, we would conclude not that no mind was involved, but that the initial conditions of the Big Bang were intentionally structured. And there simply would be no serious chance that a mind was not involved there, regardless of what the causal history might have been. Given the character of the phenomenon, we see partway into that mind, and recognize it as mind because of the specific structure and conceptual content that we find the phenomenon generating in us.

Attractor Patterns

Although not nearly so blatant, the grid case seems to exhibit a type of mind affinity which is at least in the same neighborhood. Agents directly recognize and agent awareness gravitates to particularly obvious, readily evident patterns. Such patterns in effect constitute *attractors* for minds in a way that, say, the roughly 104-degree angle between the O and the Hs in a water molecule does not, despite the mathematization of that latter relation and its importance for understanding some of the molecule's characteristics. That is an indication that the special mind correlativity in question is deeper than that required simply for scientific understanding of natural phenomena. Historically, such attractor patterns were often specially marked out as being, for example, "pleasing to the mind."[12]

It could be argued that such patterns could be generated without any mind involvement anywhere even in their primordial history, and that claim would not in this case be as prima facie implausible as would be the same claim concerning the first category. That suggests a weaker evidential force, but that is very different from absence of evidential force.

Specific Isomorphisms

An artist might deliberately and painstakingly produce an exact replica of an urban garbage heap, perhaps as some sort of social commentary. Although both the original and the replica would be unmistakable artifacts exhibiting undeniable counterflow, and although the replica would be an intentionally produced artifact, neither of them would *on its own* exhibit any properties that would constitute marks of design in any straightforward sense. The replica garbage heap would be deliberately produced in accord with an idea, and might be said in that sense to be designed; but the idea itself would not carry design in the more fundamental sense. However, the deliberately produced isomorphism between the original and the replica would exemplify mind correlativeness, and is why the term *design* would be appropriate in this case.[13]

Means/End Adjustments

Agents, nearly by definition, act toward preselected ends, and typically employ instrumental means in the pursuit of those ends. Adapting and implementing the appropriate instrumentality is simply one of the primary things rational agents do. Of course, to be effective the means chosen have to be appropriately adjusted to the end. That this adjustment has a mind-correlative character is evidenced by the fact that we typically draw inferences concerning the adjusting mind from the character and quality of the adjustments employed.[14]

However, the evidential force of a bare instrumental relationship between a starting point and some resultant point is minimal. Virtually every actual phenomenon has been brought about by a long, wildly improbable sequence of events, causes, and intersectings, and had any of that sequence gone even slightly differently the phenomenon would not have occurred. Had any of a billion things gone differently from the Big Bang to the present, the exact moon crater jumble would not be there.[15] Down to some extremely fine level of detail, the instrumental means have thus been precisely those necessary to generate exactly that consequence. But that fact—that precise instrumentality—does not seem to suggest design.

The problem is that we tend to doubt that the crater jumble was really an end. Despite the narrowness of the path from Big Bang to crater jumble, despite the exact requirements for *that* jumble being realized, that does not strike us as constituting a genuine adjustment of means to an end. Thus, although means/end adjusting is both a characteristic agent activity and is deeply mind correlative, a key requirement for using means/ends adjustments as evidence for design is the identifying of the outcome as actually being an end—indeed, typically a preselected end. How that might be done will be discussed shortly.

Aesthetics

One very characteristic activity of agents (humans, anyway) is the appreciation of beauty, elegance, and the like. Not only do we experience and appreciate it, but we sometimes attempt to produce it, and often attempt to incorporate some aesthetic dimension into things we are doing for other reasons entirely. In fact, the aesthetic sometimes seems to have an attractor effect similar to that discussed above, and exhibits a similar type of mind correlativeness. Were we to land on some alien planet and to discover that in some places flowers were in groupings where colors complemented, fragrances blended in particularly nice ways, shapes were set off attractively, accents were provided by naturally textured stones, and so forth, we might reasonably begin to wonder if it was all intentional.

Of course, aesthetics is tricky. It is possible to argue that it is all subjective, that "perceiving" beauty involves so high a degree of agent input as not to qualify as genuine observation, that aesthetic experience is not genuinely cognitive, and so forth. It can even be argued that the aesthetic is merely the conscious presentation of some hidden evolutionary lessons learned by our primate ancestors—that pleasant aesthetic experiences are merely how evolutionarily useful stimuli triggered by various phenomena around us present themselves to our awareness. On this view, just as a need for fluids presents itself to us as a prickling in the back of the throat, just as the shapes of certain molecules present themselves to us as the smell of coffee, certain evolutionarily learned assurances concerning our environment present themselves to us as aesthetic pleasure.

I think that those claims are not prima facie silly. But the fact that aesthetic sensibilities have played an important, substantive role within science itself prompts two brief responses.[16] First, that genuine, successful science has employed aesthetic sensitivities provides some presumption that (a) aesthetic perceptions are at least indirectly linked to something real, (b) that there is some (perhaps buried) cognitive aspect to the aesthetic dimension, and (c) that rejecting the aesthetic out of hand while maintaining a commitment to the legitimacy of science may be problematic.

Second, that aesthetic experiences may be presentations of other, deeper matters may cut several ways. According to some, a genetically based need to propagate presents itself to us emotionally as love. According to others, a resentment of parents or siblings presents itself to us as an inclination to smash things. In similar fashion, it may be that deep mind correlativity sometimes presents itself to us as a perception of theoretical beauty, a sense of an elegance in nature, a feeling of rightness when we get a particular theoretical perspective on some aspect of reality.[17] I'll have a bit more to say about this issue later, but if theoretical beauty is a veiled experience of deep mind correlativity, that plus the fact that aesthetic considerations in science have something of a track record of scientific success might constitute part of the answer to one standard objection to design explanations in science—the objection that design explanations are devoid of any practical scientific content or implications.[18]

Cases: Second Set

Although deep mind correlativity will be a key component of design projects, it is not the whole story. Consider one other set of examples. The "natural reactor" at Oklo was discussed earlier, and it was noted that we know of no reason to suspect either agent activity or design, despite the fact that the initiating and sustaining conditions for the reaction were quite complex. The episode involved multiple causal streams that had to intersect in exactly the right way in the right sequences at the right times, and were hugely improbable as well. (No other such event may ever have occurred in the entire history of the entire cosmos.)

Now compare the following scenarios. First, suppose that Oklo occurred, but had no noteworthy effects at all. Second, suppose that the radiation from Oklo had one effect—it triggered a mutation that resulted in all descendent cockroaches having a slightly tighter curl in their antennae than they otherwise would have had. Third, suppose that the radiation triggered the rise of primates.[19] Finally, suppose that Oklo was at the single precise window of opportunity and triggered the explosion of intelligence in human ancestors, and that without Oklo that wouldn't have happened.[20]

Despite the complexity of the Oklo event, the first case above suggests little if anything concerning design. But the last is a bit different. Was that last just a monumentally lucky (for us) coincidence? A really fortunate accident? Some undiscovered but wholly fortuitous natural necessity? Or was the complicated episode set up *for* the actually produced result? Was that incredibly unlikely and complex event an exquisite preadjustment of means to an end? That is a sensible question to ask, regardless of what we decide the answer is. It is a prima facie plausible question in a way that asking the same question about the cockroach antennae is not.

If there is a progression in the plausibleness of the Oklo cases vis à vis design, what underlies that progression? There may be some differences in probabilities or in some technicalities of complexity, but, as in the moon crater examples, that does not appear to be driving our intuitions here.[21] What is that progression tracking?

The progression is not in any obvious way just a progression in mind correlativeness, as were the crater cases. A natural reactor that curls cockroach antennae does not seem to exert a stronger cognitive tug than a natural reactor that doesn't. Something else is going on here. Recall that something being designed involved agent *intent* to produce some mind-correlative pattern. Perhaps we should look for factors that are *intent relevant*.

That some phenomenon is the sort of thing that agents do (or that an agent would or might do) clearly counts (even if only slightly) in favor of suspicions that perhaps an agent did do it. Now obviously, there are virtually no limits to what an agent might do, if the circumstances are bizarre enough. But we do have some fairly reliable intuitions about what can be reasonably attributed to agents, and about the sorts of things agents do.

William Alston claims that part of the very definition of *personal agent* is "a being that acts in the light of knowledge to achieve purposes, a being whose actions express attitudes and are guided by standards and principles."[22] To act for a purpose is to act deliberately with the intent that the action be instrumental in the realization of a specific *value*. As that suggests, virtually all agent activity is linked to some type of value. Some things we value for their usefulness in promoting the realization of more basic values, but other things we take to have intrinsic value, and it is these latter that are of present concern. Recall the fourth Oklo scenario. The generating of intelligence strikes us as something that an agent might find worth doing. It strikes us so because we see intelligence as something inherently significant in a value sense.[23]

Given the deep connections between (perceived) value and deliberate agent activity, value is frequently a key component of and clue to intent.[24] In the Oklo cases, neither complexity, improbability, instrumentality, nor tight production constraints do much by themselves. And by itself, the bare existence of values may carry little intuitive force. But link improbability or complexity or instrumentality or tight constraints to the production of those values, and they can take on a new significance. When a value is produced by a long, tricky, precarious process, when it is generated and preserved by some breathtaking complexity, when it is realized against all odds, then intent—even design—suddenly becomes a live and reasonable question.[25] And other things being equal, in a given context the degree of reasonableness of a question is an indirect measure of the relevant evidential status of the phenomena prompting the question.

In general, just as secondary marks in concert with artifactuality typically constitute evidence for design (and intent, and purpose), so *secondary marks linked essentially to the production of value* provide similar evidence of design.[26] (Remember that the issue at the moment is simply evidential status—not degree of evidential strength.)

What might the relevant values be? With respect to human agents, a number of categories are recognizable. We value beauty, elegance, and other things of a general aesthetic nature. We value truth, knowledge, understanding, and a variety of other things epistemological. We tend to see an inherent value in life, personhood, and intelligence. Most humans take happiness, peace, freedom, and shalom to be valuable intrinsically.

It can be argued, of course, that values cannot constitute substantive evidence for anything whatever. After all, it might be claimed that values are purely subjective, that they do not mirror any genuine feature of the real world, that they are fundamentally noncognitive, that relevant alleged "experiences" are actually reactions driven by past evolutionary events whose true significance lies in some long-buried fitness enhancement of our primate ancestors, and so forth.

As in the aesthetics case, I shall not unduly worry about such objections further. For one thing, it is not even close to evident that such objections are correct. But more to the present point, the ultimate issue being pursued concerns what is or is not legitimate within science as best we understand what science is. And some values are essential to the operation of science itself, while others constitute key motivations for science and crucial principles underpinning the pursuit of science. (This general topic will be discussed in some detail later.)

In any case, given the perhaps definitive role that value plays in agent activity, identification either of the realization of significant values by nature, or of the maintenance in nature of the essential conditions for such values being realized by other agents, *could* constitute some evidence of design.

Secondary Marks Alone Inadequate

In whatever way mind affinity, values, and such secondary marks as complexity, improbability, and production constraints ultimately work together, it is evident that secondary marks alone just won't do the job of supporting design cases. So long as the deeper factors (e.g., value) are absent, complexity (e.g., the arrangement of sand grains on a beach) will never constitute evidence of design, *no matter how high the degree of complexity or how low the probability.* So long as these deeper factors are absent, improbably tight constraints (e.g., a particular proton from a particular point in the Big Bang being at a specific location above the Eiffel Tower) will never constitute evidence of design *no matter how narrow the instrumental path or how tight the constraints required.*[27]

Neither complexity nor improbability nor tight causal constraints are located on a scale that at some point crosses over into either this deeper mind correlativity, value, or any other crucial factor. They are simply different concepts, and thus merely intensifying them or heightening their degree will in general have no significant evidential consequences for the designedness of phenomena with natural causal histories.[28]

Consider the crater jumble case again. The complexity is enormous. The improbability of exactly that array and all its characteristics being produced is arbitrarily high. The constraints on initiating structures required to get the exact jumble by natural means from the Big Bang are nearly impossibly tight. Yet, we have no suspicion of design at all. Why? Because it exhibits nothing specially attractive to cognition, and nothing of any apparent special value significance.[29] Lacking either sort of feature, it simply does not seem like a preselected end that the actual instrumental means were chosen, shaped, and adjusted for. The same goes for the first Oklo case, and nearly the same goes for the second. The results simply do not seem to be of a significance commensurate with the demanding care that the actual production path would have represented had the actual production path been a deliberate means.[30]

Design Cases

We can now draw some preliminary conclusions concerning phenomena in nature— phenomena produced by natural means, lacking all counterflow and other indications of direct agency. First, in such cases secondary marks such as complexity, improbability, precise instrumentality, tight constraints on production, and so forth, do not by themselves provide strong, obvious evidence for design. Second, patterns and phenomena that exhibit a deep mind correlativity—mind affinity—can constitute varying degrees of evidence for design. In some cases (phenomena with clear conceptual content) the evidence can be extremely powerful. Such evidences are relatively independent of secondary marks, not necessarily in the sense of lacking them but in the sense that the evidential force does not derive from those marks.[31] Third, complexity, improbability, precise instrumentality, or tight production constraints when operating in the service of producing value can constitute evidence for design.[32]

So concerning purely natural phenomena—phenomena produced by nature and in the absence of counterflow:

1. Secondary marks alone (complexity, improbability) generally do not constitute strong design evidence
2. Deep mind correlativity (mind affinity) can constitute evidence (sometimes powerful) for design independent of secondary marks[33]
3. Secondary marks instrumental in production and preservation of value can in conjunction with that value constitute evidence of design

Secondary Marks Again

Regardless of whether they take design intuitions to be legitimate, and regardless of what they identify as the basis of those intuitions, most of those involved in design disputes historically have felt that the kind of complexity and improbability associated with the eye, living organisms, and so forth, demanded some special kind of explanation.[34] (That itself constitutes further indication both of the intuitive evidential power of certain types of complexity, and of its intuitive recognizability as mind correlative.) Responses to that perceived demand have fallen into roughly five basic categories.

a. *direct agent activity.* The basic idea is that unaided nature could not produce such systems, that the existence of such represents gaps in nature, and that direct agent activity is thus the only reasonable—or possible—explanation. This position has been popular among creationists.

b. *indirect agent activity.* The view here is that the extreme mind correlativity of the systems in question requires an ultimate design explanation, that the systems are produced by natural means (no gaps), and that the required agent activity is thus primordial, involving selection of initial structures.

c. *overpowering the odds*. On this view, the chances of unaided nature producing the systems in question are arbitrarily small. However, those odds are swamped by arbitrarily large numbers of trials. This is the solution offered by, e.g., many-universes hypotheses. The complexity or order in question is natural in the sense that no agent activity or preplanning is required for its production, but it is not inevitable or guaranteed by law in any given world. In fact, the overwhelming majority of worlds will not exhibit such complexity. But given the number of trials, the existence of such complexity *in some world or other* is inevitable (and, of course, agents seeking explanations will be in some such worlds).

d. *denying the odds* The idea here is that far from being long shots requiring some specially tailored explanation, relevant order and complexity are the virtually inevitable, utterly normal, highly probable results of emergent processes dictated by fundamental physical laws. That such complexity will arise in spontaneous, law-governed ways (via, e.g., autocatalytic processes, self-organizing criticality) is simply one of the deep rules of nature. This view is associated with, e.g., Stuart Kauffman and other members of the Santa Fe Institute.[35]

e. *eroding the odds*. On this view, high degrees of complex order are produced by a natural selection mechanism which preferentially preserves, accumulates, and propagates tiny increments of complexity which are themselves produced by chance. Improbabilities are neither denied nor swamped— merely sieved by natural selection and outflanked. The most prominant advocate of this position is probably Richard Dawkins.[36]

f. *beating the odds*. With sufficient luck, it is possible to beat huge odds on the first throw. On this view, that is what happened—there is one cosmos, and it just happened by chance to be one of those which not only could but actually would experience the emergence of stability, life, intelligence, etc., against wildly huge odds. In effect, this position provides no real explanation.

The first is widely considered to be scientifically illegitimate, the second to be scientifically irrelevant. The remaining four are frequently advanced as *alternatives* to design, the implicit idea being that if any of them were correct, secondary marks would constitute no evidence for design. Indeed, some argue that the correctness of specific ones of them would provide positive evidence for the absence of design.[37]

But if sheer complexity, improbability, apparent adjustment of means to ends, and the like, have minimal evidential force on their own (as [1] above asserts and as [c]–[f] are frequently taken to imply), why have they historically (and presently) been so popular as bases for design cases? One fairly popular answer is: ignorance historically and blindness presently.

It's not that simple. Although complexity, improbability, and so forth, are usually the explicitly cited bases, that often does not in fact capture the real operative intuitions.[38] For one thing, historical cases almost always tacitly involved value. Whatever the surface focus, the specific examples chosen for discussion almost invariably involved something implicitly considered to be of value (usually something contributing to surviving or flourishing). For another, the explicit focus was often exclusively upon the coming together of a multitude of interacting factors, that complex meshing constituting the evidence for design.[39] But here again, the specific examples told a bit deeper tale. The complexity was not just sheer complication, but typically involved some structure intuitively exhibiting mind correlativity—for example, a particularly elegant way of getting something done or of solving some adaptive or functional problem. In effect, what was actually being endorsed was something like principles [2] and [3] above.[40]

A Special Complexity

But we can go even a bit deeper. The historically most influential cases of complexity were an *operative* complexity, a *functional* complexity.[41] Consider traditional examples, from life itself to "organs of extreme perfection" (as Darwin called them—e.g., the eye) to cells to blood coagulation cascades.[42] In all those cases, there is some kind of active functioning and, typically, there is some kind of active stability—*active* maintenance either of such functionality, or of structures, relationships, or conditions essential for the existence and continuation of such functionality (homeostasis, and not just the static stability of a Martian titanium cube).[43]

Indeed, in the nineteenth century Bridgewater Treatises, the *working together of multiple factors* is sometimes cited as the most basic of design evidences.[44] Paley's examples follow this same pattern.[45] And, of course, the whole area of biological adaptation of means to ends, which has been one extremely (perhaps the most) popular category of evidence, has to do with both active functionality and maintenance (preservation, maintenance of stability).

But a bare complexity of this sort is not yet enough. The solar system is an actively functioning, actively stable, self-correcting system, yet it does not raise intuitions of design to the same degree that life, the eye, or the intricacies of the cell do. What exactly is the difference?

The difference does not initially appear to involve value. The existence and operation of a solar system might have a high value—either because of its intrinsic beauty or as a site for life, or for any number of other reasons of which we might have no idea. But in some intuitive sense, the solar system is not nearly so complex as the eye or a living cell. Evidently, then, what seems to prompt design intuitions in the eye case is not just active functioning and maintenance, and not just complexity, but the two conjoined. And the greater the intricacy and complexity of a functioning, actively stable system, the stronger the intuition. Thus,

4. Active functionality and maintenance of high degrees of stable complexity intuitively suggest design.

But why should this combination raise intuitions so powerfully (as the history of design cases indicates)? I think that the answer is that these sorts of systems suggest both mind correlativity and value (or more generally, purpose). Agents do construct things that function—things that produce intended results, things representing solutions to problems, things adjusted to specific ends.[46] Intentions, solutions, adjustments, and the like, are all indications of mind correlativity. Indeed, pursuit and production of perceived values are among the most basic of the things agents characteristically intend to do. In the context of agent activity, an actively functional and stable system would provide nearly conclusive evidence of deliberate designedness. Given PDR, even outside the context of agent activity, such a system would still constitute some evidence of designedness. Any such system, then, is at least a provisional candidate for designedness.

A candidate system being associated with value would raise the evidential force markedly. But here we run into some possible new difficulties. For value to be of any epistemological significance in the present situation, we have to be able either (a) to reliably identify particular values or (b) to reliably recognize the pursuit of value even when the value pursued is unknown, unidentifiable, or otherwise unrecognized. But if a candidate system within nature is designed, the designer is a supernatural agent. And just as there was earlier no guarantee that we could recognize patterns evident to a supernatural agent, there may be no guarantee that we can recognize some of the values relevant to supernatural agent intentions.

It is perfectly possible that some of what we classify as values really are genuine values—that is, their being objectively valuable is a real truth about the way reality is. Such values might be identifiable even when produced naturally. But would there be any way to recognize the pursuit of value in cases involving values we were unable to identify? It seems clear that in some cases the answer might simply be 'no'.

But other cases might not be completely beyond reach. In the context of agent activity, function is a good indication of—and substantial evidence for—*purpose*. And in the context of agent activity, increasing intricacy and complexity of functional and maintenance structures suggest increasing degrees of care. Degree of care—investment—in structuring, generating, and maintaining, is a reasonable indication of valuing. So *in the context of agent activity*, active functioning and self-maintenance of stable complexity would constitute substantial evidence of care, intent, purposiveness, and designedness, and actual function would provide evidence of what the purpose might be. Indeed, such cases are nearly conclusive in any practical sense.

Would such a system outside the context of agent activity constitute evidence of value pursuit? Two lines would suggest that it would. First, as indicated earlier, the properties of such a system would be design relevant (according to PDR). Given the close connection between designedness and value, evidence for designedness very nearly constitutes evidence for valuedness. Unfortunately, that would not help much in the present case, since value was being sought as support for design. However, it is not entirely implausible to think that a value-oriented version of PDR may be true on its own—a *Principle of Value Relevance*.

PVR: something which is evidence of valuedness in the context of direct agent activity is value-relevant simpliciter.

Although I shall not push PVR further, I believe that it does have some plausibility. Systems of the type described above are indeed the type that a valuing agent would construct in a variety of circumstances. That is not claimed to be in any sense conclusive. The point is merely that consideration of such systems is not just irrelevant to the larger question.

In any case, actively functioning, actively stable, complex systems do exhibit a degree of mind correlativity. Beyond that, many such systems in nature are essentially linked to things we take to be of evident value—life, intelligence, consciousness, and so forth. Furthermore, such systems are perhaps of a value-relevant sort, and that value relevance may be recognizable apart from identifiability of the value in question. If this last is true, then the historical (and present) popularity of these systems as design evidences can be easily understood. Such systems not only exhibit various striking secondary marks (complexity and so forth), which are generally admitted to require some special explanatory attention, but the brand of complexity they exhibit is both mind correlative and plausibly connectable to value (or to the pursuit of value).

Conclusion

With respect to phenomena produced by nature, secondary marks alone do not generally support strong design cases, although secondary marks essentially tied to the production of value may do so. However, due to their plausible suggestions of care, high degrees of active, self-maintaining, functional complexity may constitute plausible design evidence. In any case, different types of mind affinity can in varying degrees generate rationally defensible design positions.

Interim Summation

We now have several preliminary subconclusions. There are several categories in which support for design explanations might legitimately be found.

a. *Counterflow* of a sort not produceable by finite agents would constitute genuine evidence for supernatural agent activity. The addition of some types of mind correlativity or value would evidentially raise such cases from agent activity to deliberate design.

b. If legitimately established, genuine *contranomicity* would constitute evidence of supernatural agent activity. As above, addition of mind correlativity or value would relocate the case into the area of design.

c. Precosmic *initial structuring* (of laws, initial boundary conditions, etc.) could provide evidence for design were such conditions either especially mind-correlative in their own right or instrumental (or essential) in the production of recognizable values (assuming the production of such values to be enormously sensitive to initial structures). Neither counterflow nor contranomicity would be involved, the relevant activity being prior to the laws and structures by which counterflow and contranomicity are defined.

d. Although generally not alone adquate, secondary marks could in some cases partially constitute evidence of design wholly independent of any causal history. This can occur either when phenomena exhibit a particularly evident mind affinity, or when secondary marks are essential to the realization of some evident value. In some special cases, a specific type of secondary mark—an actively functional, actively stable, high complexity—could itself constitute design evidence even in the absence of any link to any recognizable value.

Were (a) or (b) firmly established, the case for agent activity (and the foundation for design) would be powerful indeed. Establishment of (c) would constitute a substantial case for deliberate design. Although in general (d) would provide weaker cases, in some specific instances (e.g., the John 3:16 case), the support for a design explanation would even here be powerful indeed. But even were the cases judged to be relatively weak, that is very different from their being wholly without evidential force.

So design explanations of structures and phenomena in nature *can* be rationally legitimate. Furthermore, concerning some things of which we are presently aware, it is probably *rationally permissible although not evidentially obligatory* to hold either that they represent genuine counterflow, or that although not counterflow, they required initial cosmic structures of a sort that indicates genuine mind affinity. The emergence of life may be among the former, and cosmic anthropic principles are built upon intuitions of the latter.[47] In addition, it is rationally legitimate to take some relevant phenomena as exhibiting genuine values—beauty, life, consciousness. Counterflow, contranomicity, selection of initial structures, and high functional and stable complexity in association with value constitutes significant evidential foundations for design explanations. Again, such conclusions are often not rationally forced, but that does not alter their rational legitimacy or rational permissibility.

Two questions remain. First, how might we assess the strength of the evidence provided? Second, even if design explanations are rationally defensible, are they scientifically permissible? Addressing the first is not my present aim. Evidential force might, for instance, be tied to the precise character and degree of the complexity involved, and determining that is a different project. In some areas, we are still in the process of learning those things. Concerning the second question, it is perfectly possible that certain types of evidence of design meet all relevant criteria of rationality without meeting empirical, evidential, or other criteria of scientific legitimacy. Addressing that question will require preliminary examination of some relevant pieces of philosophy of science, involving just what the criteria of scientific legitimacy might be. It is to such issues we now turn.

III

BOUNDARIES OF SCIENTIFIC LEGITIMACY

7

Beyond the Empirical

There is currently nearly unanimous agreement that reference to the supernatural—and that includes divine intelligent design—is completely out of place in scientific contexts. But the illegitimacy of the supernatural in science certainly wasn't obvious to many major historical figures in science. Some, such as Newton, made explicit reference to divine activity and design in their scientific theorizing, and the theology of others, such as Boyle, Maxwell, Faraday, and Herschel, played formative roles in the shaping of their scientific theories. Obviously, views concerning the boundaries of scientific legitimacy have shifted substantially. What underlay that shift?

The nature and boundaries of scientific legitimacy were neither found carved in stone somewhere, developed purely a priori, nor just always known innately by humans. Rather, conceptions of science, scientific method, and scientific legitimacy that we currently take to be correct have histories and have developed along with science itself. Indeed, the history of science is a history not only of discovery and growing understanding of nature itself, but also of discovery and growing understanding of how to approach nature, of how to put questions to nature, and of how to construe nature's answers. In indirect, complex, and still incomplete ways, human scientists have had to learn from nature herself some of the outlines of how to conduct a viable science of nature. That process is highly indirect and complex because, contrary to the old positivist and inductivist dreams, nature does not speak directly and unequivocally in terms we understand.

It is, of course, widely assumed that what nature does say is said in empirical terms. Thus, insofar as we can manage, our scientific dealings with nature are (at least supposed to be) empirically based. That empiricalism developed historically as an important component of scientific method—that is, of science's deliberately structured attempt to hear nature's voice as free of distortion as possible. But exactly why was something as formal as a deliberate method needed?

Subjectivity-Proofing Science

Scientific method has historically often been held in extremely high regard. That method appeared to allow us to dig out the hidden secrets of the universe—to even, as Kepler put it, "think God's thoughts after Him." But the methodology did not merely provide essential toe-holds on the climb to scientific truth. It also served a crucial preventative function. One driving subtext of many conceptions of scientific method has been a distrust of unregulated human intuitions, and in particular of anything colored by human subjectivity. During this century, human philosophies, politics, intuitions, preferences, psychologies, agendas, and, especially, religions, have all been seen as seriously unreliable and as having disastrous epistemological effects. The roots of that distrust go back several centuries, and partially constituted some early justifications for science having a stringent method.[1]

So, one major task of scientific method was to screen human subjectivity and biases out of science, allowing nature's authoritative voice to be heard undistorted.[2] Empirical observation, which was seen as untainted by humans, uninfected by theory, and experienced in common by all who honestly investigated nature, provided the secure foundation for science, and descriptive and explanatory structures were set on that foundation in accord with some type of logic—a logic which, properly employed, was also free of human subjective taint. If the foundations and building materials of science were pure and nature-dictated (empirical, observational data), and if the procedure for constructing theories on that firm foundation, from those untainted materials, both preserved that purity and were reason-guaranteed (a strict logic of scientific inference), then there simply was no place for human subjective contamination to seep in. That, at least, was the perceived ideal.

That basic ideal persisted even though specific conceptions of scientific method underwent substantial changes over time. For instance, according to some early conceptions, the scientific logic in question was inductive (e.g., Bacon), while according to others it was deductive (e.g., Descartes), and according to yet others it might be some combination of those two, or might vary in different areas (e.g., Newton). Or at some historical points it was thought that proper scientific theory could be logically inferred from data, so that the means of generating the theory from pure data also provided the desired epistemological guarantees. Inductivists are obvious examples here.[3] Others, skeptical of the view that source could constitute warrant, held that regardless of origin or means of generation (whether above reproach or beneath contempt), nature could still exercise final authority over the fate of scientific theory via pure data and pure logic. Thus, a rigorous empirical evaluative process still apparently offered at least some part of the desired guarantees, whether from the positive side (hypothetico-deductivism) or from the negative (falsificationism). But through all such changes, the persisting aim and hope were the same—ending up with secure results through a method that ensured that objective reality and not unreliably subjective human factors would have whatever final say might be possible within science.

Recent Turnings

As it happens, this whole cluster of ideals has largely come unraveled. That unraveling has been precipitated from two directions, one (underdetermination) having long historical roots, the other (spotlighting human factors) being much more recent. Brief discussion of each follows.

Underdetermination

It is more or less universally recognized now, and was suggested as far back as late Medieval times, that the empirical by itself radically underdetermines any interesting theoretical science. Any body of data, no matter how extensive or complete, is always in principle consistent with any number of possible explanatory theories (whether we can think of any or not).[4] The data thus do not and cannot uniquely either logically imply or conclusively confirm (or even conclusively falsify all the competitors of) some specific theory which can then be identified as the true theory. In fact, data cannot even strictly establish some theory as uniquely probable. This cluster of effects is generally referred to as the underdetermination of theory by data.

Underdetermination, by denying us the possibility of rigorously generating theory out of empirical data, confronts us with two broad categories of options. One is to hang on to some form of the old ideal of science as involving only a pure empirical base and what can be rigorously constructed and securely justified on that base. In light of the fact that no logic can rigorously bridge the gap from data to theory, this first option requires that we simply bite the bullet and reject the theoretical, restricting science to the merely instrumental or to a forever provisional empirical adequacy. The other primary option is to hang on to some form of realism—for example, to insist that theories are legitimate and that sometimes we even have rational grounds for thinking that particular theories might be in some specified sense true. In light of the fact that there can be no logically rigorous empirical justification for that selection of a particular theory, this second option entails that whatever process we employ in singling out particular theories will of necessity involve "extra-empirical" factors—factors beyond the purely empirical.

Underdetermination, then, presents us with a forced choice between empirical purity (at a cost of the theoretical) and theoretical legitimacy (at the cost of empirical rigor). Historically, there has been some dispute over which way to jump. But despite widespread staunch suspicion of anything beyond the purely empirical in science, the history of philosophy of science in this century can in a broad sense be viewed as a history of progressive, albeit stoutly begrudged, recognition of the limited power of the empirical, and the consequent unpleasant necessity of choosing either to reduce the status of purely empirical science toward a thin empirical adequacy or to preserve the richness of the theoretical by granting ever-increasing legitimacy to admission of the nonempirical.[5]

In any case, the ideal of a full-blown empirical, rigorously ironclad, theoretically rich science is an impossible one, and the underdetermination that lies at the roots of that impossibility confronts us with a choice that is both a nonempirical philosophical choice, and one that is forced upon us. Although there have been disputes, the bulk of the scientific community historically and presently has in practice chosen the second option—deliberately embracing specific theories as true or approximately so. (Some, having adopted this option without recognizing the accompanying ramifications, vociferously espouse the truth of favorite theoretical principles while simultaneously claiming that science is purely a matter of empirical observation and logical rigor.)

Taking this second, realist, option (which I believe to be the preferable one) will have implications for the boundaries of scientific legitimacy. If taking theories as not only scientifically legitimate but as true, approximately true, or even rationally warranted in science requires at least tacit dependence upon extraempirical factors (as underdetermination guarantees), then there are extraempirical matters that are legitimate and even essential within science. And that seems unproblematically true. One simply cannot do significant science without presuppositions concerning, for example, what types of concepts are rationally legitimate, what evaluative criteria theories must answer to, and what resolution procedures are justifiable when those criteria conflict, as well as answers to deeper questions concerning aspects of the character of reality itself, concerning the nature and earmarks of truth and of knowledge, concerning what science is about and what it is for, concerning human sensory and cognitive and reasoning capabilities, and other matters that will arise later.

Science cannot be done without a substantial fund of nonempirical principles and presuppositions. But again, that does not automatically constitute any problem for science. Certain specific presuppositions, of course, might be illegitimate, unproductive, or destructive of science, but that implies only that the criterion for scientific legitimacy for nonempirical presuppositions runs through the nonempirical category—not simply along its boundary. The questions that will have to be faced later, of course, are first, What exactly is that criterion? and second, Is it or is it not possible for the concept of supernatural design ever, under any circumstances, to meet that criterion?

Humans Again

If any single idea has dominated conceptions of science in recent decades, it is that various human factors are inextricably infused into some essential processes and products of science. Although cases have been sometimes overblown, evidence for that general idea has come from historical, sociological, philosophical, and psychological investigations of science itself. Political, economic, social, gender, and other such factors have all been alleged to irremovably operate deep within science itself.[6]

But perhaps the most influential manifestation of that recognition is in terms of a conception of science as fundamentally value freighted, and its pursuit as involving an attempt to optimize such values.

The values in question come in roughly two waves. The first wave is an inescapable consequence of underdetermination. As noted above, underdetermination entails that singling out specific theories as true, approximately true, or probable must involve nonempirical inputs. Intuitively, the inputs most often cited do not seem subversive of the larger character of science, but include normative values— characteristics of good theories—such as empirical adequacy, accuracy, breadth, elegance, coherence, fruitfulness, simplicity, beauty, explanatory power, and the like. The underlying idea is that although extraempirical, such factors do constitute *indicators* (albeit defeasible indicators) of truth. For example, a simple theory that accounts for the data is widely accepted as more likely true than a wildly complicated theory covering the same data. These values are thus, on this view, neither arbitrary nor subjective, but are truth-relevant, *epistemic* values, and are thus legitimate within the scope of the larger alethic aims of science.

But the present point is that even if claims of epistemic relevance seem plausible, such values are not empirical matters, nor is their appropriateness and worth (much less their connections to theoretical truth) straightforwardly established by purely empirical considerations.

Getting Fuzzier

As relatively harmless as all that appears, the color of the horse shifts just a bit when we probe a little deeper. Like values of many sorts, even the above plausibly epistemic values come in a wide range of degrees, often come into conflict, can be given a variety of relative weights, rank orderings, and so forth. In fact, from, for example, Kuhn on, the foundational dynamic of key operations of science has widely been conceived as driven by applications, conflicts, compromises, and judgments of value. If correct even in gross outline, this picture virtually guarantees that science, being driven toward value optimization, will require employment of decision principles that go beyond not only anything purely empirical, but beyond the apparently harmless epistemic values above.

Three things need be noted. First, at least some of those values have an irremovable human tint to them. For instance, what is identified as simple is notoriously affected by background assumptions, theoretical stances, and even various personal characteristics. And one would anticipate that other sorts of beings with different cognitive makeups would find very different things to be simple than we do—if they even had the relevant corresponding concepts (or even concepts). So as harmless as the values in question might be, even they undercut any notion of science as human-free.

Second, not only in those epistemic values but also in the necessary principles of ranking them and resolving conflicts among them we find nonempirical considerations. Since these principles partially *govern* directions, decisions, and theory competitions within science itself, they cannot be simple results either of the empirical or even of the larger structure of science. And there are other human factors that affect directions and lie near the surface of science as well.[7]

Third, here is another place where some grounds for determining legitimacy are required. For the fact is that not only has the list of "approved" values changed historically, but there is no current complete consensus either. Some deny that explanatory power belongs on the list (or claim that explanatory power and empirical accuracy are mutually exclusive).[8] Some scientists are inclined to give simplicity and elegance pride of place, while others consider such features to be mere surface decoration.[9] There is a spectrum of positions concerning where the relevant lines are when depth requires sacrifice of breadth.

But again, theory assessment, resolution of theory conflict, assessment of data, and decisions concerning which theories to accept as parts of the orthodox scientific picture of reality cannot be done without at least tacit intuitions concerning such values and their proper application. But what values do and do not count as legitimate is neither empirically decidable, easily settlable, or currently settled. The same may be said for specific definitions even of agreed values. For instance, many agree to the inclusion of simplicity, but cannot agree on what it *is*. If Kuhn and others are right that hands-on training is an essential part of science education, the relevant values may not even all be *expressible* but may be part of the "feel" that guides a significant part of scientific activity—what Knorr-Cetina calls an "action/cognition mesh."[10] And applications of value—value judgments—are not only disputable, they are not rule governed, rigorously empirically driven, or neatly axiomatizable. They are *judgments* of relative *values*, and human judgments of humanly chosen values at that. But science cannot be done without them. And given that the very direction of science and that what is or is not eventually accepted as scientifically respectable sometimes tracks back to such value decisions, they are far from trivial matters.

Other Considerations—Human Perception

But there are other areas of nonempirical, human, "subjective" influences as well. One area under recent discussion has been perception itself—the process which in earlier views was supposed to provide the pristine, objective bedrock of science and scientific method. It has perhaps never been very controversial that interests, mindset, enthusiasms, expectations, and so forth might affect what was perceptually noticed, attended to, or singled out as significant. But at present many believe that some human factors are partially constitutive of the very experiences themselves. And that represents a major shift.

In centuries past, it was widely supposed that perception was a passive process, involving nature "out there" simply imprinting objective, nonnegotiable information through transparent senses onto the mind. Of course, there were some challenges to that view (e.g., Kant), and the necessity of certain restrictions was generally admitted (Galileo, Boyle, and many others).[11] Still, there was a basic stratum of primary qualities which were not only the (mathematizable) foundational characteristics of nature itself and thus essential to science, but which the phenomenological content of our perceptual experiences accurately mirrored.

But that general picture of perception as ultimately passive came under serious question in recent decades. As presently conceived, perception involves more of the observer than merely mechanically operating sensory faculties, and some of that additional involvement is active. Such activity can grow out of anything from very specific theory-based expectations through broader conceptual commitments, Kuhnian "paradigms," or background mindsets, to full-blown worldviews. And, again, it is not that such factors merely direct or filter perception, but that they partially shape the very content of some perceptual experiences. Thus, when veteran telescopic observers draw detailed diagrams of canals on Mars, when reputable professional physicists write technical papers reporting properties of the lines generated by their N-ray difractors, when professional followers of Darwin discuss observations of Bathybius haeckelii, or when early microscopists produce sketches of homunculi, we need not necessarily dismiss it all as just invention, self-delusion, or deceit. And when the two sides of nineteenth century disputes over heredity systematically report different observed behavior of chromosomes during meiosis, or when opponents in the open/closed-universe debate report correspondingly different density measurements, we need not necessarily attribute it either to incompetence or to desperate efforts to save face by the losing side. If perception is indeed an active process, it may well be that in all these sorts of cases, the scientists in question were perfectly accurately reporting the actual content of their own observational experiences.[12]

Mindsets, worldviews, and the like would generally be categorized as "subjective" factors, in some broad sense. And if such factors are both essential to and constitutive of perception, then there is clearly a risk of subjective subversion at the very heart of science.[13] And if, as some argue (a la Kant), the constitutive activity of the subjective is preconscious, so that even our most basic perceptual experiences are simply presented to us already actively shaped and completed, then there is little prospect of self-correction.[14] We not only might not have access to the actual process, but might have no way of determining what parts of our own perception were generated by such preconscious activity and which were not—even if we *could* separate our perceptions into relevant components.

Here is where another putative role of scientific method emerges. Science is typically done by communities of scientists. A range of different, conflicting subjectivisms will be represented within such a community, and standard demands for replication of results by other observers will virtually guarantee that any individual subjectivity molded into specific results will eventually be exposed through direct conflict with other conflicting subjectivisms. So the communal aspect of science will filter out subjective intrusions, even if such intrusions can be neither prevented nor even spotted by individual human observers. (Of course, this will work only if the subjective aspects can be separated from the core of "pure" observation.)[15]

Of course, even if that is right, that will have no effect whatever on subjective infusions into human perception which are common to all humans (perhaps as a result of our history and makeup as a species). In such cases, there would be no communal conflicts which would reveal and correct. Indeed, there is no guarantee that we would even realize the existence of preconscious subjective activity in perception. (Kant, of course, finessed the whole matter by simply defining objectivity to be any subjectivity that is universally shared.)[16] But that hardly helps here. It is, in fact, hard to see how the necessary conditions of human perception could fail to have potential formative implications for perception.

In any case, the older view of perception as passive, and as constituting potential protection from the subjective because of that passivity no longer seems quite right. That creates opportunity, if not inevitability, for infusion of some subjective, or at least human, factors in some degree into perception itself.

Even Further

But humanness may go even deeper in a number of essential areas of science, in ways that are hard to specify. I will briefly mention suggestive features in one such area, without pursuing any rigorous explication.

Among key tasks of the scientific enterprise, perhaps none is more fundamental than that of making parts of the world understandable. Such understanding is typically seen as involving certain sorts of empirically supported explanations. That seemingly simple idea pitches us headlong into a variety of philosophical and historical thickets, but of present interest are apparent connections to human subjectivity, social structures, philosophical presuppositions, and other such matters.

Understanding

The concept *understanding* is extremely difficult to explicate. Indeed, the standard *Encyclopedia of Philosophy*, which isn't usually troubled with timidity, doesn't so much as have an entry on the concept. But the basic idea is straightforward: understanding something involves removal of at least some of its mystery. The process of coming to understand something involves a transition from mystery to sense making. It is a coming to see an answer to a particular sort of "Why?" question.

Of course, what kinds of things strike us as mysterious, and why, involves all sorts of deep roots in, for example, human nature, cognition, specific context, and perspective. All those matters are structured in terms of human concepts, human experience, and the human condition generally.[17]

What seems to make sense is, of course, tightly connected to such important epistemic factors as background beliefs, conceptual matrix, theory commitments, paradigms, and even worldviews. What seems to make sense is also notoriously dependent upon psychological circumstances, mental condition, levels of various substances in the brain, and so forth. Both batches of factors provide some potential for subjective, human intrusion into the process.

But there may be something even more fundamentally human at work here as well. There is an internal phenomenal, experiential dimension to things appearing sense-making, and the presence of that feel, that seeming, that seeing, may be the most fundamental component of something's making sense to us. And we cannot get behind or underneath it to examine its credentials.[18]

It appears relatively clear that that dimension can be triggered by any number of (suspect or completely unsuspected) human factors. Things that make intense sense in dreams, or to the intoxicated, or to the mad, are often utterly indescribable in ordinary discourse. (We've all had dreams that made starkly clear sense at the time, but which were only fleetingly and sketchily even thinkable in ordinary waking states of consciousness—if at all.) Not only is this "sense" faculty thus not infallible, but there is apparently no noncircular procedure for justifying reliance upon it. Any such case, to have any chance of being convincing, would have to employ resources and procedures the justification for employment of which would ultimately track back at least in part to the faculty itself. And there is, obviously, no hope whatever for an empirically based case of the required, noncircular sort.

There is thus apparently some internal faculty of human cognition upon which we cannot escape placing a crucial dependence, but into whose inner workings we cannot look. That is not to say that it does not work, is unreliable, should be ignored, is irrational to trust, or anything of the sort. I believe none of those to be true. (Indeed, we seem to be in exactly the same circumstance with respect to it as we are to not only our other cognitive faculties, but even to our perceptual senses.) But its workings seem to be largely involuntary, we have little clue as to how it works or why the things that trigger it do so, and it seems to be both profoundly human and inevitably (maybe even essentially) affected by a wide variety of human factors and foibles.[19]

Thus, one of the foundational aims of science may not even be definable in human-free terms. Ultimately, we are unable to avoid taking the deliverances of some human cognitive capacity or function as reliably given, and we simply go from there. There is no other alternative. And neither rigor, the empirical, nor formalisms will get us out of that.[20] *Something* has to be fundamental in even the most rigid axiom system (along with the givenness of some notion of proof, rigor, etc.), and even mere coherence still demands reliance on some ultimate identifying of coherence (and upon some principle linking coherence to the relevant epistemic characteristics aimed at, upon some value assignment to that characteristic, etc.).

So the whole idea of understanding (scientific or otherwise) rests upon an involuntary endorsement of the objective legitimacy of specific *human inner phenomenal experiences* associated with particular things having a genuinely sense-making appearance. That we are not dealing here with some "objective" human-free process seems amply clear.[21]

Explanation

Understanding, then, is (or at least involves) the experiencing of sense-makingness. Something makes sense when we see how and why it occurs, or why it is as it is, what meaning (if any) it has, what role it plays in some contextual setting, and so forth. But not only is that "seeing" itself mediated by its embedding conceptual context, the relevant sense of seeing something is deeply experientially psychological, involving hard-to-define cognitive connections that may simply be causal results of our human cognitive structure. And the conditions of that experience seem nearly unmanageably rich. We have only the spottiest ideas of what go into it, which may be why our references in this whole area are almost always metaphorical—"see," "light," "grasp," and so on.

Explanations are what supply the materials that allow that seeing.[22] And a good explanation must supply the sort of materials that, in the complicated human cognitive context in question, will trigger that shift from mystery to sense. Different sorts of explanations may do that in different ways in different contexts. Very generally, explanations supply such materials by formally, narratively, or otherwise displaying a field of background causal webs, patterns, events, conditions, laws, and/or historical developments within which the phenomena in question fit organically, so that the phenomena become integrated, constituent parts of some larger pattern or flow. (Formalizing such intuitions is, of course, where numerous philosophical bodies are buried. I shall leave them there.)[23]

Such shifts and such integrations are mediated by a complicated, enmeshing system of outlooks, stances, theoretical commitments, expectations, sensitivities, and the like.[24] Many of the relevant factors we can easily identify. Indeed, some of them are constraints that we deliberately impose—empirical constraints of some sort on "scientific" explanations, for instance. But not all may be explicitly identifiable. One hint of that is the fact that many explanations from past eras (in science and other areas) have such a peculiar feel to us, and we often cannot fully say what it is about those bits of past science that strikes us as so out of whack. It often isn't just that we have better data in hand and can thus uncover empirical difficulties, but that there is just something ineffably *wrong* about the whole setup. But that would suggest that here too there are components not reduceable to the empirical. Furthermore, explanatory regresses must stop somewhere, and locating and identifying what constitutes epistemically satisfactory stopping conditions also involves complicated judgments that are not data dictated.[25]

Support

We sometimes categorize types of explanations by the constraints we impose upon them. Of present relevance, it is widely stipulated that scientific explanations must have specific ties to the empirical. However, more or less every attempt in this century to say something both rigorous and right about what sorts of ties those might be has come pretty much unhinged. A serious problem facing all such logic-framed attempts—inductive, deductive, retroductive, hypothetico-deductive—is the apparent fact that there is no such general logic.

As it turns out, assessing the relationship between theory, explanation, and data involves judgment calls that are frequently not formalizable, are not rigorous, and are shaped and directed by the cognitive matrix within which they are formed. The influences of different background slants on data assessment are often fairly subtle within science, but not always. The differences in taxonomy between lumpers and splitters—all of whom subscribe to the same broad theories, all of whom are working with the same data—are nearly legendary. And even in disciplines as rigorous as contemporary physics, one can find cases where one group takes a specified theory as "well confirmed" by the exact body of data taken by another group as conclusively falsifying that theory.[26] Obviously, something a bit beyond, for example, simple *modus tollens* is afoot here. In the actual scientific trenches, relation of theory to data (and even acceptance or rejection of data) often involves human-generated decisions of a sort that does not readily lend itself to formal algorithms, and which provides—perhaps even requires—input from a human context.[27]

Upshot

So we should not be particularly surprised when across cultures even as closely linked as English and French, we find different scientific assessment and reception of Newton and, later, of Darwin. That some of the ethos of post–World War I Germany might seep into the quantum mechanics born there should not be a shock. That field theory should arise during a time of Romantic insistence on the interconnectedness of all that is, probably should not astonish. Nor should the parallels between seventeenth century science and seventeenth century social theory, or those between Victorian cultural themes and Darwinian evolution. Nor need it make us uneasy that some thrusts of the English Revolution were echoed in directions of newly emerging science.[28]

After all, empirical data and logic alone cannot do the scientific job. And where can other materials come from except the humans who do the science? Theoretical concepts and connections are brought into science only by human beings. The only concepts in human science are concepts that humans have thought of and can deal with, and the only principles, patterns, and schemas that can gain entry into science have the same source and conditions. And some of those materials will have histories—histories with roots well beyond the domain of the laboratory. After all, nature cannot simply dictate theoretical concepts or theories. And as Dirac once remarked, "Nature's fundamental laws . . . control a substratum of which we *cannot* form a mental picture without introducing irrelevancies" [my emphasis].[29]

A frequent response, of course, is that despite all that, only those resources that pass the empirical muster of nature can *remain* in science. But although containing important truth, by now it should be clear why that answer in any unvarnished form will not work. The "muster" is extremely nonrigid. In the very perception underlying observation, in decisions concerning data, in assessments of data/theory relationships, in choice and application of values in such assessment, in directions and aims defining overarching constraints upon science—in all of those areas (and others as well) human factors play roles. Even the most extreme and barren positivist antirealism cannot purge humanness from science. It can only purge explanation, theories, predictive power, sense making, breadth, depth, and other things that make science interesting. And still humans will be peering up from the bottom of the mug.[30]

Implications

Science is a much less rigid enterprise than was previously thought or hoped. Its procedures do not provide quite the airtight protection from human subjectivity previously thought, and its processes are not somehow immune to the conditions of other human pursuits. Scientific method is not a human-free zone, and neither are the products of that method. Historically, many have wanted science to be as completely mechanically algorithmic and as devoid of the taint of human input as possible. In some cases, the motive has been quasi religious—to make science a worthy object of near worship, or to elevate its masters (us) to some cosmic pinnacle from which we would have to neither look up to nor bow to anyone or anything higher. In other cases, the motive has been only to epistemically purify science, to guarantee its trustworthiness by ridding it of all contamination of human subjectivity. Neither of those attempts had any chance of succeeding. Science has a serious, incurable case of the humans. Even so staunch an empiricist as Hume remarked " 'Tis evident that all the sciences have a relation, greater or less, to human nature; and that however wide any of them may seem to run from it, they still return back by one passage or another. Even Mathematics, Natural Philosophy, and Natural Religion are in some measure dependent on the science of MAN, since they lie under the cognizance of men, and are judged of them by their powers and faculties."[31]

But this case of humans isn't necessarily a fatal case.[32] None of the foregoing implies that just anything goes. Nor does any of it imply that science cannot get us toward theoretical truths about nature. Despite some claims to the contrary, antirealism and relativism are not automatic consequences of discovering humans and even human choosings in science. Nor does it follow that there is no distinction between science and nonscience. Nor does it follow that human "subjective wishes" are the primary operative factor in science.[33] There are in science constraints—*epistemically relevant* constraints. Those constraints are perhaps tighter and in some sense less arbitrary than in most other human intellectual disciplines. The relevant extraempirical factors will still need some sort of legitimation, although that cannot be "scientific" in any simple sense. Science is committed to limiting and neutralizing subjective (and other) taints to the extent reasonably possible. Efforts in that direction involve among other things, barring certain sorts of concepts and the principles containing them from scientific theorizing and trying to objectify observation by replacing human perceptual judgments with instrument readings. That generally means that the barred concepts are viewed as not sufficiently "empirical," which means that the scope—or more often, perhaps, the potential scope—of the human streak in them has crossed some intuitive but generally unstateable (and historically unstable) line, presumably creating too great a risk that experimental and observational procedures cannot grip them quite tightly enough to force them to behave in ways accepted by scientists and others as appropriate.

So any boundary (or zone) between scientific legitimacy and illegitimacy does not fall along a simple empirical/nonempirical divide, or along a human-free (objective) or human-tainted (subjective) break. It isn't nearly that easy. The implication of immediate relevance is that blanket prohibitions on concepts or imposed limitations on content within science—such as stipulated bans on the supernatural—must have more behind them than merely the residual momentum of insufficiently nuanced empiricist conceptions of science. What must be sought is some separation running through the nonempirical and the human-shaded realms, and which distinguishes the scentifically legitimate from the scientifically illegitimate within those realms themselves.

8

THE LEGITIMACY CRITERION

Absent any possibility of a method capable of automatically generating explanatory theories, the primary function of scientific method is frequently seen as exclusionary—eliminating inadequate theories and keeping subjective intrusions (inter alia) at bay. However, complete exclusion of human factors is not achievable, and even if it were, the consequences would be fatal for science. Although somewhat suspicious in the past, the scientific community has begun to accept such views. For instance, in a recent publication the National Academy of Sciences described as "highly prized" such theory traits (values) as internal consistency, accuracy of prediction, unification of disparate observations, simplicity, and elegance, and then continued:

> Other kinds of values also come into play in science. Historians, sociologists, and other students of science have shown that social and personal beliefs— including philosophical, thematic, religious, cultural, political, and economic beliefs—can shape scientific judgments in fundamental ways. [Despite potential (and occasionally actual) problems] it is clear that values cannot—and should not—be separated from science. The desire to do good work is a human value. So is the conviction that standards of honesty and objectivity need to be maintained. The belief that the universe is simple and coherent has lead to great advances in science. If researchers did not believe that the world can be described in terms of a relatively small number of fundamental principles, science would amount to no more than organized observation. Religious convictions about the nature of the universe have also led to important scientific insights.[1]

That does not, however, entail that screening such epistemologically active infusions to the extent reasonably possible is not nonetheless epistemologically appropriate or even essential.

But subjective factors are not the only significant exclusions tied to scientific methodology. For example, it is widely considered axiomatic that science cannot formally consider the existence, character, or activity of the supernatural. A common justification for that blanket exclusion is that *by definition* science deals only with the natural realm, considers only natural causes, and proposes only natural explanations. For instance, Eugenie Scott:

> To be dealt with scientifically, "intelligence" must also be natural, because *all* science is natural. [A]ppeal to . . . SETI is fallacious. SETI is indeed a scientific project; it seeks *natural* intelligence. Any theory with a supernatural foundation is not scientific.[2]

But, surely, appeal to a definition cannot be the whole story. Surely, that prohibition is not just capricious and arbitrary as, say, would be a definition according to which science dealt only with the realm of pink things. But while not arbitrary, the proper definition and prohibitions of science were not simply discovered carved on stone somewhere either. So exactly what might be the rationale behind the alleged definition?

The answer might well involve questions concerning the fundamental character and aims of science. One possible aim of science might be to discover what we can about the structure, governing principles, and operation of the purely natural realm. But a different possible aim might be to discover what we can about the structure, governing principles, and operation of the actual world. There is, of course, no a priori guarantee whatever that either those aims or their results will coincide. There is no necessary requirement that the natural and the real be identical. Disagreements on this aims question might thus have significant ramifications for other aspects of science—including what scientific theories are accepted as confirmed, or even as legitimate candidates.

There is not even any a priori guarantee that the natural realm coincides with the *empirical* realm. There is no compelling reason to think that the sensory and cognitive faculties with which we have been equipped or whose evolution to their present state has been driven by random and arbitrary contingencies (and which provide the foundation for the very definition of the empirical) are directly or indirectly adequate to absolutely everything that exists, even should it turn out that everything *is* purely natural. In fact, a case would be needed for thinking even that either the empirical or the natural is wholly contained within the other. One might simply define anything empirical as natural, but given at least the possibility of visible miracles, that move would need some support. And the prospects for a definition of everything natural being empirical (all nature just happening to fall within the range of our faculties) seem equally dim.

If science is by definition an attempt to discover as much as possible concerning the inherent, autonomous structure and operation of the purely natural realm, then prohibitions on the supernatural within science make some sense. But even in that case, that policy would not be an automatic given. If phenomena around us involve a mixture of the natural and the supernatural, then even the attempt to understand the natural part on its own terms might require some means of identifying and separating the natural and the supernatural, in order to prevent matters not properly belonging to the natural realm getting mistakenly included in investigations of that realm, leading to mistaken scientific conclusions. Thus, one *essential* procedure of such a science might be identifying the supernatural.[3]

However, if one takes the second option—science as an attempt to discover as much as possible concerning the structure, operation, and history of actual reality, whatever that reality may be or include—then the situation is very different. In particular, prohibition on the supernatural does not even superficially appear to emerge out of the definition or primary aim of science. In fact, under this second conception, science—aimed now at the truth, whatever the truth turns out to be— might be required to think about the possibilities of supernatural causation and phenomena within even the empirical realm.

At least prima facie, the above two overall aims and the pictures associated with them are quite different. Some people, however, seem prone to conflating the two. But to take the aims mentioned as identical is simply to presuppose philosophical naturalism. Indeed, to take science as by definition restricted to the natural while taking all potential results of such a restricted science as true also comes very near an endorsement of philosophical naturalism.[4]

Clearly, attempts to simply stipulate prohibitions on the supernatural involve some rather deep and tricky waters. But I do not think that most prohibitionists mean to rely on arbitrary stipulation. There is, I think, a fairly common, prima facie sensible, and more respectable underlying intuition.

That standard intuition is straightforward and goes roughly as follows. Science aims at generating explanations, understanding, and truths. In that pursuit it has a method that is alethically reliable and competent *for a particular category* of things (natural, material). Thus science cannot, on pain of conceptual muddle, try to deal with or pronounce on things beyond that realm. Given then that (by definition) the supernatural is not part of that realm, it must be consistently excluded from scientific cognizance. That does not necessarily mean that science must deny the existence or activity of such agency—science must merely tend to its own (natural, material) business and withhold comment on anything else.

But, it might be asked here too, if the supernatural does exist and does act in the cosmos, does not that "natural only" decree open up at least the possibility if not the guarantee of incompleteness and even serious error—for example, spurious "natural" explanations of phenomena that actually result from supernatural activity and thus have no natural explanation at all? There are three standard responses here. One is simply a stipulation (sometimes tacit) that philosophical naturalism is true, and that thus a restriction of science to the natural is merely a "restriction" of science to the realm of truth and rationality. The alleged risk, on this view, just doesn't exist.

Notice that in this response, part of the justification for an allegedly scientifically essential methodological presupposition is purely philosophical.

A second response is a variant on the first—that whether or not there is a supernatural realm, it has no relevance to or implications for (scientific study of) the natural, material realm. If that is the case, then the natural realm is closed and, on its own level, complete. So again, excluding any recognition of the supernatural from science will involve no epistemological risks. There is a theologically based, Leibnizian variation on this theme also: that for various reasons agents in the supernatural realm would not violate the inherent integrity of the natural realm, so that although philosophical naturalism fails, it fails in a way that poses no risk for scientific method. But again in this type of response, we are given philosophical (and in the variant form even theological) justification for a methodological stipulation advanced as scientifically essential.

The third response is, in effect: yes, there is a risk but it cannot be helped and is worth it anyway. The background intuition here is that nonnatural things operate in ways beyond the grip of any empirical method (and perhaps any other method as well), and that, consequently, such concepts could operate in ways beyond any reliable (i.e., empirical) methodological controls, checks, or constraints. For instance, any (subjectively disliked) theory or result could be repudiated, or any (subjectively favored) theory or result protected by unconstrainable hypothesizing of supernatural activity. Such hypotheses would be unconstrainable due to their empirical unfalsifiability and even untestability. Scientific method simply would lose any means of gaining a firm hold, and nature would lose any objectifying authority in science. Trying to evade the risk of error or incompleteness by opening the doors of science to such concepts ultimately results in *everything* coming unhinged. So ignoring the risk is the best pragmatic strategy and has in any case been strongly vindicated by the success science has had while enforcing the prohibition.[5]

It is worth noting here that should it turn out that the supernatural were scientifically relevant in a way that would render science systematically wrong (or systematically at risk of being wrong), the widely accepted "self-correcting" character of science would not function at all effectively. Given a "natural only" policy, even if there were supernatural causes generating effects within the empirical realm, science would as a policy be committed to refusing to consider supernatural explanations, and would be forced either to leave the relevant phenomena unexplained, or to propose natural explanations that would be *ex hypothesi* simply wrong.

But exactly what is it about the supernatural that seems to place it beyond the scope of scientific method? More generally, what would put anything beyond that scope? Scientific method, as typically construed, is a procedure for keeping or discarding theories on the basis of what nature tells us about them. Doing that requires an approach that embodies *sensitivity* and *accountability*. The method must be adequately sensitive to register what nature is or is not in fact indicating, and then theories must be held accountable to that. Although sensitivity and accountability are tightly intertwined, and are no more completely separable than are data and theory themselves, in practice a rough, ready, and useful intuitive distinction can be drawn.

Sensitivity is a more prominent issue in matters of experiment, experimental design, and broader data-related decisions, while accountability concerns features more visible in matters involving "scientific inference" (confirmation, falsification, theory construction) and in determining the nature and fate of theories (pursuit, evaluation, acceptance, protection, rejection, modification).

A requirement of sensitivity to nature generates some obvious conditions, among them the following three. For instance, (i) we must correctly *recognize* nature's voice via our method (and not confuse it with some other voice, with our own voice, or with noise); (ii) we must adequately render the substantive *content* of that voice (not taking 'no' for 'yes', '2.317' for '2.318'); and (iii) we must isolate the *focus* of nature's answers (identifying exactly what question the voice is in answer to).

Concerning (i), it is typically assumed that nature speaks always and only in the empirical—that nature thus does not speak on topics that cannot be linked directly or indirectly to empirical matters.[6] Method, designed in significant part to enhance our hearing of nature's voice, thus requires assumptions both that fundamental natural truths are being expressed via the empirical, and that however partial and limited our capacity, we can and do register genuine expressions of nature. Without such assumptions, there simply could be no science as we usually conceive it.

Concerning (ii), it is typically assumed that nature always speaks consistently, uniformly. Indeed, Hume, Kant and others argued that we *cannot* think that a nonuniform voice is authentically nature's voice. *Law* or *natural necessity* is the measure and guarantee of that consistency, which in turn provides the justification for inductive and other inferences. Without such assumptions, logics and strategies for establishing general scientific principles would be hopeless, as would be science itself without the fundamental generalities. So when effects are not replicable, or results are not repeatable, it is presumed that either the method got tuned to some other voice or the investigator garbled or (perhaps inadvertently) manufactured the empirical transcript(s). Concerning (iii), a key aim of experimental design is the isolation of, and the confining of nature's answers to, single, focused, specifically posed questions.

Accountability generates its own demands also. Accountability to nature is generally construed in terms of giving nature as large a say as possible in the ultimate fate of scientific theories. (Of course, given underdetermination and other issues discussed in a previous chapter, nature cannot deliver a complete and final say in such fates.) Of course, a theory cannot be held accountable to what nature says if it operates in some area where nature does not speak or to which nature pays no attention even, so if nature speaks only via the empirical, any properly scientific theory must lie at least to some degree in the realm of nature's cognizance, that is, in the empirical domain. So (iv) only theories to which *nature is sensitive* should be entertained. Further, if nature is to have a say in the fates of theories, then (v) theories must be put *in empirical harm's way*. And, of course, for there to be any substance to accountability, (vi) science must at least in the long run take some kind of active notice of nature's input.[7]

Those assumptions and aims are not, of course, dictated by any empirical results. But neither are they simply arbitrary. They are, rather, linked to a number of interesting deeper considerations connected to human limitations which must be dealt with in some way or other if there is to be any even remote prospect of science. To see a bit into where that leads, let us look at one set of factors tied to all of the above facets of method.

Ceteris Paribus Clauses

Science, again, is fundamentally in the business of producing understanding and explanations by reference to nature's empirical pronouncements. Given the complexity of nature and the finiteness of human beings, human resources and human knowledge, maintaining even a prima facie sensitivity and accountability requires that explanations nearly (if not absolutely) always operate within the context of implicit ceteris paribus clauses: for example,

All else being equal, this is what naturally happens in that situation and why.

The "all else" in specific cases involves factors not expressly accounted for in the explanation in question. Of course, in the humanly unmanageable complexity of nature, all else never is *equal*. So (as, e.g., Cartwright has argued)[8] the functional, practical thrust of the tacit clause is really something like

All else being *irrelevant*, or *absent*, or *right*, this is what naturally occurs in that situation and why.

As a stopgap approximation, that sort of ceteris paribus qualification has historically proven productive, which is fortunate given its unavoidability. We simply have to assume that what we can get a manageable empirical handle on is a reliable reflection of some stable reality. Given inescapable human limitations, science must at least attempt to epistemically neutralize the unknown (and the unknowable), of which there is at any given point a staggering quantity. We have to be able to plausibly suppose that all else is irrelevant or absent or right.

Scientifically essential procedures of *idealization* and *abstraction* are conceptual attempts to realize the ceteris paribus condition. Influential historical conceptions of scientific method were built upon practical neutralization attempts. For instance, Bacon's inductive procedures were designed primarily to methodically strip away complexities overlaying nature's basic simplicities. Aristotle's (and Galileo's) inductive faculties were supposed to be a means for penetrating through obscuring complexities to the fundamental generalities of nature. Such essential neutralization attempts are, of course, routinely unsuccessful.[9] But that isn't necessarily regrettable. Scientific discovery sometimes takes the form of a recognition that some things long thought to be irrelevant really were not irrelevant after all, or that some things totally un-suspected to that point are neither irrelevant nor absent. (The discoveries of X-rays and neutrinos, and the aftermath of the Michelson-Morley experiments are particu-larly well-known examples.)

But despite a history of frequent and fruitful failure in specific cases, this ceteris paribus clause is indispensable in science. Indeed, it may be as fundamental a meth-odological presupposition as there is in science. If so, anything which would render that presupposition indefensible even in principle would represent a massively serious problem for science.

What sort of thing would represent such a threat? Well, suppose that it were true that

   (i) there are potentially relevant factors, assumption of the absence of which is never even in principle reliably warranted

or, in other words, that

   (ii) there are potentially relevant factors that could never even in principle be reliably equalized or neutralized

(i.e., they might or might not operate regardless of boundary conditions, experimen-tal controls, and constraints).

Under these circumstances, the ceteris paribus clause—this key methodologi-cal presupposition that underpins justification of confidence in most scientific results—would cease to warrant even provisional confidence. Suppose that some experimental or observational data seem to confirm some theory. If it is not even in principle reasonable to believe that all relevant factors are accounted for in the experimental situation, what grounds for confidence might there be for taking the theory to be thereby supported, rather than the result being some uncontrolled factor producing a "false positive" for the theory in question? Similar problems arise with apparent falsification. Some other uncontrolled but nonetheless relevant factor might have intruded into the situation, itself producing the problematic result.

It thus looks as though anything that would constitute a systematic potential challenge to every application of the ceteris paribus methodological presupposition would generate methodological chaos for science. There might be any number of ways that that sort of systematic challenge might get generated or expressed. But I think that when the objection goes to ground, the ultimate problem involves causal agencies that are *simultaneously unrecognizable and capricious*. Although the position is almost never fully stated, I think that the common instinct is that science could not effectively function in an epistemological environment containing potentially relevant causal factors which were both

> a. not reliably recognizable (or detectable or non-arbitrarily assignable to or identifiable with that agency)[10] and
> b. not reliably uniform (unpredictably variable or intermittent).

Each of the above characteristics in isolation is problematic but not automatically scientifically fatal. For instance, effects of a causal agency that acted capriciously and intermittently could be dealt with on a case-by-case basis were the activity of such an agency straightforwardly detectable and identifiable when it occurred. On the other hand, were there no way to directly detect the activity of some causal agency (or to nonarbitrarily assign or link effects to that agency) the effects of that agency's operations could in some instances still be systematically screened out, or compensatory precautions taken, were the effects uniform and their character known.

But a capriciously intermittent, unrecognizable causal factor is a very different matter. In fact, there are two potential threats to science here. The first is that such agencies could introduce effects that could be screened neither systematically nor episodically, leaving little prospect of finding underlying laws governing nature. The character and generality of laws would always be at direct risk of being masked by irregularities introduced by the agencies in question. So research with even the most upright of intentions would likely be stymied.[11]

The difficulty here ties in with the sensitivity and accountability requirements mentioned earlier. If some causal agency is not recognizable as such, or effects are not nonarbitrarily attributable to it, then either our method is not adequately sensitive (perhaps even in principle) or is perhaps sensitive to things to which it should not be. And if the results of some supposed causal agency are unpredictably variable or intermittent, it is difficult for a science seeking stable, underlying uniform principles to be properly accountable to those unreliable effects.

For example, prior to the recognition of isotopes, the most precise measurements of atomic weights varied unpredictably over otherwise apparently pure and chemically indistinguishable samples. There was no way for early atomic theory to be accountable to that unpredictably (and unaccountably) variable data. Accountability, in this case, required an altered sensitivity (made possible by a theory modification) so that the old data could now be seen as an answer to a previously formally complex question. (Or in other words, the presence of varying mixtures of different isotopes had ensured that other relevant factors had been neither absent nor right.)

The second threat associated with simultaneous unrecognizability and unreliable variability goes back to the earlier matter of human subjectivity. And in the context of causal factors whose individual instances were unrecognizable as such and whose operations were capricious, there would always be the uncontrollable potential for human circumvention of any process of falsification or confirmation. While empirical data cannot rigorously falsify scientific theories, data can at least generate severe problems and embarrassment for theories. But if causal agencies whose activities were neither directly recognizable, detectable, nor regular were admitted unconditionally into scientific discussion, theories out of harmony with empirical data would not even have to blush. Advocates could always attribute apparent failure of a favored theory (or apparent success of an opposed theory) to actions of the agency in question. Here again, of course, would be nearly unlimited scope for human subjectivity, prejudice, agendas, and so forth—the very things science has striven for centuries to at least control, if not eliminate.

These sorts of threats to science would arise regardless of the nature of the agency in question. Suppose that some scientist proposed that there were mischievous sprites who were finite, fallible, and limited—not divinities of any sort—but who had the ability to render themselves and some of their activities undetectable, and who delighted in sticking subtle wrenches into experimental gears. Suppose that this scientist further proposed that it was the perverse activity of such sprites that made the scientist's favorite theory appear to be empirically refuted even though it was in fact true—in short, that in that particular case, other things were not equal (or absent, or right), that an otherwise unaccounted causal agency had stepped in. Such "sprite defenses" of favored theories would have to be either rejected or controlled if the scientific project was to be pursued at all. (Note that the protected theories would not themselves necessarily be inherently empirically unfalsifiable, involved with the non-natural or anything of the sort.) Should these sprite abilities be exercised, science would have no defense against the complete ineffectualness of the essential ceteris paribus condition. Essentially the same sorts of problems ensue if appeals to sprite activity are given free rein within explanatory theories. In general, if there is no way of ever determining whether those abilities have been excercised or not, then the project is more or less hopeless.[12]

It might be objected that sprites are in fact supernatural, in some sense of the word. But exactly the same sort of case can be constructed with merely very advanced—perfectly natural—aliens who, for reasons of their own, choose occasionally to interfere with human scientific endeavors. The alien defense would operate just as would the sprite defense, and would raise similar considerations.

The foregoing considerations suggest that one component of any fundamental boundary (whether a line or a fuzzy zone) between scientific legitimacy and scientific illegitimacy, is defined by factors linked to the methodologically inescapable ceteris paribus principle, and that its only scientific justification is practical and methodological.[13]

Ceteris Paribus and the Supernatural

This chapter began with the general question of what underlay prohibitions against the supernatural in science. The most common answer, exemplified in the opening quotation from Scott, is that science by its very essence is restricted to the natural. But why *that* restriction? Why *that* conception? The answer, I have argued, rests on pragmatic ceteris paribus considerations.

There are, of course, other popular answers to the original question. Such prohibitions against reference to the supernatural in science almost invariably rest upon some conception of science according to which science has some essential, normative characteristic that is violated by reference to the supernatural. But such answers typically reduce to or are parasitic upon the above. Following is brief discussion of how that cashes out in one case.

Testability

It is frequently claimed that science requires testability, and that the supernatural lacks such. But what exactly does that come to? The necessary conditions for testing include (i) that the theory (or other object of testing) be linked in specifiable ways to some identifiable, recognizable phenomenon interpretable as a consequence of (among other things) the causes or other factors stipulated by the theory, and (ii) that that link, and causal or other relevant factors in the situation be reliably stable, so that some determinate meaning can be given to the test results. Without (i), whatever was being tested, it would not necessarily be the theory in question, since the results could not be pinned to the theory. Without (ii), whatever the results were, they would have no interesting implications for the theory, since there might well be no basis for stable expectations against which to compare those results. That all amounts to requirements that all relevant factors be recognizable and that none operate only sporadically—which, again, are simply the ceteris paribus implications identified above.

Conclusion

If prohibitions are to be genuinely defensible, let alone scientifically normative, there must be something about the supernatural, about design, or about the combination of the two that undercuts the scientific project and from which the scientific project requires protection. That "something" must involve violation of *ceteris paribus* conditions. The emerging question, then, is Does supernatural design truly constitute systematic, invariable, irremediable violation of such conditions?

IV

THE PERMISSIBILITY QUESTION

9

CASES FOR IMPERMISSIBILITY

It was argued in the previous chapter that *if* supernatural design concepts are impermissible in science, their illegitimacy must arise out of their undercutting of methodologically essential ceteris paribus conditions. In the present chapter, I wish to look more closely at specific cases for rejecting supernatural design concepts within science. In the next, I will address the ceteris paribus question with respect to such design directly.

In the last century, supernatural design theories have been criticized and rejected on a wide variety of counts. It has been claimed that such theories violate the very definition of science, that they are insufficiently empirical, are untestable, hyperflexible, and lack genuine content. In some cases, the character of supernatural agents underlies the purported difficulties, supernatural agents being uncontrollable, subject to no relevant constraints, capable of circumventing natural law, able to introduce the miraculous into events, and having various types of infinitude.

Familiarity has given some of those objections such an air of conclusiveness that arguments are typically taken to be unnecessary—merely stating the charges is taken to constitute refutation. However, in what follows I shall argue that the situation is perhaps not quite so simple as such appearances suggest.

Definition

It is frequently claimed that science must by definition exclude the supernatural. A number of related issues were raised in the previous chapter, but it is worth noting that appeal to a definition of science here is going to be a bit problematic because there simply is no completely satisfactory formal definition available to appeal to. Defining science turns out to be one of the nastier problems within philosophy of science. And some of the informal or partial definitions provide little comfort to would-be prohibitionists. For instance, science has recently been defined in one court simply as "what scientists do." That does not in principle rule out anything at all. *Whatever* this group of humans (scientists) decided to do—including developing theories which appeal to the supernatural—would turn out to be science. In their popular writings, some scientists define science as "an attempt to get at truth, no holds barred." "*No* holds barred" is about as antiprohibitionist as one can get. Others define science as "organized common sense." But if there is anything that has been considered common sense during human history, it is the existence and activity in nature of the supernatural. Again, barring the supernatural purely on definitional grounds thus turns out not to be a straightforward matter.[1]

Empiricality

It is widely alleged that only the empirical is scientifically legitimate, and that, not being appropriately empirical, the supernatural is inadmissible in science.[2] There are two things to be noted here. First, as indicated in earlier discussion, claims of the purity of science's empirical grounds are overly simplistic. The empirical does indeed play a profound role in science, but it is neither untouched by human factors in itself nor is it the only thing at the foundational level of science. A substantial body of nonempirical factors and principles also operate essentially and indispensibly within the foundations and at various points within the hierarchy of science. Thus, even were it true, the mere fact that principles concerning the supernatural are not empirical principles will not provide grounds for prohibition, since exactly that same nonempiricality characterizes a variety of scientifically essential principles. If there is a distinction to be made here, it must be in terms of some additional requirement which various other nonempirical principles meet, but which principles concerning the supernatural do not.

But is it even true that the supernatural is nonempirical? What exactly would that mean? Within the scientific context, all that is required for something to be a legitimately empirical matter is for it to have appropriately definable, theoretically traceable empirical consequences or effects or connections. Those connections can be exceedingly indirect, and they typically are not direct consequences just of the theoretical matters in question, but only of those matters in conjunction with a variety of other principles (sometimes referred to as "auxilliary" or "bridge" principles). It is by that means that even such exotica as quarks and the deep past get included within the empirical realm. But although a supernatural being could obviously have untraceable effects on nature, surely it cannot be claimed that a supernatural being simply *could not* have traceable effects upon empirical matters.[3]

As philosopher of science Philip Kitcher noted in his anti-creationist *Abusing Science*, "Even postulating an unobserved Creator need be no more unscientific than postulating unobservable particles. What matters is the character of the proposals."[4] If Kitcher is correct (as I believe he is) then ruling the supernatural out of science on this ground will require establishing what the special character consists in, then arguing that the supernatural inevitably fails on that count.

Observability

Related to the last objection, it is sometimes claimed that science deals only with the observable, and that supernatural design fails that requirement. The most obvious response is that the word observable has a very specialized sense in science. Indeed, when physicists speak of deeply hidden phenomena being observable they typically mean only that there is an indirect but theoretically traceable series of connections between the phenomenon in question and some phenomena observable in the intuitive sense of "observable" (e.g., a pointer reading). Specific theories involving supernatural design could obviously, at least in principle, meet this sort of observability requirement in exactly the same way as could theories involving advanced aliens.

Design might even be observable in some more straightforward, intuitive sense. What exactly is observation? In its broadest sense, it is a perceptual judgment (experience, conviction) arising usually involuntarily out of the normal operation of our cognitive and sensory faculties. Perceptual judgments of this sort—for example, that something is green—are obviously scientifically legitimate.[5] Observation is simply the eliciting of normal perceptual and conceptual cognitions under appropriate sensory circumstances—whatever the content of those experiences and whatever the normal means turns out to be. Consequently, if cognitive experiences of design in nature are naturally elicited by normal perceptual events, then design would be as much an observational matter as would greenness. As Larry Wright put it (speaking of recognizing purposes):

> To be objective enough to function in an experimental test, all that is required of propriety judgements is that they be as repeatable and intersubjective as the run of more orthodox perceptual judgments.[6]

The bulk of humans historically and presently, and even the bulk of scientists historically have believed that they observed design in nature. Perhaps they were mistaken (although that would require a case). Even so, if stable and intersubjectively shared sensory-generated cognitive experience or conviction constitutes observation in the relevant sense, design in nature may well be in that sense observable. I shall not, however, pursue this position.

Falsifiability/Testability

It is widely held that the supernatural is impermissible in science because claims concerning supernatural agents and supernatural agent activity are unfalsifiable, whereas only falsifiable claims are permissible within science. Falsifiability was proposed as a formal scientific norm over half a century ago, and the intervening years have revealed some difficulties with that stipulation.[7] But even disregarding such problems, falsifiability requirements turn out not to generate prohibitions on the supernatural in any straightforward way.

As indicated above, science has no choice but to count indirect, properly mediated connections to the observable as constituting empirical character. Rejecting that would basically deprive science of the ability to say anything significant about the entire theoretical realm. That conception of empirical character, conjoined with the interrelatedness of the various components in the conceptual structure of science, has some interesting ramifications for falsifiability.

Science attempts to allow nature, through empirical data, to have a say in the fate of scientific theories—either endorsing to some degree or objecting to some degree. The aim is to give nature as much of a say as reasonably possible, at least in the long run. But since nature's objections are never rigorously decisive, and since key scientific matters—even data—have nonempirical threads woven through them, the scientific fate of theories is shaped to some (often subtle) degree by those nonempirical factors.

Some of those additional factors historically have had to do with philosophical views concerning proper structure of scientific theories, proper procedures for interpretation of data, the nature of proper theory/data relationships, the character of admissible explanatory concepts, external constraints to which theories are subject, the structure of legitimate evaluative procedures, and so forth. Scientific theories operate within a context partially formed by such matters, and their relations with nature are assessed in such contexts. When those relations, mediated by that context, do not live up to the expectations stipulated within that context, the theory in question may be abandoned. That abandonment is generally described as the theory's having failed its empirical encounter with nature.

But there are other alternatives—for example, giving up part of the mediating context.[8] There are numerous instances of that in the history of science. For instance, Ptolemaic astronomy operated within the context of the normative Platonic philosophical principle that the basic motion out of which any acceptable theory of the heavens had to compound observed motions was circular. (Departures from apparent circularity were what required explanation.) Although rejecting Ptolemaic astronomy, both Copernicus and Galileo accepted that normative principle and conducted their theorizing accordingly, albeit in importantly different ways. Newton, of course, rejected that philosophical assumption, adopting instead the normative principle that the basic motion out of which any apparent motion must be compounded was linear. (Departures from apparent linearity—which includes virtually all motion in the cosmos—were what then required explanation.)

Here's another example a bit closer to the present. For virtually all of scientific history, it was held that any proper scientific explanation had to be deterministic.

That stipulation was, of course, philosophical. But that philosophical preference was abandoned earlier in this century, in part because theories operating within that context were not behaving in their (context-mediated) interactions with nature in ways other parts of that context stipulated as normative.

Both of the above cases—the transition to Newtonian physics and the subsequent transition to quantum physics—are nearly universally held to be episodes of scientific progress. But those transitions crucially involve replacement of (parts of) one set of philosophical prescriptions by another. If they constitute cases of genuine scientific progress, and if scientific progress is empirically driven, then it looks as though when the "nonempirical" is tied into the scientific, the empirical can be brought to bear upon those nonempirical elements and the nonempirical is not immune to the empirically driven change. That at the very least blurs the line between the empirical and the non-empirical upon which the present case for prohibition depends.

The empirical does not, again, rigorously destroy scientific theories. But when a theory is repudiated because its context-mediated relations to the world do not meet context-stipulated norms, then the theory is taken to have been empirically refuted. But since the relevant nonempirical factors were as essential a part in structuring and assessing the confrontation with the world as was the theory itself, then if, in identical circumstances, some part of the context content had been repudiated instead of the theory (or had both been abandoned), it would seem equally proper to consider relevant parts of the nonempirical context principles to have been empirically challenged. Both are essential to the confronting of the world by science, and both are potentially subject to the same fate on exactly the same grounds. To consider the one alternative but not the other to be "empirical refutation" seems arbitrary at best.

There really isn't much room to maneuver here. If the philosophical transitions noted above are not linked in some sense to the empirical, then we have to conclude that in some crucial historical cases, scientific progress was in essential respects philosophical—not empirical. But that would seem to undercut the claim that the supernatural is scientifically illegitimate merely because it is not empirical, since this position would amount to an admission that some things that are not empirical are scientifically essential. On the other hand, a claim that the essential philosophical transitions were legitimate because they were in fact empirically driven, constitutes an admission that the empirical *can* have a bearing upon the nonempirical.

One could, of course, simply bite the bullet and claim that the moves to Newtonian dynamics and to quantum mechanics do not represent scientific progress, but that seems too high a price to pay. And denying that the nonempirical is essential to science is simply no longer an option. Nor can it be seriously claimed that the philosophical changes were purely arbitrary and had no relevance to the scientific changes. The theoretical changes could not have been achieved without the accompanying nonempirical changes. If science had good empirical reasons for the theory changes, it had indirect but still legitimate and still empirical grounds for the accompanying nonempirical changes.

So given the nature of science and its operations, and the interconnectedness of the empirical and the nonempirical within the scientific context, the nearly inescapable conclusion is that the empirical can not only come to some sort of grips with some nonempirical matters, but can trigger changes in scientifically incorporated nonempirical positions, and can do so in circumstances and by means which make it proper to say that the nonempirical positions in question were empirically at risk.[9] And being empirically at risk is all that is required for something to be both falsifiable and testable.

The risk facing nonempirical principles in science is typically subtle. The normative philosophical principle that all natural explanations had to be ultimately deterministic faced some degree of empirical risk, although that risk was tenuous enough for that principle to withstand it for several centuries. But the risk was real, as evidenced by the fact that the principle did finally fall to (deeply mediated) empirical results.

Controllability

It is sometimes claimed that the problem with the supernatural in science is that the supernatural cannot be controlled. For instance, Eugenie Scott says:

> Science has made a little deal with itself; because you can't put God in a test tube (or keep it [sic] out of one) science acts as if the supernatural did not exist. This methodological materialism is the cornerstone of modern science.[10]

But exactly what does "control" mean in this context? The term *control* is used in two apparently different ways in scientific contexts. It can refer to the ability to experimentally manipulate some phenomenon, or it can refer to the ability to protect experimental procedures from the effects of some phenomenon by holding the phenomenon at experimental bay, screening out its influences, or compensating for such effects. As it turns out, however, the two uses ultimately relate to the same underlying concern.

Manipulation

We cannot at will produce or prevent things like supernovas (much less things like the Big Bang). And the difficulty is not necessarily merely one of technology. We cannot at will cause or prevent quantum events—we cannot manipulate some of them even in principle. Yet supernovas, the Big Bang, and quantum events are not beyond scientific bounds, so something beyond mere failure of manipulability must underly the perceived problem with the supernatural. Exactly what is the problem?

At the core of the perceived problem is the fact that by very definition the supernatural is not governed by law or any other form of natural necessity. A supernatural agency can override law, is not subject to the boundaries defined by law. But experimental manipulation of any sort depends essentially upon the reliable operation of laws. When we manipulate some phenomenon, we basically implement conditions in which the system in question undergoes a law-driven (or law-conforming) transition from the initial imposed state to the target state. For instance, to boil water, we place water in conditions (applied heat, etc.) in which by purely natural processes, the boil ensues. The conditions we impose may be highly artificial, but once we initiate the conditions, the rest occurs naturally—we appropriate the relevant processes by initiating those conditions. But in the case of the supernatural, there are no relevant governing natural laws that can be used for manipulation, and there are no uniform behavior patterns to which the supernatural is obliged to conform. There are then no uniformities through which the activity of the supernatural can be identified, or through which effects are reliably attributable to the supernatural. Here, then, we have violation of both ceteris paribus conditions. Thus, it is claimed, there is no prospect at all for genuinely *scientific* investigation of the supernatural. Genuine experiment requires law-based manipulation, and that is out. (It should be noted that uncontrollability is not a characteristic only of divine agents. We would face similarly problematic conditions with sprites, leprechauns, etc.) Of course, scientific investigation of things beyond manipulation can sometimes be done via opportunistic observation, as in the case of supernovas, volcanoes, and other such phenomena. But even there, the possibility of fruitful investigation depends crucially upon those phenomena being law-governed—which is precisely what is missing in cases of supernatural activity.

Screening (Controlling For)

One specific aim of experimental design is eliminating, screening out, or compensating for all but one or a few specifically identified causal factors, so that the phenomenon in question can exhibit the effects of those factors (or can exhibit the autonomous behavior patterns of the item in question under those conditions) with other obscuring effects suppressed (i.e., those things being absent or neutralized). But there is, presumably, no controlling for the supernatural. That was the thrust of the remark that one can not force the supernatural either into or out of test tubes. That allows for one of the worst of scientific nightmares—the intermittent effect. And if such effects are unrecognizable, the result is the removal of any hope of meeting ceteris paribus criteria. On this view, regardless of what we do in the scientific context, the supernatural may or may not be acting, and we never know which. That is, obviously, just a variant form of the "undetectable and intermittent" criterion identified in the previous chapter.

However, the attempt to generate a prohibition on the supernatural in science on this basis seems to rest upon a simple logical confusion. Suppose that it is granted that science cannot cope with phenomena that are both unrecognizable and unpredictably intermittent. And suppose that there were extremely advanced aliens who could affect certain earthly events in ways we could not trace, and that they did such things in a totally random, sporadic manner. It would not in the slightest follow that we were violating basic criteria of science (let alone of rationality) were we to attribute the Martian titanium cube to alien activity. That case we can easily and quite properly identify as a result of alien agent activity. Similarly, suppose that it is granted that supernatural agents can act in ways both unrecognizable and unpredictably intermittent. No *general* prohibition follows from that at all—certainly no prohibition on attributing phenomena to supernatural design in cases where such design *was* identifiable.

Of course, a general prohibition would follow were it established that all supernatural agent activity was unrecognizable and unpredictably intermittent. But I know of no such case, and making such a case would involve deep excursions into theology—an odd place to find most of those advocating the prohibition in question. But without such theological doctrines, attempting to extract a general ban on the supernatural in science from the fact that a supernatural agent *could* act in intermittent, unrecognizable ways embodies a trivial logical mistake. In the absence of reasons for thinking that supernatural activity is never recognizable, the prohibition amounts to the counsel that, since there could be such activity without our knowing it, we should resolve to ignore such activity even should we recognize it. Anyone wishing to turn that into a *normative* epistemological principle has some work ahead of them.

Hyperflexibility

One frequent objection is that divine activity or design has no stable core content, and since it is thus so flexible that it can be bent into any desired explanatory shape, it has no *real* explanatory significance at all. Hyperflexible theories in a sense represent the flip side of underdetermination. Given underdetermination, nature can escape any attempt to pin her down to a single theory, and can do so without having to deny any of the data in question. A hyperflexible theory can escape any attempt of nature to nail it with refuting data, happily absorbing the data in question.

But exactly what is the problem with such theories? The problem cannot be that such theories cannot be true. And the problem isn't a failure of sensitivity to nature. Since hyperflexible theories are consistent with any empirical data that might arise, they face no threat whatever from such empirical data. They thus have no investment in nature saying one thing rather than another, and can be perfectly happy with even the most strenuous efforts to get the data right, whatever they turn out to be. Nor does the problem involve failure to be consistent with available data. Hyperflexible theories do that superbly.

It is sometimes thought that the problem is that such theories are too vague and general. But that is not quite right. For instance, psychologists of a particular school might be able to produce a detailed, specific, technical-jargon-laced explanation for virtually any specific behavior by virtually any specific person in virtually any specific circumstance. And if it then turns out that the behavior report was mistaken and that the person in question actually did exactly the opposite of the behavior just meticulously explained, an equally detailed, specific explanation of that opposite behavior will be immediately forthcoming. The problem here is not a lack of explanatory specificity.

But contrary to common intuitions, hyperflexibility is not a difficulty in and of itself. Exactly this type of hyperflexibility is to be found in every legitimate scientific discipline. For instance, the following story was told at a professional conference on evolution:

> When I was in Cambridge, we were working with two species of British vole.
>
> We had a little test in which an object moved overhead; one species would run away and the other species would freeze. Also, one species happened to live in the woods and the other happened to live in the field. This was rather fun, and, not really being a zoologist, I went up to see some of my zoologist friends and I reversed the data. I asked them, simply, why a species which lived in the field should freeze and why one that lived in the woods should run away (when the converse was the case). I wish I had recorded their explanations, because they were very impressive indeed.[11]

Does this obvious malleability indicate some deep problem with evolutionary theory? Not at all. Indeed, that point was made later at the same conference by biologist C. H. Waddington:

> The criticism was that if an animal evolves one way, biologists have a perfectly good explantion; but if it evolves some other way, they have an equally good explanation. So what is the good of all this explanation? If I find Jupiter has six moons, the physicists have a perfectly good Newtonian explanation; but if I find it has seven, this doesn't do anything to Newtonian physics which can easily produce a slightly different explanation which explains that just as well. This is exactly parallel to what is going on in evolution theory. This means that the theory is not, at this level, a predictive theory as to what must happen. It is a

theory which tells you in what terms to analyze the contingent events you happen to come across; [it is like Newtonian physics at this level, which] simply tells you in which direction to look for the explanation.[12]

Waddington's key phrase is "at this level." Science embodies a conceptual *hierarchy,* including philosophical, axiological, epistemological, methodological, and other principles. Within that hierarchy, different components essential to science function on a variety of levels, in a variety of ways, and with a variety of degrees of distance from and accountability to empirical data.[13] In present terms, Waddington's response is in effect that the core structures of evolutionary theory and Newtonian physics operate far enough up their respective hierarchies that demands that those core components have *direct* ties to the empirical are inappropriate. That is not their role. Their function is to define general boundaries (metaphysical, ontological, episte-mological) within which specific explanations are to take shape.

I think that Waddington is clearly right. The ability to account for virtually any number of moons of Jupiter does not count against Newtonian physics. The ability to account for virtually any contingent evolutionary path does not count against evolu-tionary theory. And that raises some suggestive points concerning supernatural design theories. The mere possibility of explaining virtually anything in terms of super-natural design theories might not count against such theories. And the inability of such theories to predict specific design features in nature might have no particular relevance either. If design theories functioned at some level of a hierarchy comparable to that of core principles of Newtonian physics and evolution, then demands for specific predictions might be equally inappropriate in all three cases. This issue will be explored further later on.

But surely there is something suspicious about the sort of flexibility exhibited by the earlier psychology case. Intuitively, the problem in such hyperflexibility cases is this. Since any warranted confidence in an empirical theory must rest upon supposi-tions that nature has been give a chance to speak, has spoken, has been heard, and has been attended to with respect to the theory in question, confidence in any theory about which nature has been deprived of a chance to say 'no' is going to be problem-atic. The situation parallels that of an "elected" official in a Stalinist country—she may have gotten 100 percent of the vote, but given the absence of any other choice in the vote there has to be just a bit of nagging doubt concerning the strength of the voters' affection. What might they have said had they been given the real opportunity to say no? Some of the affirmative votes might have been wildly enthusiastic, but it is difficult to be confident of that. Similarly, a theory's hyperflexibility removes any possibility of nature saying no to that theory, making any positive empirical instances substantially less significant than they otherwise might have been. Hyperflexibility, then, is problematic *below a certain point on the hierarchy.* For design theories to face difficulties here it must be established not only that they are irreparably hyperflexible, but that they exhibit that at specific, problematic levels. I know of no attempts to do that.

There is one small twist here. Barring supernatural design theories from science as a matter of policy deprives nature of the opportunity to say "design." That prohibition not only endangers the "self-correcting" character usually attributed to science,[14] but it also automatically turns *naturalism* into a hyperflexible principle—complete with whatever problems that might generate.

Content/Prediction

Darwin and many others have thought that supernatural "explanations" of empirical phenomena are ultimately empty. The suspicion is that the claim that, for example,

    a. species are distributed as they are because God wanted them distributed that way

conveys no empirical information concerning the natural realm, reveals no pattern or mechanism in nature, and has no hint of explanatory power or anything else of scientific relevance. And making the claim more specific merely makes that scientific emptiness more starkly visible. The claim that

    b. species are distributed in specific manner D because God wanted them distributed that way

does indeed convey genuine empirical information—that species are distributed in specific manner D. But the reference to the supernatural is now merely a detachable bit of theological decoration. The larger statement is merely, on this view, a theologically ornamented restatement of the other. The theological reference does no real work—all reference to the supernatural can be removed, leaving utterly intact and complete every part of the description or explanation that has any substantive implications for the empirical, observable, material, nomic, and causal. The additional clause neither adds to, subtracts from, nor in any way affects the scientifically relevant content of the core empirical statement. In fact, this apparent emptiness often amounts to hyperflexibility—no matter what the distribution of species turns out to be, the same claim would arise—that species were distributed in that way (whatever it was) because God wanted things to be that way.

But why is that a problem? Absent a case for atheism or philosophical naturalism, the claim that species are distributed as they are because God wanted them distributed that way could certainly be true. In fact, that claim has precisely the same logical status as the corresponding claim that species are distributed the way they are because that's how nature happened to work things out. That latter is widely held to be a normative presupposition of science. Since neither of those general principles has specific empirical content, if the latter has a legitimate place in the scientific conceptual hierarchy, then the problem with the former cannot be merely that it lacks empirical content.

Indeed, there are all sorts of scientifically essential principles that have no specific empirical content whatsoever. The principle of the uniformity of nature is as good an example as any. By itself, that principle has no specific empirical content. It does not tell us what to expect. No matter what nature presents to us, we would never abandon that principle. Nature could not do anything to induce us to consider that principle violated—we would simply conclude that we had misconstrued what nature had done previously. Or again, it is surely crucial for scientific theories ultimately to be internally coherent. Appeal to that principle in scientific discussion is inarguably legitimate, and can even be the occasion for tossing theories out of science entirely. It does not, however, have the slightest empirical content, provides no substantive guidance in the lab, or anything of the sort.[15]

But surely something is worrisome in this general vicinity. The potential difficulty involves predictive power. It is widely held that genuinely scientific theories must have some predictive capacity, and if supernatural theories (including design theories) are actually devoid of independent empirical content, they seem to lack that capacity.

Predictive capacity is scientifically important for several reasons. Without it, theories typically lack falsifiability, testability, and any resistance to hyperflexibility. In addition, given the minute, nearly vanishing fraction of the total time and extent of the cosmos that we have or can examine, any theory that only followed in the footsteps of already acquired data would be very nearly scientifically useless, especially given the usual presupposition that science is largely interested in general laws, principles, and explanations. As a matter of near necessity, then, theories cannot meekly *trail* data—they have to leap very nearly blindly beyond data, making horribly vulnerable claims about totalities of phenomena based upon examination of a percentage of them roughly indistinguishable from zero. (The justification for such projections is another area in which nonempirical, philosophical, and, historically, even theological principles have played formative roles in science.) Theories are typically proposed in light of data already in hand—so proposal of theories usually follows in the wake data make—but if a theory never passes the data and never gets out ahead of the data curve (i.e., makes *pre*dictions), it has little use. (That, incidentally, was another of the gaffes of some versions of positivism. The view, held by some, that theories were mere summations of data already in hand guaranteed the logical security of such theories at a cost of guaranteeing their explanatory and predictive uselessness.)

Science assumes, of course, the strict uniformity of nature, and that assumption constitutes part of the justification for these logically spectacular and risky leaps. But a science explicitly including supernatural activities would apparently have to make comparable leaps without the comfort of the same sort of uniformity, because a key factor in such a science would be actions that were both free (and thus flexible in ways that behavior of natural phenomena seem not to be) and unconstrained by natural principles (and thus flexible in ways beyond those even of free actions of humans, sprites, and aliens).

In such a situation, what could a theory do but cautiously trail the data? Any theory that did trail the data really would constitute nothing much beyond a restatement of the data (which is not scientifically promising) and any theory that did not would seem to be tacitly employing at least some theological principles concerning supernatural activities (which is fraught with its own difficulties).

But that may represent less than the whole picture. First, design theories are, ultimately, theories involving agency. And, with respect to agents, theories and explanations often must trail data. We are often in positions of utter inability to predict specific human actions, but such actions once observed may be readily and quite legitimately explainable. It might be maintained that we can never be in a similar position with respect to supernatural agents—that we can never provide legitimate explanations for supernatural agent activity. Why that should be so is not clear. But at the very least, anyone wishing to establish such a claim will have to engage in some serious theological work.

Second, it seems fairly clear that not all theories involving the supernatural need be otherwise empty restatements of data. The claims that there is exactly one supernatural creator of nature and that that creator works according to a principle of uniformity of natural design might jointly imply that we should expect to find a single basic DNA dictionary in the cosmos. That implication might turn out to be mistaken (as also have most genuinely scientific theories over most of history), but it is not a mere statement of data already in hand. Those claims might have other sorts of problems, but empirical emptiness is not one of them.

Third, the empirical content and predictions of supernaturally linked theories can be as precise and technical as one likes. Suppose that one has sound, rational reason (perhaps via revelation, perhaps via thousands of years of scientific research) to believe that in fact:

    i.   supernatural intervention was necessary for the origin of life.

Suppose further, that it is scientifically established that

    ii.   life would arise spontaneously if some specific sequence of chemical steps occurred spontaneously and that

> iii. every one of those steps except the 27th could—and frequently did—occur spontaneously.

The straightforward implication of those three statements is that

> iv. chemical step 27 does not occur spontaneously.

And that step can be as technical, precise, and detailed as one wishes.

Of course, it might be argued that there is no rationally legitimate way that one could come to know (i). However, prospects for such an argument appear problematic. One might try to establish the rational illegitimacy of (i) on theological grounds, but that route does not appear promising. It is not at all clear why a supernatural being could not create a world in which life could not or would not occur by spontaneous natural processes, or why a supernatural being having done so would be unable to devise a way to provide finite creatures with that information in some rationally legitimate way. Prospects for establishing the unknowability of (i) on purely epistemological grounds appear equally dismal. In fact, there appears to be no reason in principle why the impossibility of the spontaneous generation of life could not be *scientifically* established on as firm a footing as is the impossibility of perpetual motion. Science does produce rational scientific cases for certain sorts of empirical impossibility, and there is no evident a priori reason why the origin of life must be in principle immune to that eventuality. (Some have philosophical preferences to the contrary, but that is a very different matter.) Were science ever to establish that impossiblilty, (i) would be rendered nearly inescapable.[16]

So lack of immediate empirical or predictive content is not necessarily a serious difficulty. (I will have a bit more to say on this topic in the next chapter.) Depending upon where in the hierarchy a principle operates, it may even be expected. Furthermore, supernatural theories need not all be empirically empty, and can in principle indirectly involve predictions which are specific in any desired degree.

Gaps

It is very widely argued that all supernatural design arguments are God-of-the-gaps arguments, locating supernatural activity and design production in gaps in present scientific understanding. It is further claimed that such gap arguments are destructive of scientific procedure and that their historical track record is a dismal one of nearly unbroken failure as gaps are successively closed.

But it should be clear from discussion in previous chapters that the initial claim is simply mistaken. Some of the more influential design arguments historically neither relied upon nor even involved gaps in natural causation or causal histories.[17] It is further evident that there is nothing in principle suspicious about the existence of gaps in nature. There are all sorts of things nature cannot do—and indeed, such perfectly respectable scientific projects as SETI depend upon that fact. There is nothing whatever problematic or even unusual about scientific cases for gaps. In fact, every scientific case for some general principle or law is simultaneously a scientific case for nature's inability to do things contravening such principles and laws.[18]

Furthermore, the basic structure of gap arguments has the great virtue of at least being logically valid. If unaided nature cannot generate some phenomenon, and there that phenomenon is in front of us, then obviously some other agency was involved. If we add the premise that humans couldn't or didn't produce the phenomenon, whereas aliens could have, we get alien-of the-gaps arguments, which is precisely what underlies SETI. If we add the further premise that aliens couldn't or didn't (and there is no principial bar to that), then supernatural agency follows. Prohibition on such arguments is equivalent to the assertion that with respect to any phenomenon we might ever observe, we are scientifically obliged to presume that either nature or humans or aliens have the capability of producing that phenomenon. That would appear to be not only a rather sweeping presumption, but an empirical one as well, and thus not an apt candidate for normative stipulation.[19]

And is it in fact true that gap arguments have the history attributed to them? Obviously, not *all* scientific gaps are closed even now.[20] And the theories and explanations accepted as closing some of the gaps may have been accepted precisely because they were the best available explanations, *given* the prohibition on design explanations. Such cases would have limited evidential force for the present claim. Furthermore, Kuhn has argued that revolutions sometimes reopen scientific issues previously thought to be closed. If he is right about that, then gap closure may be an unstable phenomenon.

But suppose that in fact all past gaps of the relevant sort had been properly closed by purely natural means. That provides only inductive support for general prohibitions, and neither provides grounds for prohibition as a norm nor entails that no identifiable gap whose unclosability is scientifically establishable will ever arise. So if, for instance, it were ever scientifically established that life could not arise spontaneously, then the inarguable and observable presence of life in the cosmos would establish the existence of a gap that could be closed neither by appeal to nature, human activity, nor 'alien activity.[21] Any stipulation that it would be scientifically illegitimate to accept the inability of nature to produce life, no matter what the empirical and theoretical evidence, has, obviously, long since departed deep into the philosophical and worldview realms.

It might plausibly be argued that scientists have a somewhat worrisome history of underestimating nature's capabilities and of tending to see supernatural activity and design where there is none, and that a prohibition is thus a good pragmatic rule of thumb, safeguarding science from that tendency.[22] But again, the existence of that tendency among scientists is an empirical claim and thus requires empirical justification. (And if it is others, and not scientists, who suffer from that tendency, then it is not clear why *science* requires this safeguard.) And even if the charge is correct, and even if prohibition is a sensible operative rule of thumb, it is only that—a rule of thumb. Over-rigid adherence to it should not be allowed to override any possible solidly empirical cases to the contrary.

Infinitude

Supernatural agents are typically taken to possess a variety of infinite characteristics— infinite power, knowledge, and so forth. It is sometimes objected that even were we able to identify design in nature, we could still have no rational warrant for thinking that the designing agent was *supernatural*—for example, that the designing agent was infinitely powerful, infintely knowledgeable, and so on.[23] Couldn't any relevant empirical design data always be accounted for by appeal to perhaps monumental but still finite power, means, and so forth, rather than infinite power, means, etc.? Isn't it a reasonable scientific rule of thumb that the least spectacular theory that will still do the explantory job is the one to pick (Ockham's meat axe)?

Not obviously, on either point. First, there is nothing inherently unacceptable about the mere notion of infinity in scientific contexts. For instance, it is in some circles presently thought that there is not enough "missing" matter to close the universe, and that consequently the universe will go on expanding *forever.* Whether right or wrong, there seems to be nothing inherently unscientific about that theory.

Second, there is nothing inherently pernicious in a theory's postulating more than is required to perform the explanatory tasks at hand. Every theory that involves any universal claim (as nearly all at least implicitly do) goes far beyond what the data in hand or any data that will ever be in hand, require.[24] And if, as widely believed, scientific laws support *counterfactuals,* then theoretical expression of such laws extend far beyond empirical necessity even into nonactual realms.[25]

Miracles

Miracles are the focus of some of the more popular objections to allowing consideration of the supernatural in science. When pursued, the intuition seems to be roughly as follows. For science to operate at all, it must be assumed that the laws and explanatory principles it attempts to extract from investigation of phenomena are actually operating in the phenomena in question. If they are not operating, or are intermittently interrupted by (unrecognizable) miracles, or if the investigated phenomena are manifestations not of the relevant principles but of (unrecognizable) miraculous actions, then those principles are not there in extractable form, and scientific attempts in those areas will of necessity fail. Aliens and sprites may do things beyond our comprehension. They may do things which appear to defy all known laws. They may be causally involved with phenomena which utterly mask the true operation of natural principles. But in all such cases, whether beyond us or not, whether masked or not, the real laws and principles are still in actual operation, and are thus at least in principle still exhibited at some level in the phenomena, and are there for at least possible extraction by proper scientific investigation.

But in the case of a supernatural being capable of not merely masking the operation of law, but of actually defying, suspending, repealing, or breaking such laws and principles at will, we no longer have any grounds for confidence that the natural laws are still, however hidden, operative in the investigated phenomena. If we continue to investigate *as if* laws are still operative, and if they are not, or if our data collection includes events that while miraculous are not known to be so, then there is essentially no chance even in principle of our scientific results turning out to be correct.[26] As will be evident, one component of the problem is that the unidentifiable and intermittent miraculous constitutes violation of ceteris paribus conditions.

This issue is a bit more involved than might first appear, and the consequences are not quite what prohibitionists frequently claim. The first thing to notice is that *if* we had some rationally justifiable means of recognizing miracles as such, the occurrence of miracles (at least the recognized ones) need cause no principial difficulty for science at all. Those miracles could be screened out of investigation of the natural, compensated for, or dealt with in some other unproblematic manner. It might be claimed that no miracles can be rationally recognizable, but prospects for such claims would not seem promising.[27]

But *if* we have rational grounds for believing that miracles can or do occur, and *if* miracles are indeed threats to science, then the rational policy for science would surely be to try to develop means for recognizing miracles rather than to adopt a blanket policy of pretending that they do not exist. And were something miraculous rationally recognizable as a miracle, demanding that science insist upon pursuing purely natural explanations of the relevant phenomenon would require more than ordinary justification, since any such explanation science generated would automatically be mistaken—and in some cases known to be mistaken.

As with other matters, humans might have a track record of too quickly classifying some things as miraculous, perhaps to the detriment of science. But to construct a prohibition from that has some of the same risks as would a policy to ignore all wolves (no matter what the empirical evidence) on grounds that some people have a tendency to "cry wolf" too quickly, too frequently, and generally mistakenly.

Second, there might be cases where there was miraculous activity which was unrecognized as such, but which was completely uniform—where the supernatural agent doing the miraculous always miraculously produces the same result in the same circumstances. Such activity might appear to us to be simply a regularity of nature. If such activity were really uniform, then there would be no problem, in principle, in achieving empirical adequacy—our theories, in being made to conform to empirical observation, would simply incorporate the imposed uniformity in question.

Oddly enough, our theories in such situations might actually be in many respects right given that the agent in question is supernatural. The uniformity at issue would be a supernaturally maintained uniformity, and it is not clear that there is any scientifically relevant difference between natural law and supernaturally maintained material uniformity. There is certainly no empirically definable difference between the two. In fact, if the world was supernaturally created and governed, then what we call "natural law" may simply *be* supernaturally maintained material uniformities.[28] Laws may just be ways in which God directs the creation to behave, in which case in doing legitimate science and in discovering natural laws we are literally, as Kepler thought, thinking God's thoughts after him. It might be objected that there is no empirical, scientifically legitimate way to tell whether or not that is true. But even granting that point, that says only that *for all science knows now*, what we take to be fundamental natural laws are supernaturally decreed uniformities in the material realm. (Perhaps quantum events are actual examples—at least, according to Feynman *we* don't know how quantum objects manage to behave as they do. And, of course, according to Hume none of us understand causation anyway.) All of that straightforwardly entails that fundamental laws being supernaturally maintained, miraculous regularities would have no negative consequences whatever for science.

Problems do arise in unrecognizable and nonuniform cases—just as would be expected in light of the earlier discussion of ceteris paribus requirements.[29] But absent a case for thinking that all miracles must fall into that category, there is no compelling ground for thinking that taking cognizance of any and all *recognizable* miracles must be barred from science.

Human Laziness

As argued in the previous chapter, a key pragmatic and methodological requirement of science involves holding at bay any factors that simultaneously fail to be reliably identifiable and reliably uniform. There is, however, one other pragmatic objection. The worry is that supernatural explanations are too easy. Were they acceptable in science, then humans being what they are, some would be far too quick to say "miracle" or "supernatural activity," thereby escaping tough scientific work, and also thereby failing to discover legitimate natural explanations in many cases where such actually exist.[30] If there is supernatural activity in nature, then the scientific prohibition on the supernatural will result in science inescapably getting some things wrong. But on this view, that risk is dwarfed by the historically demonstrated danger on the other side—of investigation halting too soon, science settling for the easier supernatural theories.

That is indeed a ligitimate concern. Boyle, perhaps as committed a religious believer as one can find in science, issued a related warning in his 1688 *Disquisition:*

> a *Naturalist,* who would Deserve the Name, must not let the Search or Knowledge of *First Causes,* make him Neglect the Industrious Indagation of *Efficients* [emphasis his].[31]

It should be noted that this concern typically claims historical justification. I'm not sure that the historical case is as clear as it is sometimes presented as being, but won't press the issue here. In any case, pinning this particular rap of scientific laziness on the most prominent believing scientists historically—Newton, Kepler, Boyle, Maxwell, Faraday, Herschel, Copernicus, etc.—does not look easy. Newton and Boyle, for instance, were known in part precisely for excruciatingly dogged empirical work, despite specifically advocating the legitimacy of supernatural explanations within the empirical realm.[32]

But even if there has been a problem of the charged sort historically, it is not obvious that a blanket prohibition on supernatural theories is the best response to that particular problem.[33] Scientists also have a (frequently unconscious) tendency to be a bit less picky toward theories they themselves have proposed as compared with theories proposed by their competitors. But that surely is not grounds for flatly barring scientists from involvement with their own theories. This human tendency is something science and scientific method can handle. Perhaps it can also handle the alleged problem of supernatural theories being overly attractive to the scientifically lazy.

Been There, Done That

Some oppose supernatural activity/design theories on the grounds that such theories had their chance historically, and simply failed. Although that perception is very widely shared, it is not beyond question. The claim is in part an empirical, historical claim, and any defense will have to be in part an empirical, historical defense. The immediate hitch is that, so far as I know, no one has actually done the required history with the required rigor.[34] But suppose that it is granted that design arguments were indeed rejected from science. Since, on this view, design was given a fair scientific chance and it is just a contingent matter that design theories failed, no basis for a *principial* prohibition on design is generated.

Darwinian evolution is typically proposed as the empirical grounds that crushed design theories. However, while Darwinian evolution may indeed have destroyed some gap arguments, it had little consequence for deeper design arguments involving, for example, the structure of natural laws and primordial initiating conditions. Any historical failure of those deeper arguments must have had a different source. Exactly what might that have been?

Science operates through a conceptual hierarchy, and changes in theory, as well as changes in methodology, norms, and so forth, can originate far up the hierarchy, at even the level of worldviews and metaphysics. And there is certainly evidence that for some scientists philosophical sentiments played a key role in the rejection of design in science. That was true for key members of the X-Club,[35] and according to Desmond in his remarkable study *The Politics of Evolution,* some of the earliest critics of design opposed it for reasons that were deeply political and social.[36] As philosopher Thomas Nagel remarks,

> Darwin enabled modern secular culture to heave a great collective sigh of relief, by apprently providing a way to eliminate purpose, meaning, and design as fundamental features of the world.[37]

And Dawkins has claimed that "Darwin made it possible to be an intellectually fulfilled atheist."[38]

One frequently cited problem with theories incorporating the supernatural is that religious or philosophical wish fulfillment may sometimes play a role in their acceptance. As the above make clear, that wish-fulfillment risk also may run in any of several other directions. Were the required historical investigation to reveal that rejection of design theories historically stemmed from antidesign worldview commitments, it is not clear what the scientific significance of that rejection would then be.

But suppose that design theories were indeed rejected historically by the scientific community for perfectly good empirical reasons. That might still not settle the issue *now.* Although it used to be thought that the advance of science was linear, and that scientific progress was via accretion, both of those views have been challenged by historical and philosophical investigation. For instance, if Kuhn is right, key episodes of scientific progress involve revolutionary replacement of one perspective by another *incommensurable* perspective, rather than simple accretion. And Laudan has argued that, historically, the path of science has sometimes *oscillated* between competing theoretical perspectives.[39] If either of those historical analyses is correct, then the fact that design theories were currently barred from science need have no permanant consequences.[40]

In any case, this attempt to base prohibitions in history requires further detailed historical work, and even if the results are exactly what advocates of prohibition hope, it would not follow that bans upon the supernatural in science were either normative or permanant. The reasons for barring the supernatural would be empirical, and there thus would always remain the open possibility of our learning something new and relevant—contrary to the implication of flat prohibitions that even in principle we could never under any circumstances learn anything that might make it scientifically reasonable to think that some parts of the cosmos were supernaturally designed.

Scientific Toughness

The fear underlying various prohibitions widely imposed upon science is that science could not do very well if not protected from various agencies against which its methods are essentially helpless. At best, from this perspective, science might merely be unable to handle the challenge. At worst, violating the protective prohibitions might destroy science. Such prohibitions almost invariably include supernatural activity, supernatural design, and so forth.

But it may be that science is both more powerful and more resilient than its erstwhile protectors give it credit for. In fact, science has a long history of surviving exposure to things predicted to be destructive, and an equally long history of successfully dealing with things thought to be forever beyond its powers. Historically, some claimed that science either could not come to grips with or could not tolerate the unobservable, or the fundamentally indeterminate, or the intuitively ungraspable. There were deep-seated prohibitions against nonmechanical processes, or noncontact forces. It was claimed that science could not probe the deep past, or that the composition of the stars was forever beyond its capabilities.

Science, of course, confronted all those challenges and did quite nicely. That often entailed changes at various points in the hierarchy—from data through metaphysics to worldview components. But that science had the resources to make the necessary changes and continue on as recognizably science, indicates first that science was not as vulnerable as had been feared, and second that the favored "scientific" metaphysics, epistemology, values, methodology, and so forth, were nowhere close to sacred. Historically, revisions of the hierarchy, of boundaries, and of prohibitions, have all been either partially constitutive of or consequences of a number of key episodes in science. Does that imply that it's all up for grabs? Absolutely not. But it does suggest that it is perhaps a bit presumptuous to think that science has seen the last such transition—to think that *our* boundaries, *our* prohibitions are henceforth definitive for all times. Of course, in the past there have generally been very good reasons for such transitions, and it might be claimed that there are no such reasons currently on the horizon. But the lesson of history is that prohibitions—like theories—are provisional and tentative, and that thus the mere citation of a prohibition as presently favored, or as representing our present best efforts and judgment, is not a permanent trump card.

Conclusion

Science must try somehow to operate around things that are both intermittent and not reliably identifiable. Supernatural agents certainly can act in such ways, but the various attempts to support blanket, normative prohibitions on even considering supernatural design in science seem without exception to fail for various reasons. Attempts to justify such prohibitions on pragmatic grounds seem to do little better. The intuition that science cannot deal with the supernatural, so must systematically ignore it, seems a bit like advising swimmers in the Amazon that since they cannot see pirhanas from the bank nor survive a pirhana attack once in the water, they should plunge right in, pretending that there are none. Perhaps better advice might be to work on learning some pirhana recognition techniques. The intuition that humans have a tendency to see the supernatural where it is not, and should thus systematically refuse to recognize the supernatural under any circumstances, seems a bit like holding that since many people seem to see flying saucers where there are none, we should refuse to admit the existence of any such, even were they to land on the Capitol lawn and proceed to blow away the Washington Monument. Perhaps better advice might be to learn what sorts of cases to ignore and what sorts to attend to.

But scientists as a group tend to be pragmatists. Although previously committed to prohibitions on action at a distance, when Newtonian gravitational theory met with enormous empirical success, scientists enthusiastically junked the prohibition and proceeded. Although previously committed to conceptually driven prohibitions on ultimately indeterministic processes in nature, when confronted with the empirical successes of quantum mechanics, scientists (more or less) enthusiastically junked the prohibition and proceeded. Similarly, I believe that *were* design theories to offer any significant scientific payoffs, most scientists (except for some philosophical naturalist "true believers") would cheerfully junk prohibitions on such design concepts and proceed happily onward. That immediately raises the question—could there be any such payoffs? It is to that question that we now turn.

10

LEGITIMACY

As argued in the previous chapter, there are no completely compelling cases for an unnuanced policy of banning from science the ideas either of design or of supernatural activity in nature. Of course, failures of negative cases do not yet constitute positive considerations in *favor* of permitting such concepts into science. Nor does that show that such concepts, once admitted, would deliver any scientific payoffs. So, are there positive considerations to be advanced? And might there be any payoffs? Let us explore those questions in turn.

Nonrealisms

First, there are a number of ways design concepts could function within scientific contexts without posing any difficulties whatever, even in principle—for example, instrumentally or heuristically. Neither use of design concepts would raise any principial issues, since in neither case would design be construed in any realist sense.

Instrumental Function

Design concepts might function instrumentally—being involved in "artificial" procedures employed solely for generating predictions, and not considered even as candidates for real existence.[1] If things in nature can appear designed, if nature can produce things that are *as if* designed, if results of natural selection function *as if* designed, then doing science *as if* nature were designed—*methodological designism*—might be a productive, rational strategy.[2] Since things employed in science merely for their instrumental usefulness have no scientific status whatever, there are no formal prohibitions on what can go into theories interpreted instrumentally. The only "risk" from design used instrumentally would be a tendency of some people to think that there might be something to design were it to actually work instrumentally.[3]

Heuristic Function

Depending on its precise hierarchical level, design might sketch a heuristic picture intuitively suggesting conceptual directions in which to look for explanatory resources.[4] Historically, design-related concepts have actually operated in this way. As one example among others, one of Faraday's biographers notes that the speculations and experiments from which field theory emerged "owe something to [Faraday's] unquestioning belief in the unity and interconnections of all phenomena [and that that] belief, in turn, derived from his faith in God as both creator and sustainer of the universe."[5] And one of Maxwell's editors has argued that the structure Maxwell meant to capture with his famous field equations grew out of his conception of interactions among the Trinity.[6] Here some theological pictures provided outlines for a structure employed in a highly technical empirical arena.

Usefulness—Possible Implications

Usefulness might raise a nagging worry for one type of prohibitionist. The instrumental is useful *exactly because* it generates empirical predictions, and the heuristic is useful *exactly because* it suggests structures, conceptions, and so forth. Thus, although some things that are instrumentally or heuristically useful might be scientifically unacceptable on various other counts (e.g., consistency, plausibility), they cannot be faulted on grounds of empirical emptiness—if they were empty, they would not be instrumentally or heuristically useful. And if some theory component construed instrumentally was functionally involved in generating empirical predictions, it will hardly have less empirical import when construed realistically.

In fact, instrumental or heuristic usefulness may in some cases carry further implications. If a theory generates fruitful (and correct) predictions, that fact counts as evidence for the theory. Perhaps similarly, if a broader conceptual framework further up the hierarchy suggests a fruitful (and correct) theory, that should count as evidence for that broader conceptual framework.[7] Thus, if design ideas have historically suggested productive scientific principles, such principles might constitute both some indirect empirical confirmation for and some of the scientific payoff from those design ideas.

In any case, some usefulness of the idea of design is difficult to deny.[8] For centuries, the engine for much biological progress was such questions as *What is the purpose of this? What is this designed to do?* Even Dawkins cannot avoid lapsing into hypothetical agent-talk when describing some features in nature.[9] And Einstein commented that "When I am evaluating a theory, I ask myself, if I were God, would I have made the universe in that way?"[10]

Explanatory Concepts—Sources

Leaving aside possible instrumental and heuristic usefulness, could design or supernatural agency in nature have any *genuine* scientific status? Could it have any *real* explanatory relevance in science? Are there even any legitimate routes by which such concepts could enter the scientific domain in the first place?

The concept of and commitment to design can gain entry to the upper levels of the hierarchy (e.g., worldview, metaphysical) in any of a number of ways. But entry closer to the empirical ground is a bit more restricted. Very broadly, explanatory concepts in science can either arise out of scientific investigation, or be brought into scientific investigation, and the same would hold for design. In the first category, design (or at least supernatural agent activity) could be nearly forced upon us via establishment of gaps. If neither nature nor any finite agency could account for some phenomena, agency beyond the natural would be essentially unavoidable. Design could also (in principle) be plausibly inferred from special types of mind correlativity even in the absence of gaps (conceptual content, for instance).

In the second category, concepts can enter scientific discussion either as explanatory (or descriptive) resource from further up the hierarchy, or as tentative (usually explanatory) hypothesis.[11] Aside from a small group having an existential commitment to the universe lacking all plan or purpose, virtually no one will claim that the concept of design is in principle impermissible at the worldview or metaphysical levels of conceptual hierarchies. Given the dynamics operating within such conceptual hierarchies, there is nothing preventing design effects from filtering down to lower levels just as, say, requirements of consistency do. Tentative hypotheses represent the simplest entry of all. Virtually anything can be proposed for virtually any reason, so long as it has some empirical, explanatory relevance. So if design had any such relevance, getting it initially onto the scientific field would pose no difficulties.

Empirical and Explanatory Relevance

But *can* design have any empirical, explanatory relevance? *Is* there any sensible way to connect supernatural concepts to empirical issues and theories?

One ready denial can be extracted from, for example, D'Alembert:

> But we have considered it our duty to abstain from this kind of argument, because it has seemed to us that it is based on too vague a principle. The nature of the Supreme Being is too well concealed for us to be able to know directly what is, or is not, in conformity with his wisdom.[12]

The implication is that we do not have a clear enough conception of the supernatural, and consequently that the connections between such considerations and the theories suggested are not sufficiently close for the concepts to get "credit" for the theories.

It may be true that the relationship between supernatural design concepts and specific scientific matters is comparatively loose. But in general, the relation between, say, metaphysical and methodological principles within the hierarchy, or between metaphysical and theoretical principles in the hierarchy, is not as well defined as that between theory and empirical predictions. Thus, the alleged looseness may not represent anything unusual for relevant levels of the hierarchy at all.[13]

But possible connections may have more structure than sometimes claimed, as we will see.

Design and Causal Histories

As indicated above, design would be clearly relevant in virtually all cases of empirically established causal gaps. But it would not necessarily be empirically or causally irrelevant even in cases involving unbroken causal histories back to the beginning of the cosmos. A phenomenon genuinely resulting from design would not have been as it in fact is had it not been designed.[14] Among other things, that means that designed objects almost invariably have *empirical* properties that are consequences of design—involving composition, structure, function, location, and so forth. For instance, in the earlier discussed meteor crater message case, the collection of physical impacts would not have the physical configuration it did were it not for design.[15]

Of course, those empirical properties must have causal explanations, and if the causes do not involve immediate agent activity, they will themselves be physical causes. But that merely pushes the issue back one step. A phenomenon whose naturally produced design was actually built into the Big Bang billions of years ago would not be as it is, had the Big Bang not had relevant necessary characteristics. The question thus arises as to whether or not those causes in turn would have been as they are, were there no design involved. Agent design activity (albeit protohistorical) may thus turn out to be part of the ultimate physical causal history of designed phenomena. Thus, the fact that there were no gaps, no nomic discontinuities, back to the Big Bang does not imply that resulting designedness is causally inconsequential. Claiming otherwise is similar to claiming that the designedness of an automated VCR factory is somehow a detachable irrelevancy in explanations involving the VCRs. One could explain the immediate electronic and mechanical structure, operation, and history of the VCRs, but the designedness of the automated factory itself is not a simple causal irrelevance, given that without that factory's designedness the VCRs would fail both to exist and to have key physical properties they in fact have. Some of the details of the causal connections have interesting implications, and to that we now turn.[16]

Artifacts and Design Inheritedness

Consider something like a VCR produced by an automatic factory. Given a complete physical description of the automated factory (structure, operation, etc.), we could generate a complete causal account of the production and physical properties of the VCR from the initial factory state. But we'd still feel that something was missing—that there was something about the factory itself, perhaps implicit in the "givens," that demanded special explanation. Suppose that it turned out that the factory had been produced by a completely automated factory-factory (a metafactory). Given a complete physical description of the metafactory (structure, operation, etc.) we could generate a complete causal account of the production of the VCR factory from the initial metafactory state. But that doesn't seem to get us any nearer to filling in the missing piece—we've only pushed things back one stage.

The underlying intuition is roughly that the VCR is clearly designed, and that appeal to the factory as accounting for the properties comprising that designedness may in one sense answer the immediate question, but in a deeper sense it merely constitutes a promissory note. The factory is really just a *pattern carrier*. Appeal to the metafactory merely tells us how the pattern carrier came to be carrying that pattern (in whatever form). Thus, an explanatory lacuna resulting from failure to deal adequately with design in the VCR is simply transmitted back up the causal chain.

That seems to be the general pattern with designed artifacts. A complete physical account from any step to the next step still leaves an outstanding promissory design note at that step—a note that never gets paid so long as explanation does not enter the realm of agency.[17] So with (counterflow) artifacts, designedness may be produced indirectly, but does not get generated de novo along the sequence. It is always *inherited*—transmitted via a series of pattern carriers from the agent to the final design-exhibiting phenomenon in the sequence.[18]

A genuinely complete causal explanation of a designed artifact must ultimately track back to an agent. And given that

  i. design has consequences for empirical, physical aspects of designed phenomena (as noted earlier)

and that

  ii. nonagent intermediate causes can only exhibit and pass on promissory notes (not pay them off),

then any purely physical causal history of an artifact is categorially incomplete. Even where no design is involved, purely physical explanations are in one sense incomplete at any given stage, since the explanation at that stage will not contain explanations for the conditions which explanations at that stage presuppose. But while the missing explanations can still be purely physical in nondesign cases, the incompleteness of purely physical explanations (at some specific stage) in design cases is different. Such explanations contain a tacit (promissory) component that is ultimately agent based, and which is not ultimately reducible to some nonagent explanation.

In any case, we sense that something is unaccounted for in any causal explanation of the production and properties of a VCR that does not mention its designedness—indeed, recognizing that particular type of unaccountedness just is to recognize it as designed.[19]

Suppose that while examining some ambiguous object on Mars we were to learn independently (in whatever way) that the object was not just a peculiar Martian mineral formation, but a Martian artifact. Learning that the object is actually a product of alien design necessitates adding an additional category to any proposed causal accounts of that object—the category of mind-correlative agent activity. Notice that it does not merely offer the possibility of adding that causal category—it *requires* it. Why is that? The answer, I believe, is that with respect to artifacts and finite design, we intuitively accept something like a parallel of the Second Law of Thermodynamics. Loosely, the Second Law says that without outside input of the right type, certain sorts of order tend to spontaneously degrade. Analogs have been proposed within information theory, and something like it seems to hold for artifactual design as well. The patterns that constitute designedness do sometimes degrade in transmission. They do not seem to spontaneously strengthen or complexify.

What that means in practice is that when we see a VCR that has been produced by an automated factory, we assume that the designedness in the VCR was carried by the factory and must ultimately track back in some form or other to some agent—regardless of the number of intervening layers of metafactories—and that it has not spontaneously arisen by purely fortuitous processes out of nonpattern, or out of some unrelated, partially related, or lower-level pattern embodied in the factory. The intuition in question is thus

> *Principle of Design Inheritedness (PDI):* Designedness in artifacts which is not produced by direct agent activity must be inherited by those artifacts (via pattern carriers) ultimately from designedness or patternedness which is so produced.

Nature and Design Inheritedness

The fundamental question that immediately arises is this: Does something like *PDI* apply to phenomena in nature? The very comprehendability of nature, recall, entails that nature embodies mind-correlative pattern. Must any reasonable account of such pattern track back ultimately to an agent structuring nature itself in mind-correlative ways? Or can such patterns in nature arise out of nonpattern, contrary to our nearly universal experience with designed artifacts?

There is a fair amount at stake in the answer. For instance, if *PDI* applied to natural phenomena, generous versions of it might warrant the followng inference. Assume that biological organisms are products of natural evolutionary processes.

a. If organisms were artifacts, they would clearly be products of design.[20]

Therefore,

b. according to *PDR* organisms have *design-relevant* properties (e.g., mind-correlative patterns) even though produced by natural laws, processes and conditions.

Therefore,

c. according to *PDI* (applied to nature), evolutionary processes (relevant laws, processes, and conditions) are *pattern carriers.*

Therefore,

d. agent activity was involved in the primordial initiation of those processes.

The above inference would constitute a version of a teleological argument.

But is the affirmative answer concerning *PDI* actually correct? It might initially seem not. For instance, surely evolutionary theory provides ample evidence that pattern (at least *apparent design*) can be generated by nondesign, nonpattern means. And even many creationists now accept *micro*evolution as generating some adaptation out of purely natural processes of mutation and natural selection. (And recall that adaptation has traditionally been seen as powerfully mind correlative.) But if that is a possibility, then cannot some degree of mind-correlative pattern be generated out of patternless resources? If so, then *PDI* apparently would not apply unqualifiedly to the natural realm.

But it is difficult to get an unambiguously noncircular case here. If nature itself were designed—or were a pattern carrier—then cases involving patterns produced by nature would not represent cases of pattern coming from nonpattern, and would tell us little about *PDI.* Thus, simple assertions that evolution demonstrates that mind-correlative pattern can come from nonpattern won't settle the issue, unless an independent case can be made for thinking that the underlying processes and laws are themselves devoid of relevant pattern intended to produce evolutionary results. Those cases are not easy to come by either.

Claims that there are no such underlying patterns are fairly common, frequently resting on the assertion that evolutionary paths and results are wildly contingent (randomness of mutation, sheer happenstance re: what avoids mass extinctions and what does not, etc.). Given that in any of a zillion instances evolution could have gone in any of a bunch of different directions, and that sheer chance dictated which was actually taken, there is apparently no significant underlying pattern at all.

But even if that is true, *establishing* that truth (including truth of the relevant counterfactuals) will be exactly as difficult as establishing the contrary—that the apparent happenstance occurrences were part of a deeper design, the aim of which we may or may not know.[21] Positions here may be at least partially constituted by philosophical preference for a deep absence of pattern over the presence of deep agency.[22]

Still, some tentative points can be made. It seems somewhat plausible that intuitively low-level mind-correlative patterns might sometimes emerge from non-patterned resources (assuming there are such). The earlier mentioned acceptance by some creationists of microevolution producing some degree of adaptation via random mutation and natural selection perhaps represents tacit acceptance of this intuition.[23]

With intuitively "higher" levels of mind-correlative patternedness (e.g., conceptual content cases), affirmative answers are much less plausible. Consider the example of lunar meteor craters forming a diagram of a mathematical theorem, where the causal history of each individual meteor back to the Big Bang is both natural and unbroken. In that case, most of us simply would not believe that the initial configuration of the Big Bang was neither designed nor a pattern carrier.

If there is a spectrum of degrees here, two questions arise with respect to pattern inheritedness, pattern carriers, and the applicability or nonapplicability of *PDI:*

a. where (at what level/type of mind-correlativity) is the applicability transition line? and
b. on which side of that line do relevant natural phenomena fall?[24]

The most basic positive design position is that

> The mind-correlativity exhibited by at least some relevant natural phenomena is of such character as to require pattern inheritedness

regardless of whether or not gaps are involved.[25] Key "relevant natural phenomena" would include cosmic fine tuning, the origin of life, the complexity of organisms, the comprehendability of nature, and so forth. I do not know how to defend very specific answers to either question. But given the clear possibility in principle that some natural phenomena may lie on the high side of the line, prohibitionists have a deeper need for answers.[26] And in the absence of such answers, prohibitions on design in science and claims that design in nature has no explanatory payoffs or significance are at best unsupported and, it seems to me, carry the burden of proof.[27]

Counterquestions

In various guises, burden-of-proof disputes have played a significant role in the design debate. Historically, advocates of supernatural agency and design positions have suggested that their opponents, in resting their own explanations on "chance" or "brute fact," have failed to get to the bottom of the matter. Lurking questions are then raised: *Where did the probability space containing the relevant chances come from? How did the relevant brute facts come to be? Where did the cosmos come from, if not from supernatural agent activity?* The opponents' reply has often been in the form of a parallel counterquestion: *What accounts for that supernatural agent?*

Those asking that latter question seem to be assuming that proponents of design think they have scored points merely by asking a (perhaps unanswerable) question concerning the ultimate foundational principle of nondesign views. The counterquestion is intended to demonstrate that exactly parallel (perhaps unanswerable) questions can be asked about an ultimate foundational principle of supernatural agent views. The intuitive implication is supposed to be that the dispute is thus a wash.

But that is not the situation. Consider this analogy. Suppose again that we discovered a ten-meter, pure titanium, perfect cube on Mars. When asked where it came from, most would answer that (perhaps previously unknown) aliens were responsible. But suppose that there were those who denied either the existence of or the relevance of aliens, claiming that the cube was just there—a "brute ten-meter, titanium cube." And suppose that when pressed a bit for some further explanation, their response was to point out that the advocates of alien activity theories, when pressed in their turn, had no clue at all as to where the aliens had come from or how they had manufactured the cube.

In that case, it is pretty clear that the inability to answer those questions would not cast the slightest shadow on the alien hypothesis. It is equally clear that the mere fact that both explanatory schemes (aliens and brute cubes) could be pursued to levels containing unanswered (or unanswerable) questions does not in the slightest suggest that the answers are on a par.[28] The alien theory is obviously superior to the brute-cube theory because of specific empirical characteristics exhibited by the cube— characteristics that make the alien theory appropriate and for which brute cube proposals are hugely unsatisfactory. The cube has characteristics of a sort left irreparably unaccounted for if agent activity (whether direct or via pattern carriers) is left out.

In the design case, design advocates are not under the wild misapprehension that their explanatory suggestion is not liable to unanswered (perhaps unanswerable) questions.[29] The claim, paralleling that in the alien-cube case, is that there are crucial empirical characteristics exhibited by various aspects of nature—patternedness of sorts which nondesign explanations must leave as unpaid promissory notes, and which are left unaccounted for if agent activity (whether direct or via pattern carriers) is left out, just as key matters of the titanium cube are left unaccounted for by brute-cube theories. And, as in the cube case, lack of answers concerning the agent in question has no automatic bearing upon the legitimacy of the original design proposal.

Legitimacy—Present Status

As argued in the previous chapter, the standard cases for prohibition are not compelling. As argued in the foregoing, when incorporated into a scientific conceptual hierarchy, design can in principle be of scientific, empirical, explanatory relevance. If all that is correct, consideration within the scientific context of design and supernatural agency in nature is rationally permissible. But such permissibility does not yet answer the question of whether or not there is any reason to act upon that permission, or whether or not there might be any genuinely scientific payoff for doing so. It is to that issue that we now turn.

11

ARE THERE ANY PAYOFFS?

Scientists have a long and productive track record of changing the "rules" and "boundaries" of science whenever they become convinced that there is some genuinely scientific mileage to be gained by doing so. The details of virtually every scientific revolution testify to that. Conservative scientific diehards invariably resist such changes, but if some substantive scientific payoff becomes visible, the doctrinaire defenders of the scientific conceptual status quo simply get left behind. That, at least, is the lesson of Kuhn and others. I have argued that even under present conceptions of science there is no clear case for blanket prohibitions against considering at least some types of design concepts in scientific contexts, and that there are some significant reasons for rejecting such prohibitions. Even were there a case for prohibitionism, given science's repeatedly revolutionary past (at all levels of the hierarchy), there is no compelling ground for thinking that our current definitions, norms, and so forth, are the final word forever. In any case, the bottom line concerning the fate of design is probably not determined by what sorts of definitional, a priori, historical, philosophical, or other sorts of arguments can be made for or against the legitimacy of design concepts in science, but by whether or not there is ultimately any prospect of design concepts producing anything of scientific substance. So is there any such prospect?

Looking at the Question Itself

Since principles have different functions at different levels in scientific hierarchies, what counts as paying off can vary at those different levels. For instance, the upper-echelon principle that specific scientific theories must eventually be consistent with other scientific theories has certainly paid off historically, but it has done so in a vastly different way than has, say, the theoretical generalization that electrons carry a unit negative charge, or the empirical generalization that all snails of a certain variety have shells that spiral counterclockwise. We must thus be fairly careful not to mix level-relative expectations when considering prospective payoffs.

When the question is asked *What are the real scientific payoffs, if any, of design theories?* the intended thrust is nearly invariably something like: *what empirical predic-*

tions does the theory make? What difference would/could such a theory make in the lab? Are there nitty-gritty implications for this particular titration? But asking such questions involves a substantive presupposition concerning how and at what level design concepts can be expected to operate, and those presuppositions may be wrong. There are perfectly legitimate—even essential—principles operating at various levels of the conceptual hierarchy for which the above questions would be utterly inappropriate.

Uniformity of Nature—An Example

For instance, consider the principle of the uniformity of nature. It is as nearly scientifically essential a principle as one can find.[1] Yet, uniformity has quite a number of interesting features. First, uniformity has its roots in the metaphysical, if not the worldview level of the hierarchy. Second, it is a principle which theories are required to respect, but it is not merely that—it is a descriptive characteristic ascribed to nature itself, which is a very different and more substantive matter. Third, predictions are not even on the horizon except in conjunction with some substantive theory specifying uniformity *in some specific respect.* Thus, fourth, given the unlimited range of possibilities of such respects, the bare principle of uniformity has basically unlimited flexibility.

Fifth, in contrast to the contingency usually attributed to scientific theories, uniformity is considered by some (e.g., Kant, Hume)[2] to be a regulative principle of human thought itself. That means that, sixth, uniformity has an odd and protected status within science. It is not clear that the notion of empirical testing even makes sense applied to uniformity, but what is perfectly clear is that uniformity is not actually at empirical risk.[3] When results are inconsistent, or when patterns in nature seem to change for no discernable reason, scientists do not speculate (at least out loud) that nature may have just now changed the rules. The nearly invariable approach is to retain unquestioned the commitment to uniformity, but to refocus the search for the relevant uniformity to some deeper level.[4] There have been historical cases (e.g., the "Allison effect") where procedures that seemed to work reliably and accurately have suddenly ceased to work at all, the apparent change remaining an unexplained puzzle to the present.[5] It is simply presumed that something has gone amiss somewhere else—*uniformity being presupposed in the very determination that there is a puzzle.*

So the uniformity of nature principle is metaphysically rooted, nonnegotiable, normative, systematically protected, immune to empirical challenge, untestable, nonpredictive, and unlimitedly flexible. Notice that in those respects it has virtually the entire catalog of characteristics alleged to render the idea of supernatural design scientifically hopeless.[6] Notice further that the uniformity principle does not by itself generate any payoff of the sort typically demanded of supernatural design—by itself it makes no empirical predictions, gives no specific guidance in the lab, has nothing to say about specific titrations.[7]

But it has had a huge payoff in that it has been a deep background part of a guiding conceptual framework within which attempts to understand the cosmos have met with significantly more systematic success than was achieved within alternative conceptual frameworks of irregularity and arbitrariness. Thus, although a demand for some prospect of scientific profit from design might be appropriate, the specific types of profit it is or is not legitimate to demand may depend on exactly where and how design might be expected to operate in a scientific hierarchy.[8]

Design Functions: Historical Foundations

Were design operating within science, what might it suggest? What influences might it generate? Again, there are few rigorous connections in this area. But neither are there rigorous links between our experiences and an external world, a past, and so on. In such cases we literally have no choice but to go with what seems reasonable.[9]

Creation

Historically, design was a subcomponent of the concept of *creation*, and it is useful as a sighting shot to look at scientifically relevant matters extracted from the larger idea of creation historically. In an extremely useful survey, John Hedley Brooke provides a catalog of historical links, among which are the following (with some representative associated figures).[10] The concept of creation provided one way of rationally justifying such key presuppositions as the uniformity of nature, the universality of natural laws (Newton), the comprehensibility of nature (Whewell), and sanctions for and justifications of science itself (Bacon). It contributed to such essential conceptual resources as *law* and *force* (visible in, e.g., Newton). It supported such basic methodological norms as objectivity and empiricality (e.g. Mersenne). It provided part of the justification for such theory-evaluation criteria as simplicity (e.g., Newton and Faraday) and beauty, and affected the shape of various plausibility structures. It factored into the context of pursuit in terms of choice of problems, and judgments concerning the acceptability of solutions. It lent credibility to specific conceptual stances (e.g., the highly fruitful machine model had roots in the conception of the cosmos as *made*). It offered "regulative" principles employed in specific disciplines— for example, anatomy, geology (Hutton), chemistry (Priestley), and paleontology. It stimulated investigation and factored into specific interpretations of data (Kepler), and occasionally even provided specific content to theories. Such contributions are not negligible.

Design

What of *design* more specifically? As it happens, the concept of creation historically involved the idea of an agent who created deliberately, purposefully, and with wisdom. Thus, design, defined earlier as deliberately created mind-correlative pattern, was already included, and it inherits much of the above list. But there are some of those to which design is especially relevant. That principle functioning at the world-view level has a cascade of plausible, possible connections. It might not *drive* all such connections, but it has historically suggested some, legitimated others, and been able to comfortably absorb the rest.

The most basic suggestion from a design outlook might simply be an expectation that the physical world would in some way make sense.[11] If the cosmos was designed, then it was an artifact, to be investigated in appropriate ways. So analogies to agent products—machines and art, for instance[12]—would be useful guides to theorizing. And thus, agent-valued factors such as elegance and beauty and simplicity might constitute effective evaluative guides. Mind-correlative patterns would necessarily be built in and could be discovered. Structures would be in principle intelligible, as with anything deliberately designed. Given that the construction of pattern was deliberate, purposes could be fruitfully sought. Expectations of coordinated functioning would be reasonable. Such functioning would be productively effective. Consistent operation—uniformity—would be reasonably anticipated, making induction a reliable procedure. Principles of order would underlay cosmic operations.

Design also could support more specifically theoretical and empirical content as well. For instance, that organisms were invariably adapted to their environment and mode of life was an expectation explicitly derived from design outlooks.[13] Other specific matters had links to design as well—for example, Descartes's principle of inertia, Boyle's rejection of nature's alleged abhorrence of vaccua, Maupertuis's "least action" principle, Newton's theory of comets.

And not incidently, the cosmos in fact being designed would rather effectively explain any heuristic and instrumental usefulness of the idea that the cosmos was designed.[14]

If we include the idea that human observers were designed for this cosmos with faculties designed to get at truth when properly employed, justifications for other scientifically essential principles emerge as well—for example, justification for the scientifically essential reliability of human senses, and the reliability and applicability of both human conceptual patterns and human reasoning patterns. Such justifications are not otherwise trivial to come by.[15]

It will of course be noticed that virtually all of the above already operate within the scientific conceptual hierarchy and thus would not seem to represent potential new payoffs of considering design now. But if those scientifically essential principles, sensitivities, and stances are indeed historical fruits of a design outlook, then to some extent the question *What would be the payoff from design?* is a bit peculiar. It may be that science is *immersed* in design payoffs—that (*a la* Moliere's would-be gentleman) science has been speaking design prose all along. As physicist Paul Davies says: "Science began as an outgrowth of theology, and all scientists, whether atheists or theists . . . accept an essentially theological world view."[16]

If various historians of science are correct about some of the theologically freighted details of the rise of Western science,[17] it may thus be that design hasn't gotten due scientific credit because we have become too comfortably familiar with the design-induced shape of science to recall that that shape was neither a priori given, obviously normative, nor always old. It wears the mask of the ordinary. A question of Einstein's might be well worth pondering here: "What does a fish know about the water in which he swims all his life?"[18]

Scientific Superfluity—An Objection

But even if design did undergird various scientifically essential principles, it would still seem to be detachable from science and scientific theories proper, and would thus appear to be strictly speaking, *scientifically superfluous.* Isn't the source of concepts and principles and theories scientifically irrelevant? And wouldn't Ockham have something to say about the scientifically superfluous? Aren't superfluous components supposed to be removed by the famous razor?

As it turns out, it isn't quite that simple. Although the furor has quieted, several decades ago a formal result known as "Craig's Theorem" was interpreted by many as demonstrating that theories themselves are logically superfluous within science. Supposing that result to be correct, given that theories are essential to key aspects of science, we are, I think, forced to the conclusion that logical superfluousness is perfectly consistent with scientific indispensibility. That suggests that care is required in this area.[19]

In any case, Ockham's razor may cut various ways through potentially design-related questions. For instance, "many universe" hypotheses are sometimes employed in attempts to spike design-friendly fine-tuning arguments. But as Davies notes: "Invoking an infinite number of other universes just to explain the apparent contrivances of the one we see is pretty drastic, and in stark conflict with Occam's razor,"[20] and physicist Edward Harrison adds: "Take your choice: blind chance that requires multitudes of universes, or design that requires only one."[21]

Design Functions: Broad Umbrellas

Suppose that near the beginnings of science, design did in fact underwrite (or at least motivate) scientifically essential principles.[22] In that case, design might have contributed essential pieces of the conceptual space in which science still operates—

again, a not insignificant contribution. But there is still a tendency to ask "yeah, but what has design done for us lately?" What sort of use is it now? Hasn't anything it might once have had to offer already been mined—and much of that already discarded?[23]

The case for design legitimacy would indeed be substantially more attractive were there scientific payoffs beyond background framework principles, essential and significant to science though they are. And there might be some. For instance, a commitment to design might generate expectations of finding deeper patterns underlying cases of apparent randomness. A design stance might suggest that perhaps the Copenhagen interpretation of quantum mechanics fell into the very error widely associated with theories involving supernatural agency—it quit too soon. A design approach might spur one to continue attempts to close apparent quantum gaps.[24]

Since (as seen earlier) finite design nearly invariably involves nomic discontinuity and since supernatural design can also in principle involve such discontinuity, another aspect of a design outlook might be a general openness to recognition of the possibility of naturalistic explantory dead ends—of gaps. For instance, it might underpin a willingness to accept the impossibility of a purely natural origin of life, should the evidence for such impossibility approach the level of the evidence for the impossibility of perpetual motion. It might mean a willingness, under appropriate scientific circumstances, to abandon any a priori insistence that some particular phenomenon was purely natural, come what empirical evidence may. There have been those who virtually defined "nature" (at least the physical realm) as being a realm of those things "which should be referred to purely corporeal causes, i.e., those devoid of thought and mind."[25] A high-level design outlook might simply consist in a willingness to allow that or other reductionistic philosophical dictates to be challengeable in suitable empirical situations, should suitable empirical situations ever arise.[26]

This willingness might never result in actual changes in the content of science—the "impossibility" eventuality in question might simply never arise. It would, however, affect the "flavor" of science, giving science at least one new degree of freedom. To some, that would not be an attraction. But it might have payoffs. For one thing, it would provide science the wherewithall to abandon persistently failing naturalistic research programs. For instance, Prigogine and Stengers claim that "Since there is no one to build nature, we must give to its very 'bricks'—that is, to its microscopic activity—a description that accounts for the building process."[27] Here on the basis of an (anti)theological supposition we are, it is alleged, forced to restrict ourselves to specific types of theories about microrealities.[28] Suppose that such attempts were consistently scientifically unproductive for centuries. That is certainly possible.[29] Evidently, on the view of Prigogine and Stengers, one would have to either continue beating a dead horse or give up thinking about basic building processes, or else—ironically enough—give up science in order to try thinking about such processes in more empirically productive ways.

In such circumstances, the above design stance would allow one both to acknowledge the message nature might be trying to display—"'tain't how it is"—and to move the explanatory search into the right region—mind-correlative agent involvement. Legitimizing abandonment of demonstrably failing research programs plus permitting relevant efforts to move into the right explanatory regions *in appropriate circumstances* are not insignificant practical payoffs.

Gaps

An in-principle willingness to consider the possibility that purely natural causes (and finite agencies) might be inadequate to some phenomena in nature leads fairly directly to supernatural agent activity and—nearly inevitably—to gaps. It was argued in the previous chapter that the possibility of and recognition of gaps need not have the destructive effects on science often alleged. In fact, such willingness and recognition might even help focus scientific investigation in specific instances. Gap questions suggest a number of lines for exploration—for example:

a. are there actually any gaps?
b. if so, where and what are they?
c. are there any regularities or patterns to gap locations?
d. are there characteristic categories of phenomena in which gaps appear?
e. are there classifiable types of gaps (a gap typology)?
f. are there characteristic clues to gaps?
g. are there patterns (signatures) to the structures of phenomena that bridge the gaps?

Notice that the answers to (c) through (g) could each provide bases for prediction. Notice that answers to those questions could be empirically tested. Notice that pursuit of those questions could perhaps uncover patterns in nature. Notice that such patterns might never be uncovered were those questions not asked. And notice that prohibitionists forbid one even to *ask* those questions in a scientific context.

As noted earlier, gap cases are nearly universally condemned as undermining the motivation for rigorous empirical inquiry. But none of the above questions constitutes counsel to short-circuit investigation.[30] In fact, were one committed to the existence of gaps, one of the better strategies for confirming their existence might be strenuous attempts to close purported gaps. Failure of such attempts would potentially have the same implications as failure of strenuous (Popperian) attempts to falsify theories—a procedure often advertised as the real core of science. Persistant survival of such trials by fire is one of the stronger endorsements a theory can receive from nature.

In any case, there is nothing irrational or subversive of science in a willingness to admit, under empirically appropriate circumstances, the possibility or the actuality of gaps in natural causation. And if any such gaps were scientifically pursued and established, the consequences could be powerful, specific, and scientifically significant payoffs.

Gapless Natural Causation

As noted earlier, it is at least possible for phenomena to exhibit mind correlativity powerful enough to push us toward design conclusions, even in cases lacking nomic discontinuities.[31] But if there are no gaps in the natural causal history of a phenomenon, then isn't that natural causal history a scientifically adequate, complete causal history? And in that case, what is to be gained scientifically from acknowledging design? It might be replied that *being designed* would still be an important *truth* about that phenomenon. That is no doubt correct. But if the immediate causal history, structure, composition, and operation of the phenomenon can be given a completely natural account without specific reference to that truth, then how could there be scientific payoffs to tacking that truth onto that description?

As it turns out, that acknowledgment might generate effects in a number of ways. In the earlier example involving examining something ambiguous on Mars, finding out that it was not an unusual mineral formation but a product of deliberate alien design might alter our questions, our conclusions, and even our mode of investigation.[32] Similarly, seeing some natural phenomenon (or the cosmos) as designed would at least add some questions to our scientific lists. For instance

a. does this phenomenon have some specific purpose?
b. what is that purpose?
c. how does subsystem s contribute to that purpose?
d. what subsystem performs function f which is essential to the purpose?
e. how does this phenomenon exemplify relevant design patterns?
f. is this pattern another instance of or a derivative of or reducible to some broader pattern?

But can we ever determine such purposes with any confidence? In some cases, probably. For instance, with a good design, purpose will be a subset of function. At the least, function will often be a good indicator of purpose. If sparrows are designed (directly or indirectly) it is a good guess that part of the purpose of wings is connected with flight.[33]

Ceteris Paribus Again

The question of recognizability brings us back to an earlier theme affecting legitimacy. It was argued that the only exclusion science required for its effective functioning was that arising out of ceteris paribus considerations—against matters simultaneously unreliably intermittent and not reliably recognizable. Design need not produce any difficulties here at all.

Gap Cases

In gap cases, effects of supernatual agent activity might indeed be irregular, intermittent, or even one-time. Of course, they do not have to be so. Recall the possibility suggested earlier of patterns and typologies in gap cases. But were gaps legitimately empirically established, then the existence of agent activity at those gaps would be straightforwardly recognizable, and thus mind correlativity, pattern, design, and even specific purpose might be relatively easily recognizable. Design in gap cases involving cognitive content, mind affinity, and the like would be difficult to deny.

And even one-time gap events need cause no inevitable difficulty. Despite popular claims about the scientific essentiality of repeatability, mere uniqueness of events does not stop science in its tracks. Every event is unique in some respects. But science addresses even some uniquely unique events quite nicely—for example, the Big Bang, the Oklo natural reactor. Even a one-time gap event could involve recognizable designedness, and given the possibility of *empirical* causal connections involving design, not only would scientific recognition and investigation of that designedness not be destructive of science, science would be empirically and explanatorily impoverished for ignoring it.

Nongap Cases

Design built into the laws and causal structues of the comos need not violate any strictures against unreliably intermittent effects. Indeed, such design could itself even constitute part of the consistencies against which intermittency was defined.

On the other hand, individual pieces of design built into the initiating conditions of the cosmos, while not constituting part of the lawful regularities of the cosmos, need not be unrecognizable. The designedness of the earlier mathematical meteor crater case structured into the Big Bang was clearly recognizable. It need not happen repeatedly for us to recognize that, and its resulting from an unbroken chain of causation back to the Big Bang does not undermine that recognition either.

Recognition and Costs

It is possible—perhaps even likely—that if the cosmos is designed, some parts of that design are unrecognized or unrecognizable by us. But that has little bearing upon the recognizability and the legitimacy of recognizing cases which are clear. As an analogy, that advanced aliens might subtly design some things in ways that we cannot even suspect does not undercut the legitimacy of our attributing the Martian titanium cube to aliens. If some aspects of nature are designed, and if in some instances that designedness is rationally recognizable, then prohibitions on recognizing, theorizing about, or investigating that designedness in science not only provides science with no useful protection, but they carry a cost to any conception of science as an attempt to get at empirically relevant truths about nature.

That cost is not merely one of explanatory gaps in science. Many, after all, stipulatively define *science* in ways that automatically place such explanatory gaps outside of science. People are, of course, perfectly free to stipulate such definitions if they wish. What no one *is* free to do, however, is to make such stipulations, erect on those stipulations various prohibitions concerning what science can and cannot consider, then claim that what science produces under those prohibitions is truth, rational belief, accurate mirrors of reality, self-correctiveness, or anything of the sort. The character of the results will be constrained by the legitimacy (or lack thereof) of the original stipulations. If nature does not ignore design and if design factors into relevant empirical structures, then any science built on proscriptions against design will inevitably fall into one of two difficulties. Either it will be forever incomplete (the *PDI* promissory note being forever passed along but never paid), or it will eventually get off track, with no prospect of getting back on track (key elements of the track having been placed beyond permissible bounds of discussion), thereby turning science from a correlate of nature into a humanly contrived artifact.

Permitting design into the scientific context may, as many hold, have risks. So do prohibitions.

Legitimacy and Payoffs—Conclusion

As indicated at the beginning of this chapter, scientists tend to be a pragmatic group. If design promised some payoff, scientists would tend to embrace it, letting others argue about the legitimacy issue and not being overly exercised about how it came out.[34] I have argued above that there are potential payoffs functioning at various levels in the scientific conceptual hierarchy. Merely admitting the discussability of design in science could in principle raise new questions, and affect the questions already asked in investigations. It could suggest directions for exploration, and affect approaches in those directions. It could affect the range of hypotheses considered, and the range of responses attributable to nature. It could permit us to see possible patterns that prohibitions might mask. It could allow exploration of those patterns, as well as construction of explanations, in the only terms that would be adequate to them. It could affect how questions were put to nature, and could allow us to hear more clearly some things nature might be trying to say.

How far down the hierarchy might effects be felt? Might design have consequences for *this particular* titration? Probably not (although recall the earlier origin-of-life example of how design implications could in principle involve almost arbitrary empirical specificity). But then, neither evolutionary theory nor uniformity principles—let alone commitments to use of differential equations—would by themselves have such consequences either.

So, in summary: first, the usual objections to design in science do not actually establish impermissibility. Second, design does not seem to violate the basic ceteris paribus conditions. Third, there are some scientifically relevant positive considerations for at least permitting exploration of the possibility of design in nature within the scientific context. And fourth, there are at least some possible payoffs from permitting discussion of design in science. Of course, those possibilities may never come off—empirical investigation may not ultimately tell in their favor. But even if so, it should not be forgotten that the medium in which science now swims may itself consist of unacknowledged design payoffs.

12

CONCLUSION

The question of whether or not concepts and principles involving supernatural intelligent design can occupy any legitimate place within science has a long and varied history. But as with many other issues, contemporary culture has on this question opted for easy resolutions. Some attempts appeal to unreflective conceptions of *science* as being simplistically empirical on the one hand and of the *supernatural* as being wholly disconnected from the empirical on the other. Other attempts consist of the claims that design theories ultimately reduce to gap theories and that such theories are inherently impermissible in science. On both views, the easy negative answers follow nearly immediately.

As I have argued in the foregoing, however, once relevant issues are pursued in any depth, the appearance of simplicity evaporates. Given the interconnected nature of the conceptual components of science, the idea that concepts intuitively more at home in upper levels of the hierarchy (including design concepts) can be systematically screened off from methodological, theoretical, pragmatic, and other factors constitutive of science does not appear promising. And "gap" objections seem mistaken on all counts—conceptual, logical, empirical, and historical.

In fact, if the preceeding investigations are correct, there is no compelling conceptual basis for any blanket prohibition on exploring applications or implications of the idea of supernatural design within the scientific context. Some design theories may be inappropriate in some instances, but that is perfectly consistent with others being in principle legitimate. It is, of course, perfectly possible that such attempts could end up wholly empty, but since every scientific research program faces at least that possibility, that hardly constitutes grounds for preemptive prohibitions.

Of course, the "preemptive" might elicit protests. It is sometimes argued that whatever the normative status of the case, design "research programs" have had their chance historically and have simply proven to be scientifically barren. Perhaps so. It is worth keeping in mind, however, that such claims are not straightforward and that establishing them is not trivial. For instance, such claims involve philosophical positions concerning just what scientific failure *is*, and concerning how such failure is to be recognized. Furthermore, establishing the precise de facto reasons for a theory being abandoned historically is far from easy, and cannot always even be done.

Determining exactly what role religion, philosophy, social, personal, and empirical matters played in the career of specific theories is a wildly complicated matter even in superficially straightforward cases. And in cases of theories rejected for partly philosophical reasons, such rejections may provide only limited evidential support for contentions of *scientific* failure.

But as noted earlier, some major historians of science do not in fact find uniform failure in the scientific historical record. Furthermore, if (as some historians argue) the very rise, contours, and structure of science itself reflect some aspects of a doctrine of creation, we must face the question How much indirect "credit" should design concepts get, even for theories that do not overtly involve design, merely by virtue of their conforming to structures initially design driven? And exactly how should that credit "count" on the question of whether or not design conceptions have been historical failures?

Of course, even were all such questions readily answerable, and even were it clear that design theories had been scientific failures historically, that would not yet constitute a *normative* case for any prohibition. For one thing, abandoned scientific pictures sometimes make comebacks, sometimes temporary, sometimes not— witness, for example, wave theories of light, atomism, and an episodic beginning of the cosmos. Suppose further that design theories not only had been failures, but were destined to continue to be failures. Even then, there would be little reason to fear exploration of them. Though widely misconstrued, surely Popper taught us that much.

There is one more, deeper cluster of considerations linked to *correlation to mind.* Key presuppositions of science—presuppositions whose content is utterly indispensible and whose legitimacy *as presuppositions* must unavoidably be simply granted—are linked to such correlation. Indeed, one key presupposition—the intelligibility of nature—very nearly just *is* a presupposition of nature's mind correlativity. And as argued earlier, the very concepts of human explanation and understanding are built around mind correlativity and our experiential recognitions of it. The rise and early development of science itself were bound up with (and perhaps even partially dependent upon) the extremely fruitful conviction that the cosmos and its contents were creations. That conviction secured mind correlativity and its implications, underpinned the legitimacy of the project, and justified not only the appropriateness of human concepts and reason as applied to nature (i.e., the objectivity of the correlativity), but even the use of human analogies which themselves essentially involved mind correlativity—for example, nature as art, nature as machine.

Thus, the structure of science, the structure of understanding, the structure of key conceptual analogies, the structure of conceptions of reality, the structure of science's conceptual underpinnings—all these contain echoes of mind correlativity. One of the key attractions of Darwinian evolution was that it provided a framework within which a significant number of scientifically relevant considerations could coalesce into a larger, integrated system. Broad philosophical outlooks, various scientific disciplines, and some isolated subdisciplines could, after Darwin, interlock in scientifically interesting ways. Given the pervasiveness of the echoes of mind correlativity just mentioned, design—with its core concept of *correlation to mind*—may have some potential for that same sort of broad, interlocking integration. Indeed, I have tried to sketch out tentatively a bit of the what and where of such potential.

But whether design theories should prove to be ultimately scientifically successful or not, there is little to be said for a prohibitionism that forbids even the attempt to pursue whatever potential there might be.

APPENDIX
DEMBSKI'S *DESIGN INFERENCE*

Readers familiar with current design debates will have noticed an apparent omission in the foregoing—absence of any extended discussion of William Dembski's *The Design Inference*. I have given little attention to that work for a variety of reasons. Among other things, primary concerns in the present work center around what the very concept of design comes to, and whether or not (and why) that concept might be either legitimate or useful in scientific contexts. Dembski's primary project is to present a rigorous rational reconstruction of the logic of a certain sort of inference to design conclusions, where "design" is understood in a specific stipulated way. Although there is only limited overlap, the two projects can be understood as dovetailing in certain ways. In this appendix, I will briefly and relatively informally explicate Dembski's main theses, indicate how our two projects relate, then briefly catalog a number of what seem to me to be significant difficulties with various of Dembski's contentions as developed specifically in *The Design Inference*.

Explication

According to Dembski, when confronted with a phenomenon demanding explanation, we implicitly work through a hierarchy of explanatory categories constituting an "Explanatory Filter." The sequence, in proposed order of precedence, is *regularity*, *chance*, and *design*. If the phenomenon in question is reasonably attributable to some natural regularity or law, we accept that and proceed no further. If, however, such appeal does not appear to constitute adequate explanation, we proceed to the next level of the filter and consider whether or not some explanatory appeal to chance (or coincidence, or randomness) might be adequate. If the probability of the phenomenon, given our relevant background information, is above some minimal threshhold, we typically chalk the phenomenon up to chance and pursue the issue no further. For instance, the odds are against getting double sixes in one throw of the dice, but the probability is not so low that when it happens we go off in search of hidden causes and meanings. So appeal to chance with respect to events of moderate probability seems unproblematic.

Events of very small probability, however, pose potential problems for "chance" explanations. Of course, low probability alone need pose no such problems, since billions of things of enormously low probability happen all the time. However, with respect to some specific low probability events we are inclined to think: this particular thing couldn't or wouldn't have happened just by chance. (Recall, for instance, the earlier case of a card dealer getting two successive royal flushes.) Obviously, then, there is something about such cases in view of which chance no longer constitutes a defensible account. In these cases, says Dembski, we move one step further down the filter and attribute the phenomenon to design.

The project Dembski sets for himself is the technical examination of this sequential series of inferences, and in particular the rigorous explication of the formal structure of the logic by which "chance" hypotheses can be dismissed, thereby triggering the final move within the filter to "design." There are a number of technical matters requiring attention–for example, identifying relevant probability thresholds. But the key task Dembski pursues is explicating the *formal* contours of the "something" which in addition to suitably low probability rationally warrants the conclusion that this particular thing wasn't a result of chance, and more specifically to identify the logical requirements and the formal structure of the inferential rejection of mere chance in the occurrence of the phenomenon.

In the above paragraph, I have repeatedly stressed the formal, technical, and logical nature of Dembski's project. It is crucial to keep that in mind, because Dembski is not attempting to give a formal analysis of what the concept of design comes to, nor is he attempting to explicate the substantive details of when design conclusions are or are not warranted. Indeed, the concept of design which he employs is given almost no positive content. Dembski himself stresses that fact repeatedly. For instance:

> To attribute an event to design is to say that it cannot be reasonably referred to either regularity or chance. [That amounts to] defining design as the set-theoretic complement of the disjunction regularity-or-chance. (p. 36)

Dembski repeats that he is "[d]efining design as the negation of regularity and chance" (p. 36). Given that design as employed by Dembski acquires its character through negation, inferences to design will have to proceed by a via negativa—that is, by elimination of the alternatives the absence of which defines design. Dembski both reaffirms that character and endorses the implication:

> The concept of design that emerges from the design inference is therefore eliminative, asserting of an event what it is not, not what it is. To attribute an event to design is to say that regularity and chance have been ruled out (p. 19)

and says that "design [is] the elimination of regularity and chance" (p. 20).

That Dembski is not employing the robust, standard, agent-derived conception of design that most of his supporters and many of his critics have assumed seems clear. Dembski further seems commited to the position that that more substantive concept of design is neither required by the design inference as he explicates it, nor is it a consequence of that inference:

> There is no reason to commit the design inference to a doctrine of intelligent agency . . . [An intelligent agent] is not part of the logical structure of the design inference. (p. x–xi)

> Note, however, that their identification of design with the activity of an intelligent agent . . . does not follow by the force of this logic. (p. 60)

> Although a design inference is often the occasion for inferring an intelligent agent, as a pattern of inference the design inference is not tied to any doctrine of intelligent agency. (p. 8)

> Taken by itself design does not require that [an intelligent] agent be posited. The notion of design that emerges from the design inference must not be confused with intelligent agency. (p. 227)

Of course, it might be thought that although the concepts of design and intelligent agency differ and thus should not be confused, and although the cogency of the inference can be demonstrated independently of any such connection, there nonetheless *is* some essential, necessary connection between them. But Dembski appears to reject that as well:

> Frequently the reason an event conforms to a pattern is because an intelligent agent arranged it so. There is no reason, however, to turn this common occurrence into a metaphysical first principle. (p. 227)

Whatever the connections may or may not be, establishing intelligent agency requires some further inferential step, involving further argumentation employing further principles. Thus, "[D]esign is a mode of explanation logically preliminary to agency" (p. 19).

So Dembski is simply attempting a formal, rational reconstruction of the logical structure of a type of inference, and is not attempting to give a full-blown account of design, to specify conditions under which design conclusions would be empirically warranted or justified in a specifically scientific context, or anything of that sort. That is why as he uses the concept, "Design . . . constitutes a logical rather than a causal category" (p. 9).

Specification

What exactly is the formal feature which, according to Dembski, undergirds the key move of the design inference—the elimination of chance as a viable explanatory category in specific low probability cases? The key formal feature is what Dembski terms "*specification*," informally characterized as follows: "Specifications are the non-ad hoc patterns that can legitimately be used to eliminate chance and warrant a design inference" (p. 13)

Approaching from a different angle, we might ask, Since we are dealing with an essentially eliminative inference, what ultimately is it that must be eliminated to reach the final node of the Explanatory Filter? Dembski's answer is basically that we must rule out ad hoc patterns as candidates for design attribution. What exactly does that mean, and how exactly do we go about it?

Let us begin with two of Dembski's examples. The first is one of Dembski's favorite analogies, involving variant cases of alleged archery skill. In the first case, a series of targets is painted on a barn, then an archer from a quite impressive distance fires one arrow at each target, putting the arrow smack in the center of the target. In the second case, an archer fires a series of arrows at the unpainted barn, then being a skilled painter manufactures a target around each arrow stuck in the barn wall. In both cases, we are presented with a series of bullseyes with arrows in the exact center, but we are inclined to attribute the first case to archery skill and the second case to attempted con artistry. Dembski identifies the first case as involving specification, the second as demonstrating fabrication.

The second example involves the resident experts from the *National Enquirer.* Upon the event of a political assasination, those experts recall having previously seen some peculiar markings on an Egyptian artifact, and expressly for the purposes at hand arbitrarily assign an interpretation to the marks, crediting them with containing a prophetic description of the assasination.

Both the target fabrication and the Egyptian prophecy cases are ad hoc in evident although different ways. The fabrication involves manipulation of (or arbitrary production of) the arrow/target pattern itself—a pattern which if not the product of an ad hoc fabrication would have been legitimately significant of archery skill on the standard criteria of such skill. The prophecy case involves manipulation of (or arbitrary invention of) an interpretive criterion intended to confer a significance onto the markings which—had the interpretive criterion in question had some independent foundation and not been merely the product of ad hoc invention formed out of the event (the assassination) itself—those markings might otherwise have had.

The first case has been inappropriately skewed by information concerning actual pattern significance criteria factoring into the production of the arrow/target pattern (or the relevant event) itself. In the second case, the significance—via the interpretive criterion—has been inappropriately skewed by information that the event in question (the assassination) has actually taken place. The intuitive question such cases raise is How might one guard against this ad hoc skewing by information of the actual?

Dembski's answer is, in effect, that both the pattern that is identified in an event and the process of that identification must be independent in definable ways from the fact of the event's occurrence. A pattern that escapes the ad hoc category must be *detachable*, where detachability is a conjunction of two more basic characteristics—*epistemic independence* and *tractability*. The first condition is met if taking account of "side information" (relevant cognitive resources available independently of any information derived from the event in question) would make it neither more nor less likely that the actually observed pattern would have been produced *had* sheer random chance been the correct explanation of the occurrence of relevant events—in short (and ignoring one technical complication for the sake of simplicity), if $P(E/H) = P(E/H\&I)$ where E is the event in question, H is the hypothesis that the event occurred purely by chance, and I is certain relevant "side information." The second condition is met if from that relevant side information alone, one could in principle construct a set of patterns of the type relevant to the event in question, E.

Intuitively, the archery fabrication case fails the first condition, the Egyptian prophecy case fails the second. (For instance, the Egyptian prophecy case involved an alleged interpretation of the markings which emerged solely for the purpose of confering post facto significance onto them, and construction of the criteria depended essentially upon and was generated out of prior information concerning the occurrernce of the assassination.)

Finally, a pattern is *delimited* if that pattern (typically characterizing some actual event) falls within the set of patterns generated under the tractability condition. A pattern that meets the independence, tractability, and delimitation conditions is a specification. According to what Dembski terms the Law of Small Probability, specified events of low probability do not occur merely by chance. Thus, any such events may be inferred to fall into the final category of the Explanatory Filter—design.

Here's a simple illustration. Suppose that SETI searchers pick up a string of microwave pulses which when transcribed as 0s and 1s turn out to be the first thirty prime numbers in binary. We would fairly confidently conclude that the string was a designed attempt at communication. Why so? We would quickly rule out any purely natural process involving either law or reasonable probability. In fact, the probability of getting any particular string of 0s and 1s of the relevant length—including the one actually received—is abysmally low. We would thus move rapidly to the "low probability" area of the Explanatory Filter. The only remaining question, on Dembski's system, would be whether or not the precise sequence received was specified. Is it?

To answer that question, we must first identify relevant side information. In a similar case, the relevant side information identified by Dembski consists of some basic facts about the structure of binary numbers, binary representations, and some very basic arithmetical facts. With that in mind, we can readily see that the binary pattern exhibited by the SETI signals is independent in the sense defined—taking that side information into account would not alter the probability of the binary string being the actual string received on the provisional assumption merely that some string or other had been received and that that string (whatever it was) had been produced by random processes. It is also tractable in the stipulated sense—given relevant facts about binary numbers, binary representation, and the like, we could easily on that basis alone produce a number of telling binary strings. Among those strings could surely be the string in question—the sequence of primes—meaning that the delimitation condition would be met. The string in question is thus specified, of appropriately low probability, and sheer chance can be ruled out as the proper explanatory category for the sequence monitored by SETI. The ruling out of regularity and chance entails design in Dembski's sense.

The bulk of the technical discussion within Dembski's book is his attempt to rigorously explicate exactly what the relevant sort of independence comes to formally (this is done in terms of probability theory), what tractability comes to formally (this is done in terms of complexity theory), and what delimitation comes to formally (this is done roughly in terms of set theory). There are a number of things of interest within those technicalities and formalisms, but I shall not discuss them here.

Incompleteness

As noted earlier, *The Design Inference* does not provide any real analysis of the concept of design. Dembski's characterization of design is essentially negative—a largely undefined set-theoretic complement with a resultant "what-design-is-not" structure. That is not necessarily a criticism, since that was not part of the task Dembski set himself. But that absence is not an insignificant one. For one thing, many of Dembski's supporters and various of his critics have failed to notice the actual boundaries of his project, with various resultant infelicitous reactions. But more significantly, the thread of that absence reaches deep into Dembski's project, and it is a gap that must be at least partially filled before Dembski's formal design inference—even if correct—can be of substantive and broad use in investigative contexts. I shall briefly try to substantiate that claim.

Both the independence and the tractability conditions depend fundamentally upon identification of the relevant side information. How is that side information identified? Here Dembski provides no real help whatever, saying only that:

> [I]dentifying suitable patterns and side information for eliminating chance requires of [the agent] S insight . . . What's needed is insight, and insight admits no hard and fast rules . . . We have such insights all the time, and use them to identify patterns and side information that eliminate chance. But the logic of discovery by which we identify such patterns and side information is largely a mystery. (p. 148)

In fact, as Dembski sees it, the relevant side information is typically identified *in light of* the specific pattern in question, and only *after* the pattern has already—on grounds that are "largely a mystery"—been identified as a candidate for a design explanation. That is made relatively clear by such claims as:

> Verifying [the tractability condition] is not a matter of formulating D [the pattern in question] from scratch. Typically, a subject S explicitly identifies an event E (whose explanation is in question), as well as a pattern D that delimits E. In particular, D will aready be in S's hands. S's task, therefore, is not so much to formulate D, as to convince oneself that S could have formulated D knowing only that D delimits some indeterminate event compatible with [the chance hypothesis], and that [side information] *I* provides information that may be relevant to this indeterminate event. Having identified E and D, S pretends E and D are still unidentified, and then determines whether the side information *I* is enough to formulate D. (p. 150, see also p. 146)

Furthermore

> Typically the side information *I* will not signify the totality of S's problem-solving capabilities, but only those items of information specifically relevant to formulating [the pattern] D. (p. 151)

Of course, relevance can only be defined relative to the pattern in question.

So typically, patterns that are likely candidates for design are *first* identified as such by some unspecified ("mysterious") means, then with the pattern in hand S picks out side information identified (by unspecified means) as being relevant to the particular pattern, then sees whether the pattern in question is among the various patterns that *could* have been constructed from that side information.

What this means, of course, is that Dembski's design inference will not be particularly useful either in initial recognition or identification of design. That is not necessarily a criticism, given that Dembski was after different game. As he indicated very near the end of the book, in a slightly more limited context: "What's at stake . . . is epistemic justification, or what philosophers who study conditional logic call assertibility" (p. 221).

Relationship to Present Work

In a nutshell, Dembski's project and the present work can be seen as distinct, indeed independent, pieces of a larger investigation of design. Whereas Dembski is in effect taking a design concept (and to some extent design recognition) as a given, focusing on the formal credentials of a certain sort of inference related to design, the present work has in effect taken the formal legitimacy of such inferences as unproblematic and has attempted to explicate some of the underlying foundational conceptual and philosophy of science matters.

Some Critical Evaluation of Dembski's Work

Any attempt at rational reconstruction is subject to a variety of possible critical, evaluative questions—e.g., whether or not the formalisms themselves pass formal muster, whether or not the reconstruction actually captures anything of the original processes, whether the formalisms accomodate or conform to relevant foundational intuitions and concepts, and whether or not the reconstruction has problematic implications. I now turn briefly to some of these questions.

Relativization and Omniscience

As indicated above, Dembski is attempting to formally explicate the logical structure of a rationally warranting inference. Rational warrant must, of course, be indexed to specific agents—what it is rational for one person to believe (in the light of their circumstances, information, and epistemic resources) may be irrational for another person to believe (in the light of their different circumstances, information, and epistemic resources). For instance, a three year old is probably not behaving irrationally in believing in Santa Claus. A forty year old probably is. Thus, considerations will have to be ultimately relativized to some specific cognitive agent, S. Dembski explicitly stipulates that:

> Detachability must always be relativized to a subject and a subject's background knowledge. (p. 17)

Indeed,

> Everything depends on what S knows, believes, determines, and provisionally accepts. (p. 147–48)

This relativization further makes clear that Dembski's project is not to analyze design, generate design-recognition criteria, and so on. Whether or not something is in fact designed is not relativized to agents. Dembski's results are thoroughly and explicitly relativized.

Things seem to go a bit astray, however, when the agent in question is omniscient. Consider tractability. Tractability is roughly a measure of how many (or what portion) of the relevant possible patterns the agent S could generate employing the indicated side information. Clearly, an omniscient agent could generate every possible pattern on the basis of any—or no—relevant information. Thus, any tractability conditions are automatically met. Further, since any relevant actual pattern will fall within the bounds of all possible relevant patterns, the delimitation condition, as defined by Dembski, will be met as well. What of epistemic independence? The independence intuition as stated informally by Dembski is:

> Two things are epistemically independent if knowledge about one thing (in this case *I*) does not affect knowledge about the other (in this case E*'s ocurrence conditional on [the chance hypotheis] H). (p. 143)

Dembski has given us no minimum concerning what goes into *I*. Now, for any event E, there will always be some minor bit of side information *I* which is epistemically independent of E, and given the infinite pattern-producing capabilities of an omniscient being, the tractability and delimitation conditions will automatically be met employing only that minimal *I*. Consequently, E will be specified, and thus for any E of suitably low probability (if any), the agent in question will, according to the design inference, be epistemically warranted in concluding that the proper explanation for E is design.

Furthermore, if one grants the very plausible premise that anything rationally warranted for an omniscient being is in fact true, it will follow that the mere existence of an omniscient being (whether omnipotent, etc., or not) guarantees that there are no undesigned events of low probability. That seems to me to be a problematic consequence. On the other hand, suppose that omniscience does factor into *I*. It seems to me that in that case the dependence condition is never met. If it is never met, then a design inference is never warranted for an omniscient agent, and given the plausible premise that what is not rationally warranted for an omniscience being is in fact false, it may turn out that given the mere existence of an omnicient being, nothing is designed. That seems problematic as well.

Content Lack (Again)

Near here, it seems to me, is a core bit of the difficulty with Dembski's proposal. The only requirement for tractability is that a set of patterns be produced, with the further requirement that the pattern in question be somewhere among them (the delimitation condition). While identifying artifactuality and counterflow involves identifying patterns nature would not produce, identifying design typically involves identifying patterns an intelligent agent would produce. Merely looking among patterns that an agent given certain resources *could* produce seems to me to lack exactly the indispensible discrimination—the "insight," which in my terms would involve recognition of mind correlativeness—required to spot design. The problem with the tractability criterion as developed is that there is no substantive discrimination among the patterns produced. That lack becomes acutely evident and the tractability requirement clearly loses all bite when omniscience expands those patterns to the set of all possible patterns. (In this connection it is worth noting that Dembski argues (p. 228) that the design inference detects information, in some formal (e.g., Shannon) sense of "information." I shall not pursue the issue here, but one prominant feature of the formal treatments of information is that the formalisms do not capture the idea of semantic, cognitive content. It is exactly that content, of course, which is the most crucial characteristic of information in the usual sense. Thus, if what the design inference does is equivalent to detecting and measuring information in the formal sense, that fact would further spotlight exactly the conceptual-content incompleteness under discussion.)

What does the lack of bite of the tractability requirement in the case of omniscience reveal? I believe that it reveals a fairly deep difficulty in Dembski's ultimate case. To see how that emerges, let us take an indirect approach. Dembski takes his principle result to be the Law of Small Probabilities, that is,

LSP: Specified events of small probability do not occur by chance. (p. 5)

It might appear that LSP involves a prima facie confusion of categories—specification is a person-relative epistemic category; whereas, whether or not something occurs by chance appears to be a thoroughly ontological matter. This minor apparent glitch might look easily remediable—for example, by recasting the entire principle explicitly into terms concerning what categorization a specification rationally warranted one in inferring. In light of the considerations involving omniscience, above, I'm not sure that the required epistemic/ontological separation is quite that easy, but will not pursue that now.

What concerns me here is a different worry. Recall that the concept of design employed by Dembski is identified not by any positive content but is a set-theoretic complement, and that the correlated inferential structure proposed by Dembski is eliminative. Recall further that for Dembski, the last eliminative step is the elimination of ad hocness. LSP presupposes that successful specification—successful elimination of ad hocness—guarantees that any pattern left standing exemplifies design. The deeper presupposition is that in low probability cases designedness and ad hocness are exclusive and exhaustive. Perhaps they are exclusive (although that may be problematic), but I see no nonarbitrary reason for thinking that they are exhaustive. Designedness in any substantive sense involves exemplification of certain positive characteristics. Ruling out ad hocness (relative to S's particular resources and side information) does not yet establish anything at all concerning the presence or absence of those characteristics. If design and ad hocness were complementary in certain ways, then by ruling out all hints of ad hocness with sufficient stringency one could be assured that what remained represented design. But I see no reason to think that ad hocness and design stand in any such relationship, especially with respect to events or phenomena in nature. *Ad hoc* and *designed* seem to be just different, and not merely inverse, concepts. Given our finite resources and side information, there is always the open possibility of a gap between finitely identifiable ad hocness (which is what specification is supposed to eliminate) and actual design in any substantive sense. Thus, a defense against adhocness is not equivalent to a recognition procedure for genuine, substantive design.

Further Limitation

As noted earlier, Dembski's characterization of design is by exclusion. That has an immediate consequence, which Dembski notes:

> Defining design as the set-theoretic complement of the disjunction regularity-or-chance guarantees that the three modes of explanation are mutually exclusive and exhaustive. (p. 36)

That exclusive character is essential to the operation of the Explanatory Filter, as Dembski constructs it, but that benefit, it seems to me, comes with a significant cost. What it immediately means is that anything produced by nature (whether by law or chance) can be neither classified as designed in Dembski's sense, recognized as designed by Dembski's Explanatory Filter, nor epistemically justified as designed by Dembski's design inference. Anything produced by natural law simply sticks at that first point of the filter. As Dembski says: "If we can explain by means of a regularity, chance and design are automatically precluded" (p. 39). That difficulty is also evident with respect to Dembski's claim that design is "patterned improbability" (p. xii). If a supernatural agent deliberately structured natural laws and regularities to produce specific, patterned phenomena, such phenomena would surely count as designed, but need not be at all improbable with respect to the relevant laws and structures of nature. It seems to me, in fact, that *designed* and *improbable* are simply orthogonal notions, and that making improbability a necessary condition for designedness, as Dembski does, is simply to mistake two different concepts.

That has a number of further consequences. First, the design inference will simply be inapplicable to (or will summarily dismiss) a number of significant historical cases for design—such as those discussed earlier, which attempted to identify evidences of design in the productions of nature—design perhaps deliberately built into the very structure and processes of nature itself. The fact that some phenomenon was produced by some natural regularity was seen—rightly, it seems to me—as a different issue than whether or not that phenomenon exhibited clear marks of designedness. The exclusionary nature of Dembski's definition of design forecloses on all that without, so far as I can see, providing any justification whatever. That means that Dembski's rational reconstruction will have no application in some of the most interesting cases. For instance, Michael Behe argues in *Darwin's Black Box* that such phenomena as electric rotory flagella motors in E. coli exhibit design regardless of whether they were produced by natural (albeit non-Darwinian) means or by supernatural agent intervention at some point in the past. If Dembski is correct, Behe is mistaken about that—an implication I think most design advocates have failed to note.

In fact, the consequences may be even more dire. Consider the earlier case of a swarm of meteors printing something with cognitive content on the far side of the moon, where the history of that event tracks back by unbroken natural processes to the Big Bang. Once that unbroken natural history were established, the exclusionary conception of design would prevent us from recognizing the designedness of the message—cognitive content notwithstanding. Such a conception of design seems to me to be significantly wide of the mark, failing to recognize that there are at least in principle some characteristics that can signal design regardless of means of production.

Second, since designedness and production by nature were not construed as exclusive by most design advocates historically, and since they are so construed by Dembski, it appears as though Dembski has changed the topic. Changing the topic is, of course, perfectly legitimate, but any benefits of the previous topic cannot just automatically be appropriated.

Third, if a phenomenon being produced by natural means precludes that phenomenon being designed, the clear consequence is that design can only apply in cases of counterflow and artifactuality. With finite beings, that is relatively unproblematic. But if supernatural agents are included, then the only design activity Dembski's system *can* recognize is God-of-the-gaps activity. As is clear from earlier chapters, I have nothing in principle against God-of-the-gaps cases. But the problem for Dembski is that his system is limited to such cases.

Sample Tilt

Dembski appeals to a number of what he takes to be paradigm examples of design reasoning in both constructing and motivating his reconstruction. However, it turns out that many of his paradigm cases are cases involving attempts by one agent to conceal specific data from another agent by mimicing nature or chance, or at least by masking specific aspects of the counterflow inevitably involved. (See, for example, the cases involving Caputo, bullseye fabrications, detection and identification of criminals, plagerism, copyright violations, data cooking, cryptography, concealed murder to collect life insurance, pseudo-random number generating, and so on.) The design inferences involved consist of attempts by the second party to uncover the presence of or specific character of the first agent's actual activity.

Those sorts of cases are, of course, perfectly legitimate, and any adequate theory of design or reconstruction of design inferences should be able to handle them. But that paradigm slant does pose some risks. It means that the key founding intuitions for Dembski's reconstruction are taken from cases within the context of artifactuality, and in some cases from within the context of known or suspected artifactuality. As I argued earlier, the evidential situations within and outside such contexts differ significantly. Might that have consequences here? I'm not entirely sure, but there are a number of possibilities. One, taking clearly artifactual cases as paradigms might be part of the reason why Dembski constructed a system that seems to be inapplicable to cases in nature—which, again, may constitute some of the most interesting cases. Two, Dembski's apparent assumption that ruling out ad hocness secures design, is more plausible within the context of artifactuality. That might explain some aspects of LSP. Third, as noted earlier, Dembski gives no real hint as to what can or cannot factor into side information. If whether or not a case falls into a general artifactual context could be a part of one's side information, then given the difference between artifactual and nonartifactual contexts, the independence condition (as formally stated by Dembski) may fail—meaning once again that the design inference as formulated by Dembski might fail to deliver design conclusions even in cases of clear and obvious natural design. If that is the case, simply modifying the Explanatory Filter (which might help in earlier versions of this problem) might not solve this version of the problem.

A similar point can be extracted from Dembski's brief discussion of coincidences. As he notes, some coincidences cry out for explanation, and some do not. Dembski briefly describes two that do not seem to cry out, and seems to classify them among "coincidences for which we haven't a clue how to submit them to the Explanatory Filter" or among those for which "attempts to . . . submit [them] to the Explanatory Filter [seem] fruitless" (p. 225). It seems to me not to be just coincidence that both these cases, which appear to be beyond the bounds of artifactuality, appear to Dembski not to fit the filter in any fruitful way.

Miscategorizations

It seems to me that there may be a third problematic consequence as well—that of simply not operating as claimed in specific cases. Two possible cases follow.

Alien artifacts—a false negative. Suppose that we land on Mars, and discover something we can easily and clearly identify as an alien artifact. Such identification is perfectly unproblematic, and identification of artifactuality would mean that we had already progressed past regularity, medium probability, and sheer improbability within the filter. According to Dembski's rational reconstruction, our rational warrant in believing this to be designed (in his sense) would depend upon our having the capability of constructing a delimiting pattern purely from side information *I*. But if the aliens are alien enough, we might not even have the concepts—even *after* examination of the artifact—to construct such a pattern. But we could still recognize—rationally—the artifactuality of the object in question, and as discussed earlier, in some circumstances we might even be able to legitimately conclude that the object was not only artifactual but designed in the full intuitive sense of the word. Lacking the relevant concepts for the alien artifact, we probably could not discover or even understand what the actual design was, but that would have no bearing upon the initial recognition.

This example, then, seems to constitute a case of rational design recognition and inference in the complete absence of specification, which is not only a necessary condition for Dembski's design inference, but which, says Dembski, "is the only means available to us for distinguishing choice from chance, directed contingency from blind contingency" (p. 64).

That appears not to be the case. The ultimate problem here is not that we get a false negative, but that it emerges in a way which seems to me to be indicative of Dembski's approach being a bit off the mark.

Tumbleweeds—a false positive. First, a story—and one that so far as I remember is true. Some years ago my family and I were driving through a long, unpopulated stretch of a Western state. A fence paralleled the road on our left for quite a number of miles. At one point, I saw ahead of us a small tumbleweed—the only one I remember seeing for hours—being leisurely blown toward the road from the right. As we approached, the tumbleweed rolled across the road in front of us and—to my delight—rolled up to the fence on our left and continued on *precisely* through a small hole at the bottom of the fence—the only hole I had noticed in the fence.

Now, it strikes me that that event had a lot in common with Dembski's arrow example (or safe combination example) of specification. There is a special, independently set outcome in each case—success in hitting the target is dictated by the preestablished location of the target, which is determined independently of the actual location of the arrow; success in opening the safe is dictated by the preestablished configuration of the safe lock, which is determined independently of the combination actually entered; success in getting through the hole in the fence is dictated by the preestablished location of the hole, which is determined independently of the actual location of the tumbleweed. The probabilities associated with the chance hypotheses (that the arrow hit the precise spot of the target center by chance, that the precise safe combination was hit upon by chance, that the tumbleweed hit the precise spot of the fence hole by chance) are not altered by any reasonable side information. Thus, independence. Given some basic side information, we could easily formulate a collection of patterns that would include the key pattern in question. The pattern of the arrow hitting the target, of the entered combination being correct, of the tumbleweed hitting the hole in the fence, all rather jump out at one. Thus, tractability. The pattern of the actual event is, of course, found within the generated patterns. Thus, delimitation. And in all three cases, the probability can be nearly as low as one likes.

Given the precise parallels, it would seem that if the first two cases involve specification—which Dembski explicitly indicates—then the third one would as well, meaning that the design inference says "design" all three times. Yet, although we would readily place the first two in the design category, except in special circumstances we would not do so in the third case. Why not?

It seems to me that here is yet another demonstration that the presence or absence of artifactuality changes the evidential situation—a differentiation Dembski's system does not incorporate. It might be replied that whether or not one is in an artifactual context would be a key component in one's side information, but if so, there may well be other difficulties in cases where whether or not one *is* in an artifactual context is exactly what is at issue—for example, in Dembski's example of a detective trying to determine if a death involved artifactuality (a subtle murder) or not (a freakish accident). A design inference structure according to which one had to know in advance whether or not the situation was artifactual would obviously be of limited use in such cases.

Subsidiary Quibbles

Although I shall not pursue them here, I think that there are a number of smaller infelicities in *The Design Inference*. For instance, I think that Dembski sometimes forgets that his official characterization of design is merely that of a set-theoretic complement—a "what it is not." He thus occasionally refers to design as an explanation, the design inference as an explanatory tool, and so forth—none of which a mere "what it is not" can very readily be, it seems to me. This occasional tendency also manifests itself in other ways (see, e.g., Dembski's remarks concering SETI, p. 31).

Upshot

As indicated above, I believe that not only are there some significant limitations on the design inference as reconstructed by Dembski, even if his reconstruction is correct, but that there are some aspects of it which are not quite on target.

On a deeper level, I do not think that the design inference as reconstructed is likely to help resolve many disputes. Aside from philosophical disputes over the legitimacy of design within the natural scientific context, what are the fundamental disagreements typically over? As I see it, they are generally over concept substance—

over whether or not some specific characteristic exhibited in some natural phenomenon really is a reliable or reasonable design indicator. On that point, it seems to me, *The Design Inference* gives no guidance—leaving that to "insight," which operates in an area of "mystery."

It seems to me further, that if *that* issue were settled, there would be little substantial quibbling about the logical structure of a general inference to design. The basic structure of the Explanatory Filter is relatively uncontraversial, and the trilemma—law, chance, design—has been discussed historically. In the case of low probability, *if* we had some settled, common, *agreed upon* "insight" concerning what separated wildly improbable chance occurrences from those for which chance explanations simply wouldn't do, I do not think it likely that substantive dispute would arise over formal inference structures. One indication of that, it seems to me, is the fact that despite all the technical formalisms, when Dembski gets to the end of his project with the results of the relevant "insight" built in as a given, the design inference as he presents it in final form is straightforwardly valid in standard predicate calculus terms.

I do not wish to play down or denigrate what Dembski has done. There is much of value in *The Design Inference*. But I think that some aspects of even the limited task Dembski set for himself still remain to be tamed.

NOTES

Chapter 1. Design Preliminaries

1. Stuart Kauffman, in *The Origins of Order* notes that "Wolfgang Pauli is said to have remarked that the deepest pleasure in science comes from finding . . . a home, for some deeply felt, deeply held image" (p. vii). A deeply held cognitive image finding a home in nature presents a fairly nice picture of one side of mind correlativity.

2. Midgeley, *Science as Salvation,* 3–14. Keller, in *Reflections on Gender and Science* notes that "For most scientists [there is] a congruence between our scientific minds and the natural world—not unlike Plato's kinship between mind and form" (p. 142). In a related connection, see C. S. Lewis *Christian Reflections,* p. 89. The congruences may extend in surprising ways. For instance, consider the following from Peat, *Superstrings,* p. 28: "Very recently David Finkelstein made what he considers to be a breakthrough in his understanding of the origin of space-time and the quantum theory. His approach is analogous to the neural nets that are currently being investigated by Artificial Intelligence researchers."

3. It is perhaps not essential to the concepts of design and designedness that the agent activity involved be free. However, in order to avoid a variety of tangential snarls (and because I find it intuitively plausible anyway), I will assume that in the cases of interest, at least some of the agent activity in question is freely undertaken activity.

4. Nothing, however, is implied concerning whether the activity in question is direct, or indirect, concerning the length of the causal chains involved, or anything of that sort. Nor are there restrictions on the type of phenomenon involved—whether physical objects, or processes, sequences, events, mathematical algorithms or other nonobjectual phenomena.

5. Richard Dawkins, *Blind Watchmaker,* p. 21. Counterfactual reference to what an intelligent agent would have done is not new with Dawkins. For example, it is employed by Broad (*Mind and Its Place in Nature,* pp. 82, 84).

6. That the *might* can in some cases be sufficient is easily seen. Nature if left un-disturbed might have produced a slightly different seedling pattern. (Some aspect of that pattern was perhaps sensitive to quantum fluctuations.) But since undisturbed nature did not in fact produce that slightly different pattern, it obviously is not true that nature if left undisturbed *would* have produced that pattern. But since that slightly different pattern would still have been natural, the *might* is in this case adequate.

7. Essentially the same concept can be found in Kant who refers to cases where "we do violence to nature, and constrain it to proceed not according to its own ends but in conformity

with ours" (*Critique of Pure Reason,* p. 521). And in Francis Bacon's *De Dignitate et Augmentis Scientiarum* (1623), Book II chapter 2, we find similar remarks:

> For I find nature in three different states . . . She is either free, and follows her ordinary course of development . . . or she is driven out of her ordinary course by the perverseness, insolence, and frowardness of matter, and violence of impediment, as in the case of monsters; or lastly, she is put in constraint, moulded, and made as it were new by art and the hand of man, as in things artificial. (p. 379 in Jones, *Francis Bacon*).

Tom Sorrell employs a similar concept in the context of artistic creation (*Scientism* pp. 114–15), and Robert Nozick suggests something similar in the conceptual realm:

> The material of the philosopher is ideas, questions, tensions, concepts. He molds and shapes these . . . This molding also involves shaping parts, somewhat against their natural grain sometimes, so as better to fit the overall pattern, one designed in part to fit them. (*Philosophical Explanations,* pp. 645–46).

See also Parker, *Creation,* pp. 13–17.

8. There will be some quirky exceptions. For instance, suppose that hostile aliens have decided that the earth deserves destruction (intergallactic space is becoming unbearably polluted with sleaze from daytime TV talk shows). The aliens' plan is as follows: Unknown to earth astronomers, space is teeming with dark-matter astroids, several dozen of which are on collision courses with Earth at any given moment. The aliens, initially quite sympathetic to Earth, have for ages been unobtrusively diverting the astroids far out beyond the orbit of Pluto, but, having finally lost patience, have picked an exactly appropriate astroid on an exactly appropriate trajectory and have made the deliberate decision to let it through their shield. Events proceed as expected. In this case we are inclined, I think, to say that the destruction was intended, and that the destruction was a result of alien design, even though their activity was nothing beyond the decision to be *inactive* where they were usually active, merely taking advantage of a fortuitious, precisely appropriate, natural contingency. In this sort of case, there will be no nomic discontinuity of the ordinary sort—the aliens, in their inactivity, did not divert nature at all. Rather, what is true is a different subjunctive: that had nature *not* been going to produce the phenomenon in question, the aliens themselves would have taken action. This is an example of what I have elsewhere described as *subjunctive supervision.* See my "Design, Chance, and Theistic Evolution" in Dembski, *Mere Creation,* pp. 289–312.

9. Some arise only in the context of divine design and will be discussed later. But others arise even here. For instance, consider the case in the previous footnote, where the intention is realized through alien inactivity. Or suppose that there is in the middle of an industrial city a completely undisturbed, preserved patch of the original grassland previously occupying the area where the city now sits. That patch itself might be perfectly natural, and it

might well be exactly what nature would have produced there had no city ever been built. But still, there is something artificial about the situation. Given the usual growth procedures of cities, deliberate effort was required for that preservation. My intuition is to say that the continued existence of that "natural" patch is artificial—even though, ex hypothesi, it might be exactly what nature herself *would* have generated had no humans ever settled that area. Again, sorting out the precise details of *might* or *would* is a bit tricky.

10. Someone might attempt to produce something exhibiting no pattern at all, or exhibiting absolutely pure chaos—say, as the international standard for designlessness. Any result would clearly be an artifact. Given the deliberate intent involved, there might be some inclination to attribute design to the product, even though ex hypothesi if the attempt was successful there would be no exhibited, mind-correlative pattern. The existence of any such artifact would certainly be by design, but further than that I'm not sure exactly what the right thing to say here is. Part of the oddity is that the intention (which is usually linked to pattern) is to produce an absence of pattern.

11. For reasons of this sort, *designed* and *artifact*, although closely related, are not equivalent.

12. Some might accept consequences similar to this. For instance, C. A. Hooker in *A Realistic Theory of Science* says that "technological development has been transforming the biophysical world . . . into a human artifact in new patterns" (p. 184).

13. For example, imagine a completely natural planet except for the presence of one bulldozer. That combined system would not be an artifact, because the bulldozer would constitute a proper subpart, removal of which would remove all the counterflow from the system, while there would be no proper subpart of the bulldozer removal of which would remove all the counterflow from the combined system.

14. In the bulldozer example, artifactuality would not extend down to the atomic level, since one could completely remove all artifactuality from the system (by, e.g., dispersing the atoms of the bulldozer) without thereby affecting any of the inherent characteristics of the atoms in question.

15. The view that natural laws, processes, and conditions are not even in principle adequate to the generating of life to begin with, so that the initiating of the history of life must involve counterflow activity has a long history, and can be found explicitly stated in Thomas Chalmers's 1834 *Power*, pp. 27ff, in Newton's *Optiks*, Book III, and elsewhere.

16. "Imitate, make it geometrical, intensify: that is not a bad three-part formula for the driving pulse of the arts as a whole" E.O.Wilson, *Consilience*, p. 241.

17. As Hildebrandt and Tomba remark, "Nature does not abhor polyhedral configurations" (*Parsimonious Universe*, p. 14). But when nature does produce such forms, they are often on a micro scale. And interestingly enough, many such examples when photomagnified, do indeed look for all the world like artifacts. The Hildebrandt and Tomba volume contains magnifications of aluminum and palladium crystals, which would make nice movie sets for alien cities (p. 14), and a photo of a "gelatinous preparation of tin oil" which, as they note,

could easily be taken for 'an aerial photograph of farmland' (p. 10). Some radiolaria skeletons, if enlarged to a diameter of several hundred yards would be dead ringers for futuristic space stations.

It is difficult to say exactly why scale should apparently make such a difference. Some, however, have implicitly denied that it does. Herschel, ignoring scale, claimed that the identicalness of all atoms of a specific sort gave them "the essential character of a manufactured article" (quoted in Whewell, *Astronomy*, p. 302). And Descartes, from his mechanistic perspective on nature, claims in *Principles* that scale is the only real distinction between various artifactual and natural phenomena:

> I know of no distinction between those things [human artifacts] and natural bodies except that the operations of things made by skill are, for the most part, performed by apparatus large enough to be easily perceived by the senses. (Miller and Miller translation, Article 203, Part IV, p. 285)

18. Thus Sir James Jeans: "The universe begins to look more like a great thought than like a great machine" (*Mysterious Universe*, p. 186). The implications of the similarities here may run deeper than at first appears. Midgeley claims that both religion and science have grown out of the same "unifying, ordering vision" (Midgeley, *Science*, p. 12).

19. I am using complexity here in an intuitive sense. Some more formal characterizations will be mentioned later.

20. For instance, an artist or a scientist might attempt—successfully—to produce something indistinguishable from some natural phenomenon, and might do so in such a way that direct observation of the agent activity in question was the only way to determine the actual artifactuality of the produced phenomenon.

21. "Designed" and "artifact," although not equivalent, are routinely equated in the literature. For example, see Herbert Simon (*The Science of the Artificial*), Laszlo (*The Systems View of the World*), and C. A. Hooker (*A Realistic Theory of Science*, e.g., pp. 184, 214) for examples. In connection with their distinctness, it is worth noting that unintended, undesigned, unwanted effects of human agency in experimental or observational situations are typically termed "artifacts"—a useage that fits with the present proposed definition. Even *intentional artifactuality* and *designed* are not quite equivalent. Someone adrift on the ocean using a can lid as a reflector to try to attract the attention of passing aircraft is intentionally producing counterflow and artifactuality (the flashes), but there need be nothing in the flashes exhibiting pattern, correlation, design, etc.

22. With finite alien beings we might be on a bit shakier ground, but could probably do respectably well in identifying alien artifactuality (since that need involve only counterflow) and might even do reasonably well identifying alien designedness (and perhaps sometimes even specific design purpose) despite possibly differing cognitive structures. But as we'll see, the situation is significantly different in perhaps unexpected ways in the case both of supernatural agent activity and design.

23. Whewell, *Astronomy,* 13–14. See also Bell, *The Hand,* e.g., p. 73. Other early nineteenth century writers also tended to take lifestyles of natural organisms as a given, then to see as *pattern* (indeed, deliberate pattern) the match between those demands and organism capacities. What I'm calling "correlation to mind" may be related to what David Wilcox had in mind in saying that "we recognize intent in artifacts by seeing them as components of larger mental templates" ("How Blind a Watchmaker?" p. 172).

24. If I read parts of Donna Haraway's *Primate Visions* right, she at least suggests that the manner in which truth attaches to scientific theories may also be of this sort.

25. Wilkinson, *The Quarks and Captain Ahab,* p. 22. Subversive as Wilkinson's claim might sound to some, it is not that uncommon. For instance, John Tyler Bonner, in *The Evolution of Complexity,* says "As has so often been pointed out in the past, a good explanation is one that gives some inner satisfaction" (x), and notes that such satisfaction is provided by different types of things for different people. Peter Kosso remarks that "the accomplishment of explanation, after all, is a psychological accomplishment" (*Appearance and Reality,* pp. 27–28; see also 179). On the flip side, A. G. Cairns-Smith, *Seven Clues to the Origin of Life,* mentions "a feeling of unease" generated by some "false picture" even when such pictures are still accommodating new evidence. See also Polanyi, *Science,* p. 9, and Putnam, *Many Faces,* p. 85.

26. Of course, like our other faculties this experiential identification is not infallible. Not only is it mediated by all sorts of other matters (both external and internal) but the phenomenology of sense making can be triggered by any number of very human factors. This issue will be discussed further in chapter 7.

27. For example, it is at least possible that the pattern in question was simply a byproduct of the actual intent. But as patterns get more involved, more powerfully mind correlative, more plausibly valued, etc., that possibility becomes increasingly less plausible.

Chapter 2. Science and Finite Design

1. That (in effect) identifying counterflow constitutes the core of SETI recognition procedures is clear from virtually all the *SETI* literature—e.g. Sagan's *Communication with Extraterrestrial Intelligence,* Asimov's *Extraterrestrial Civilizations,* and even such NASA publications as *SETI* (NAS 1.83 114/990) p. 23. In fact, in nearly all such publications, the initial aim is simply to identify artifactuality. See also Beck, p. 4.

2. Some aspects of the SETI project touch on speculative alien psychology. In *The Evolving Universe,* Donald Goldsmith says:

> The water hole concept [having to do with the specifics of deciding what parts of the microwave spectrum to monitor] depends on most civilizations' recognizing water as supremely important to life, and drawing the same conclusions from this fact as we do." (p. 516)

3. An interesting parallel concerning human artifacts is found in John Stuart Mill's essay "Theism":

I should draw the inference no less confidently from a footprint, as from any relic however insignificant which experience has taught me to attribute to man; as geologists infer the past existence of animals from copralites, though no one sees marks of design in copralite. (*Nature, The Utility of Religion, and Theism*, p. 168)

4. Sagan, *Broca's Brain*, p. 320, "There is *no difficulty* in envisioning an intersteller radio message that unambiguously arises from intelligent life."

5. For just such reasons, some scientists have advised against responding to any such signals.

6. This situation even arises with human artifact. Some primative hand axes are only subtly different if at all from rocks chipped and abraded by natural processes, for instance. In this connection, see, e.g., Trigger *History* pp. 52–54. See also p. 47 and p. 382.

7. For some additional cases, see Regis, p. 176. See also Trigger, op. cit. p. 47.

8. Fred Hoyle and Chandra Wickramisinghe are among the best known of this group. See, e.g., their *Evolution from Space*. Others who have discussed the possibility of life originating elsewhere and then spreading to Earth by various means include Crick, Orgel, Gold, and even some nineteenth century figures such as Arrhenius and Kelvin.

9. Despite the legitimacy (in principle) of such explanations, they would likely not be the first choice of scientists in cases where the evidence was at all equivocal. While not denying their legitimacy, Sagan describes explanatory appeals to aliens as "the explanation of last resort, when all else fails" (*Communication* 228). Dyson simply asserts that "every object must be assumed natural until proven unnatural" (*Communication* 189). There is presumably a fear of "alien of the gaps."

10. David Lewis, "Causation," pp. 556–67.

11. Sagan (*Communication* 366) claims that extremely old and technologically advanced civilizations "will have discovered laws of nature and invented technologies whose applications will appear to us indistinguishable from magic." That could generate some initial confusion. This view is sometimes referred to as the "Heinlein principle." A related point is made by Peter S. Stevens, *Patterns in Nature:* "As our mathematical models and fabrication techniques improve, we can expect that man's structures will resemble natural forms even more closely" (p. 77).

12. There are some advocates of antirealisms who would deny this. However, I do not think that those denials are consistent with how the overwhelming majority of scientists historically have conceived their project, so am taking comprehendability assumptions as essential.

13. Einstein is quoted in Margenau and Varghese, *Cosmos, Bios, Theos*, p.1; Wigner, "The Unreasonable Effectiveness of Mathematics in the Natural Sciences" p. 1, 2; de Grasse Tyson, "Romancing the Equation" p. 80; Paul Davies, *Are We Alone?* pp. 121–22. June Goodfield, *An Imagined World*, mentions "the God within" as "the name the Greeks gave to the power of man's mind to reach out and understand the world in which we live" (p.144).

14. Theological themes played formative roles in the theorizing of Newton, Boyle,

Maxwell, Faraday, Herschel, Descartes, Pasteur, and others. For instance, Newton's views or time, space, the character of matter, and the quantity of matter in the cosmos were all shaped by his theology. The literature on this general point has grown substantially in recent years. See e.g., Brooke, *Science and Religion,* chapter 1.

15. I think, however, that the general intellectual ethos (b) supports is more deeply operative within science than often recognized. In this connection see Davies, *Are We Alone,* p 138.

16. Things like that are sometimes even stated explicitly—see, e.g., Futuyma, *Trial,* p. 169. Eldredge and Ruse have made similar claims.

17. "Pandas," p. 2.

18. That is an extraordinarily strong claim, entailing (as it apparently does) that there is no logically possible empirical evidence that could provide *any* empirical support to the proposition that God initiated life on this planet. The only alternative would be to hold that even if the claim that God initiated life was legitimately supported by empirical data, such empirically supported conclusions had to be barred from empirical science.

Chapter 3. Supernatural Design: Preliminary Basics

1. Some minor qualifications might be necessary for formal reasons. However, nothing of substance hangs on any of them.

2. Designed products of human activity are sharply constrained by the natural order itself, and human production of design involves redirection and harnessing of lawful processes. We do not so much breach natural order as bring together nonnatural combinations. A Boeing 747 violates no natural laws, either in its production, existence, or operation. Rather, it depends upon them, but it depends upon a combination of them that never comes together in that way in undirected nature. And never will. As Hoyle first noted and as many creationists are fond of pointing out, a tornado in a junkyard will never produce a 747. (Of course, only a cynic would classify a junkyard as natural.)

3. For instance, I see no reason in principle why there could not be laws built into nature having to do with the evolution of states of infinite energy—states which, although thus covered by natural law, no finite agent could initiate.

4. Paley was already onto general points of this sort. As he said: "Nor can I perceive that it varies at all the inference, whether the question arise concerning a human agent, or concerning an agent of a different species, or an agent possessing, in some respect, a different nature" (*Natural Theology,* p. 4).

5. Newton held that whenever God's purposes could be achieved through use of natural law, that was the means God employed. See Brooke, *Science and Religion,* 147.

6. Some would term the present general category of activity "the miraculous." The connections between supernatural agent activity and natural law may be much deeper than often realized. See my "Nomo(theo)logical Necessity." A supernatural creative agent could also

change the laws of nature at a given point in history, or could generate the same result by intervening *contranomically* at every causal moment to bring about some effect other than that which would naturally occur. (In fact, if laws simply are uniformities in the supernatural governance of the cosmos, those two possibilities are actually equivalent.) Since changes in law is not a picture that has been seriously considered historically, I shall not pursue it further.

Calvin College physicist David van Baak tells me that there is, however, a tradition among physicists that every physicist after death gets to change one law of physics so long as the new law is still consistent with every experimental result ever obtained up to that point. This would be a practical application of underdetermination of theory by data, about which more later.

7. Nomic discontinuity will not be invariable, for reasons discussed later.

8. It might, of course, be argued that if such an object actually existed, then it would by definition no longer be contranomic, since its very existence would entail that the law it allegedly violated was no longer a law. I'm not entirely unsympathetic to such an argument, but if that argument is right, that simply opens a different supernatural contranomic possibility—that of *changing* previous law. The response to *that* might be that laws by definition cannot change. It is more difficult to see whether that is plausible or not. But it is clear that things indistinguishable from law changes are at least logically possible, and if so an omnipotent supernatural being could bring those things about. For instance, laws with built-in temporal indices involving differing results after the time in question, might in some formal sense be the same laws, but there would be an apparent change in the consequences of the law.

9. At least, the means actually employed are forbidden by nature.

10. I am classifying this as contranomic, since the supernatural agent is bringing about (in some sense) the decay; whereas, according to the usual (Copenhagen) interpretation that presumably cannot be done—at least not in any known lawful way.

11. It might be argued that probablistic laws do not permit the sort of foreknowledge required in this case. But I doubt that. Such laws might not permit rigorous predictions on the usual basis—laws and boundary conditions—but that is very different from barring omniscient foreknowledge. And it seems clear that there *is* a truth to be known. Whether caused or not, predictable or not, or determined or not, when the dust has settled either the particle will have decayed or not. Either this will be and always will have been a world in which that particle decays, or it will be and always will have been one in which it did not. An omniscient agent knowing what world this is, and knowing all the truths to be known in this world can know that one as well.

12. This parallels a case discussed previously involving aliens.

13. Similar types of cases are discussed in my "Design, Chance, and Theistic Evolution."

14. As before, there might be no legitimate reason for identifying it *as* supernaturally produced. But the situation is a bit more complicated in that respect than the previous cases. *If* we had rational scientific reason to think that some object could only be produced out of initial conditions flatly forbidden by natural law, or *if* we had rational scientific reason for thinking

that it could not be produced except via infinite power, then we might be able to conclude that this obvious artifactuality required supernatural activity for its production. Of course, it might be argued that we could never even in principle have such reason. But here, unlike the previous categories, the topic of empirical evidence of supernatural design does arise.

15. This latter is linked to a major intuition underlying prohibitions on the supernatural in science. That issue will be discussed later.

16. Physicist Edward Harrison has speculated that suitably technologically advanced finite agents could perhaps trigger quantum bubbles that would expand into closed universes. Were such agents able to control various bubble parameters they might be able to determine what would *look* like natural laws to those *inside* the bubble. See his *Masks of the Universe*.

17. This distinction and the fact that the two factors might function differently in design cases was recognized at least as early as the early nineteenth century as will be seen shortly.

18. For instance, Feynman defines beauty in terms of simplicity (*Character of Physical Law*, 173), Weinberg variously in terms of symmetry and simplicity (*Dreams*, p. 135ff., 148ff.), and Herman Weyl, in terms of symmetry (*Symmetry*, p. 3). Similar identifications can be found historically—e.g., Whewell speaks of the "beautiful symmetry of relation" to be found in natural laws (*Astronomy*, p. 381).

19. Polkinghorne, *Quantum World*, pp. 57–58.

20. For example, E. O. Wilson, *Consilience*, pp. 70–71; A. Zee, *Fearful Symmetry*, pp. 3–31; Weyl, *Symmetry*, pp. 3, 8, 133; and Wilczek and Devine, *Longing for the Harmonies*, p. 229. Some authors cite the importance of small *departures* from symmetry—e.g., Heinz Pagels, *Cosmic Code*, p. 305; Ferguson, *Fire in the Equations*, p. 19; Stenger, *Not by Design*, p. 155.

21. Matila Ghyka, *The Geometry of Art and Life*, p. 10. See Ghyka also for discussion of how even some very informal, nontechnical aesthetic judgments are linked to deep mathematical matters. Weinberg (*Dreams*, p. 149) says that the beauty found in nature "is a beauty that is spare and classic, the sort we find in Greek tragedies." Wilczek and Devine quote Einstein as claiming that "Both music and scientific research are nourished by the same source of longing" (*Longing for the Harmonies*, p. xi).

22. Weinberg, *Dreams*, p. 131.

23. Discussion can be found in the Bridgewater Treatises—see Whewell, *Astronomy*, pp. 9–10 and Chalmers, *Power*, vol. 1, pp. 16–21, 49.

24. Thus, Chalmers, *Power*, Vol. 1, p. 19: "It is in the dispositions of matter more than in the laws of matter, where the main strength of the argument lies." Similar remarks occur over the next ten or so pages.

25. For instance, if we did not know the relevant laws of the cosmos, the former pattern might still be directly recognizable as pattern, but the latter might be recognizable only via observation over time of the developing results.

26. I do not know if there would be such consequences, or how to determine what they would be if there were—but it is at least possible.

27. I am not trying to make such a case, but only to raise it as a possibility.

28. This idea was applied not just to the biological realm, but to the physical realm as well. For instance:

> Faraday's . . . second assumption was that while some forces (such as gravity) act instantly and perpetually, others remain latent or hidden, becoming active only when the appropriate enabling conditions are present. He explains these cases of "delated" action as manifest "wonderful instances of wisdom in the creation" because if such "quiescent" forces such as affinity or cohesion were perpetually exerted . . . there would be a continuous, chaotic transmutation of substances, perpetual chemical change, and no stable materials useful for the provision of life. Thus the constraining of the action of a force is a necessary instrument of divine purpose, and a continual reminder of its work. Science discovers such constraints as laws of the exertion of force. (David Gooding, "Metaphysics versus Measurement," p. 29)

29. There is one possible exception to that generalization, involving supernatural fore-knowledge of counterfactuals involving future spontaneous quantum events. That case is discussed in my "Design, Chance, and Theistic Evolution."

30. These structures have recently been the center of discussion generated by Mike Behe's work—*Darwin's Black Box.*

31. Historically, many took such design to be superior to design that required subsequent intervention. For instance, Boyle, in *Free Inquiry into the Vulgarly Receiv'd Notions of Nature* (1685–86) says:

> It much more tends to the illustration of God's wisdom, to have framed things first, that there can seldom or never need any extraordinary interposition of his power. And, as it more recommends the skill of an engineer to contrive an elaborate engine so, as that there should need nothing to reach his ends in it but the contrivance of parts devoid of understanding, than if it were necessary, that ever and anon, a discreet servant should be employed to concur notably to the operation of this or that part, or to hinder the engine from being out of order; so it more sets off the wisdom of God in the fabric of the universe, that he can make so vast a machine perform all those many things, which he designed it should, by the mere contrivance of brute matter managed by certain laws of local motion and upheld by his ordering and general concourse, than if he employed from time to time an intelligent overseer, such as nature is fancied to be, to regulate, and control the motions of the parts. (reprinted in Hall, *Robert Boyle on Natural Philosophy,* p. 150–51).

Charles Babbage, in his unofficial *Ninth Bridgewater Treatise: A Fragment* says:

> We cannot for a moment hesitate in pronouncing that that which, after its original adjustment, no superintendence was required, displayed far greater ingenuity than that which demanded, at every change in its law, the intervention of its contriver. (p. 40)

Even Darwin, in the B Notebook (fol. 101, p. 195.9), written in the late 1830s, says (in the clipped prose of his notebooks):

> Astronomers might formerly have said that God ordered each planet to move in its particular destiny. In same manner God orders each animal created with certain form in certain country, but how much more simple and sublime power let attraction act according to certain laws such as inevitable consequen [sic] let animal be created, then by the fixed laws of generation, such will be their successors.

The intuition is neatly captured by Mother Cary in Charles Kingsley's *Water Babies:* "anyone can make things, if they will take time and trouble enough, but it is not everyone who, like me, can make things make themselves" (p. 273).

32. This supernatural creation category is where many of the most influential nineteenth-century natural theology arguments fit. In the Bridgewater Treatises—e.g., Whewell's *Astronomy*—it is frequently stressed that it is the production of specified results via the remarkable cooperating of multiple natural laws and processes (and not evidences of special supernatural intervention or anything of the sort) that is the basis of design conclusions. The allegation that design arguments are typically gap arguments seems to be, historically, simply false.

33. The deeper intuition of counterflow—that *something* is *somehow* different than it otherwise would have been—does in a sense still hold in the supernatural creation case. The laws are as they are because of that supernatural activity, and without that supernatural activity they would not have been as they are. But there may well be no way that they *would have* otherwise been. More specifically, given a structure of nature, there may in fact be something that nature would have done had there been no relevant agent activity. But there might have been no specific state S such that had the present laws not been chosen, then S is what would have obtained. That sort of counterfactual does not necessarily have a defined truth value on all analyses of counterfactuals.

34. Although that is the standard reading, for reasons I will not go into here I do not believe that it is the proper reading of Paley.

Chapter 4. Identifying Supernatural Deisgn: Primary Marks

1. There is also the possibility, noted in chapter 1, of direct observation of the agent activity itself. It is not clear that this really is a possibility in the supernatural case. Most conceptions of the supernatural entail the impossibility of direct observability. And according to John 1:18, "No man has seen God at any time." It might be possible for a supernatural, omnipotent agent to endow a finite being with the capability for direct observation of the supernatural, and for the supernatural agent to do so in such a way that the observation generated genuine knowledge that the agent being observed was indeed supernatural. Were that the case, then at least some supernatural matters would become observational matters, and

barring them from science would take substantially more argumentation than usually provided. Something along this general line is perhaps to be found in the work of Thomas Reid.

2. Again a supernatural being could produce the result in question by additional means not available to any finite being, but that is a different issue.

3. And, obviously, a supernatural agent could have the capability of producing such a factory. Many would not *expect* a supernatural agent to do that, but that is an entirely different matter. Even Sagan recognizes some of the hazards of placing limitations by human fiat on supernatural activity (*Broca's Brain*, p. 334 footnote).

4. That is possible even with purely human activity. Humans have engineered a bioluminscent tobacco plant, and although nature could have done that, she did not in fact do it. However, given nature's capability, there is nothing in that result that suggests counterflow, so if that plant escapes and its humanly engineered history is forgotten, future generations will perfectly sensibly take it as natural and will pay little heed to anyone trying to argue for ancestor-design on the basis of that plant.

5. Not all physicists hope for this. Freeman Dyson, for instance, indicates that he would be disappointed "if it should turn out to be that the whole of reality can be described by a finite set of equations" (*Infinite*, p. 53).

6. See again "Some Counterflow Correlations," page 12, chapter 1 for explication of the distinction.

7. Obviously, neither the existence nor the fabrication of large Tupperware vats would violate any laws of nature. Indeed, we could do it ourselves. And it cannot seriously be claimed that it is a law of nature or a conceptual necessity that biological life begin by purely natural, unaided means. That may be the philosophical preference of many, but that is a wholly different matter.

8. Not even advocates of the strongest anthropic principles would claim that our existence now could retro-cause the primordial existence of Tupperware vats and Beatles records.

9. For reasons to be discussed in chapter 5, there is nothing inherently scientifically impermissible in science choosing that alternative. In a related connection see Quine's claim that "no statement is immune to revision" (*Logical Point of View*, p. 43).

10. This is a variant of the pulsar oracle example discussed by Dembski in "Possibility."

11. Although of a different sort, the counterflow would be at least as evident as would that in the Martian cube case. Indeed, the involvement of agent activity would be even more evident in the code case than in the cube case. One might be able to imagine some purely natural, agent-free process that would generate the cube, but it would be much more difficult to envision an agent-free process that generated Morse code conversations. There is an additional important characteristic of many phenomena that carry deliberately structured information. In ordinary cases, we recognize counterflow first, and that recognition grounds our recognition both of artifactuality and design. (The steps are often so small and closely linked that we do not even notice them.) But in communication cases, it is often reversed—only via recognition of

intelligibility (communication, information) that we can distinguish signal (and thus artifactuality) from static.

12. For present purposes I am adopting the standard position that quantum events lie outside of ordinary principles of causation, and in particular that, e.g., particle decay is neither governed nor governable by anything beyond specified probabilities. That being the case, supernatural agency causing, preventing, or changing the probabilities of such decay would be contranomic. On the other hand, given that the relevant quantum laws are fundamentally probabilistic, in any instance and at any moment either decay or failure to decay is completely lawful. So the *causing* of the event is contranomic, but the event—whatever it is—is not.

13. The history of science is extremely interesting here. For instance, historically it was widely assumed that determinism was an absolute conceptual philosophical requirement of science. Einstein, DeBroglie, Bohm, and others resisted the transition from classical to quantum physics because it required abandonment of that philosophical demand. But that deep philosophical intuition (and others) was given up. Similarly, there is no rule of science forbidding the abandonment of the favored metaphysical conception of natural laws as inviolable (even by supernatural agents).

14. The question of scientific legitimacy will be explored later. The present issue is recognizability.

15. And as evidenced by, e.g., recognition protocols of SETI projects, identification of counterflow would be the initial means by which purported alien artifacts would be distinguished from background natural phenomena. As discussed earlier, recognition of alien artifacts need not depend upon understanding alien procedures, abilities, intentions, concepts, etc. An interesting exercise is to write a list of instructions for the first astronauts landing on another planet, setting out procedures by which they are to distinguish alien artifacts (if any) from things produced by nature on that planet. I think that anyone actually doing that exercise will discover that counterflow is the fundamental operative concept, and that the human-scale geometric properties discussed in chapter 1 are easily the most intuitive indications of counterflow.

Chapter 5. Identifying Supernatural Design: Secondary Marks

1. There is a third alternative, which I will not pursue here. It is possible that what we call "natural laws" just are regularities consisting of the ways in which a supernatural agent interacts with the material cosmos. For example, it is possible that particles of matter tending to move toward each other ("attraction") is simply a description of a supernatural agent's moment-by-moment direct governance of matter. There would in that situation be no counterflow—what "nature" does just is supernatural agent activity. This view has a relatively long history within the Christian community. As it turns out, this sort of view solves a number of sticky problems concerning the character of natural law—e.g., the ability of law to support counterfactuals, and the logical status of laws as falling between logical necessity and mere

accidental generalization. Although I will not pursue this view here, I have explored it in detail in "Nomo(theo)logical Necessity."

2. *Opera Omnia* IV 260–62. Quoted in Hurlbutt, p. 12. Boyle, in *Disquisition,* p. 176, makes a similar remark: "The Structure of the Nests of Wasps . . . I have observ'd to be very Curious and Artificial." This use of "artificial" in connection with natural phenomena is surprisingly common. For instance, Darwin, in his *Beagle* diary, refers to the hunting methods of the lion ant as "so beautiful, so simple and yet so artificial a contrivance" (*Metaphysics, Materialism and the Evolution of Mind,* p. 178). See also, for instance, Samuel Butler *Evolution, Old and New,* p. 16, 20. Chester Dewey, in "On the Polished Limestone of Rochester" comments on a particular geological phenomenon as follows: "The surface was not made thus originally; it has been done *artificially,* though by nature, by some mighty power" [his emphasis] p. 242. Even contemporary authors sometimes use related terminology in this way— e.g., Woodfield, in *Teleology* refers to, e.g., spider webs as "artifacts" (p. 27–8). Remarks of Herbert Simon are also of interest in this connection:

> The adaptiveness of the human organism, the facility with which it acquires new strategies and becomes adept in dealing with highly specialized environments, make it an elusive and fascinating target of our scientific inquiries—and the very prototype of the artificial. (*The Sciences of the Artificial,* p. 127)

3. A supernatural agent might contranomically produce some phenomenon, then contranomically remove any indications of the original contranomic activity. That might seem to produce counterflow absence, but that is not quite correct. Prevention of even hidden marks that otherwise would have arisen is still by definition counterflow.

4. The term is from Peter van Inwagen. A similar idea is found in Davies *Are We Alone?* p. 25.

5. One type of qualification may be necessary. For instance, suppose that a supernatural and omniscient agent knew that were the cosmos to be begun via initiating structure S, that humans subsequently would emerge and that those humans would eventually freely choose to construct the CERN accelerator. That supernatual agent could choose to create S for the specific pupose and with the deliberate intention of the CERN accelerator—primary marks and all—coming into existence. Thus, given the appropriate counterfactuals of freedom, an omniscient supernatural agent could initiate the cosmos in such a way that without subsequent supernatural agent intervention, intended phenomena bearing primary marks should subsequently come to be. (There is a significant literature on counterfactuals of freedom, beginning with Alvin Plantinga's *Nature of Necessity.*) The above case is a variant of some cases developed in my "Design, Chance, and Theistic Evolution" and is a type of the "weak actualization" idea found in Plantinga.

6. It might be argued that chance plays a key role in evolution, and that results of chance processes cannot be interpreted as intended, deliberate, or designed. That is mistaken for several reasons. One indication that caution is required here is that detonations of nuclear

weapons can be intended, deliberate, and designed, even though such events depend crucially on irreduceably chance quantum events. But more immediately, there can be contingent truths concerning what chance events will take place tomorrow, or concerning whether or not a specific particle will decay during the next few minutes. Those might be unknowable to finite agents and to science, but in such cases there is a truth of the matter, and that truth need not be in principle unknowable for an omniscient supernatural agent. Such an agent could take advantage of foreknown chance contingencies by making present choices in the light of the way those chance events were going to go. For further disussion, see my "Design, Chance, and Theistic Evolution." For a game-theoretic case that in some situations the optimal rational strategy incorporates randomness, see Steven Brams, *Superior Beings,* p. 145ff.

      7. It would be quasi *natrifactual* since only a supernatural agent could be involved in activity determining the initiating structures of the cosmos.

      8. Quoted in Whewell, *Astronomy,* p. 358.

      9. Whewell, *Astronomy,* p. 349.

      10. It is further evident from such cases that historical design arguments were not always God-of-the-gaps arguments.

      The fact that design beliefs have remained influential despite perceived difficulties with some design arguments might suggest that design beliefs do not ultimately rest on arguments. The situation is in some ways similar to that of beliefs in an external world. Alleged *proofs* for the existence of the external world are regularly shown to be logically suspect, and just as regularly, such suspicions do not make the slightest difference to anyone's belief in that world. A Reidean explanation—that belief in the external world ultimately rests upon a belief-producing faculty rather than any argument—may be worth exploring in the design case as well.

      11. This is often cited as exactly the point of the Genesis creation account. Communication of course need not be obvious. Walter ReMine, for instance, in *Biotic Message* argues that there is a message subtly incorporated into some biological structures—a message we did not even have the capability to recognize as a message until historically fairly recently.

      12. Even Sagan has commented on the oddity of placing arbitrary limitations on what a supernatural agent could do. *Broca's Brain,* p. 334 footnote.

      13. For instance, Whewell: "When we collect design and purpose from the arrangements of the universe, we do not arrive at our conclusion by a train of deductive reasoning, but by the conviction which such combinations as we perceive, immediately and directly impress upon the mind. 'Design must have a designer.' But such a principle can be of no avail to one whom the contemplation or the description of the world does not impress with the perception of design. It is not therefore at the end but at the beginning of our syllogism, not among remote conclusions, but among original principles, that we must place the truth, that such arrangements, manifestations, and proceedings as we behold about us imply a Being endowed with consciousness, design, and will, from whom they proceed" (*Astronomy,* p. 344).

      14. This failure to conceptually distinguish the two has led to various confusions in design discussion. For instance, it is one of the things that underlies the mistake of thinking

that if the case for agent activity within nature (intervention) is removed, the case for design collapses as well.

15. In this connection, I suspect that if we discovered simply that the first members of the basic phyla had appeared instantaneously, we would likewise conclude deliberate agent activity.

16. Otherwise we would be left with the sheer, unexplained niftiness of the fact that the little pointy things went around exactly synchronously with the solar day.

17. This point was noticed by Paley. See, e.g., *Natural Theology*, p. 9.

18. There are other interesting considerations in the general area. For instance, few would deny that not only watches but even organisms, had they with their characteristics come into existence *de novo* and instantaneously, would be products of design. Some contend that means of production should have no particular bearing upon whether or not the relevant characteristics in and of themselves indicate design. As Le Gros Clark puts it: " . . . if, on the theory of direct creation, we were justified in our inference of an intelligent Creator, surely we cannot hesitate to adopt the same conclusion, if we accept the theory of evolution" (introduction to *Paley's Natural Theology*, p. 8).

19. I think that there are other principles in the neighborhood which would bear upon strength of evidential support. For instance, in the context of artifactuality, the greater the degree of complexity, the stronger the case for designedness (and not just artifactuality). Thus, degrees of complexity apparently have some evidential relevance to design. For reasons paralleling those behind PDR, we would expect that if bridge properties came in degrees that had evidential relevance in artifactuality contexts, then even beyond such contexts the degrees of those properties (those properties being design-relevant simpliciter by PDR) would also have some evidential significance. They might have less significance than in the artifactuality case, but that is a different issue.

20. Using the introduced terminology, any bridge property that justified the conclusion that some natrifact was designed would also support the conclusion that any pronatural phenomenon exhibiting those same properties was also designed.

21. It cannot seriously be denied that were eyes known to be results of agent activity, it would be reasonable to take their complexity, functional integrity, etc., as evidence of design. Nearly every competent pre-Darwinian thinker held that, and even Darwin himself was sensitive enough to the force of that reasonableness that the eye made him "shudder."

An intuition similar to PDR is at least implicit in some more contemporary work. For instance, Andrew Woodfield, in *Teleology*, says, "The central difference between natural function 'in order to' and purposive or artefact function 'in order to' is that the latter relies on a mind to weld the elements" (p. 206), and then refers to " . . . 'artefact function' [as] implying that [the artefact did A] because its designer wanted it to (be able to) [do A]" (p. 207). So the *same* function being shifted from the natural to the artifactual realm brings with it implications of deliberate intent—a designer who *wanted* it to behave in that way—which is approaching *designedness*.

22. It is also crucial to remember that the mere fact of alternative possible explanations

does not remove all evidential force. If two theories, Ta and Tb, both propose explanations for some phenomenon, the fact that we prefer Ta, or even that Ta is true, does not imply that the relevant data provide no support for Tb. To assume otherwise commits one to the mistaken view that data entail theories.

23. Producing a specific phenomenon from initiating structures alone would intuitively seem to be more demanding than producing that same phenomenon through interventions along the path of its development. For instance, the task of constructing laws, constants, and primordial conditions capable of producing the complexity and functional integrity of the eye through a multibillion-year wildly indirect path, which itself requires literally millions of appropriate and appropriately timed inputs, would appear to be more demanding than the task of producing an eye by direct intervention by a multitude of orders of magnitude. It thus might appear that *if* a phenomenon were designed via initiating structures, then the planning required was of a higher order than were it produced through interventions. That might even partially counterbalance the commonly assumed effect that discovery of a relevant natural process reduces or destroys any evidential force for design. Suppose that some property P were a bridging property. According to PDR it is thus also design relevant simpliciter. Discovery of some natural process that could produce P would mean that P was not only evidence for design, but evidence the production of which was even more demanding and involved tighter constraints than would P as a bridging property. Intuitively, the tighter the constraints for producing something, the more implausible its happening without agent involvement. Thus, the discovery of some purely natural means for producing a bridging property would not remove P's design-evidential force, but would *increase* the plausibility of agent involvement in P's (indirect, primordially based) production. So again, even if one effect of discovery of natural means was a lowering of one aspect of evidential force, that might be partially counterbalanced by other considerations.

24. An earlier qualification is again necessary. It is possible that what we call "natural law" actually represents the moment-to-moment governance of the material realm by a supernatural governing agent. If that were the case, then discovery of a "natural" process capable of producing some phenomenon would amount to discovering some uniformity in the governing activity of that agent, and thus obviously would not be inconsistent with supernatural activity in the producing of that phenomenon. It is only if natural laws are conceived in terms of capabilities inherent in nature or in objects themselves that a phenomenon being produced by "natural" processes would be in conflict with its being a result of intervention or direct supernatural agent activity. Whether or not nature had such "active powers" was, of course, a topic of dispute historically.

On a related front, *PDR* might require exclusion of logical necessities. For instance, prior to any familiarity to their mode of generation, it might be intuitively reasonable to take Mandelbrot pictures as designed. In fact, were their structure artifactual I suspect that we would so construe them. But, of course, their structure is a result of mathematical necessity, and some would argue that necessities cannot be products of agent activity and design.

25. If secondary marks in nature were indications of counterflow, they would by

themselves constitute plausible support for design in nature. After all, as indications of counterflow they would automatically provide the counterflow context that would provide themselves—as secondary marks—with the inferential and epistemic resources to support a design conclusion.

The intuitively recognized mind correlativeness is, again, why analyses of natural phenomena in engineering terms are so intuitively useful, and why some authors define *design* in nature in terms of counterfactual activity of "intelligent and knowledgeable engineer[s]" (Dawkins, *Blind Watchmaker,* p. 21).

26. It seems to be widely held that the alleged inability of nature to produce some phenomenon unaided is the only evidence ever advanced for designedness of natural phenomena. But that is a fairly serious historical confusion, as even brief examination of major traditional works (e.g., even Paley) will make clear.

27. For example, Whewell, *Astronomy,* pp. 4–5, 109; Bell, *Hand,* p. 45; Chalmers, *Power,* vol. 1, pp. 13–16, 34, 52.

28. One additional reason I am suspicious of complexity-based definitions of design is that I doubt that complexity provides a unique index. For one thing, complexity is sensitive to conceptualization. As Herbert Simon notes in a slightly different context, "There is no reason to expect that the decomposition of the complex design into functional components will be unique. In important instances there may exist alternative feasible decompositions of radically different kinds" (*Sciences of the Artificial,* p. 149).

29. Improbability is an extremely weak support for design. Extreme improbability might not even provide evidence of design in the context of artifactuality. The improbability of the exact relationship of the cuts on an idly whittled stick might be enormous without anything beyond just artifactuality being established.

Beyond that, improbability is not a property that an object, characteristic, or process has in and of itself—much less an observable property. Something is improbable only with respect to other considerations, and in the cases usually advanced as evidence for design, the improbabilities in question, when tracked to their source, generally involve improbability of initiating conditions relative to the normal flow of nature—i.e., they constitute indirect attempts to establish counterflow. Even if successful, that would imply only agent activity and would not automatically establish designedness.

Chapter 6. Design in Nature

1. The creationist claim that if there are gaps within nature then those gaps can be filled only by supernatural agent activity is certainly right. That is a different question than whether or not they are right in their identification of what is or is not genuine gap. And that is also a different question than whether or not conclusions of supernatural agent activity are legitimate within science proper. But so long as the counterflow was identifiable as such, the identity of the agent involved would be irrelevant to the design conclusion.

2. It is sometimes claimed that the deepest mystery of existence is that there is something rather than nothing. If that mystery requires an agent-based solution, it may be that the very fact that there is a cosmos already puts us into an agent-activity context.

3. Michael Behe in *Darwin's Black Box* has been widely misunderstood on this point, and has been generally mistakenly placed in the first of the above categories, as holding a gap view. Behe's view is that any Darwinian means that is both gradualist and selectionist cannot account for what he calls "irreducible complexity." His conclusion from that is *not* that *nature* could not produce irreducible complexity, but that if (perhaps since) nature has produced it then Darwinianism (as gradualist and selectionist) is simply wrong. (Behe does not even necessarily reject common ancestry—that is not really his issue.) I do not believe that Behe wishes to rule out supernatural intervention, but it is not essential to his more basic contention, which is that certain types and degrees of complexity (irreducible complexity) in and of themselves constitute evidence for design regardless of how they were produced.

4. *Compressibility* of information is used in some contexts as a measure of order. There is no settled definition of *complexity*. Indeed, according to some, there are over thirty distinguishable definitions (see John Horgan, "From Complexity to Perplexity").

5. That entails, incidently, that not all secondary marks constitute bridge properties.

6. In fact, given random quantum fluctuations, etc., it is not clear that there even *is* some initial structure that would naturally guarantee the development of exactly the present jumble.

7. This does not mean that the jumble complexity constitutes evidence on its own of designedness. In particular, PDR will not imply that result, since even an assumption of agent activity does not raise the jumble out of the idly whittled stick range. The jumble does not raise artifactuality, or natrifactuality, to designedness. But this case does indicate that *given* agent activity, secondary marks which have no inherent mind-correlative character can sometimes provide evidence concerning the capabilities of the agent involved. (That sort of inference occurs frequently in natural theology contexts.)

8. Nearly everthing in this whole area comes with possible twists. For instance, even though the crater layout seems to be simply a jumble, were we to discover exactly the same layout on a number of other moons, we would certainly begin looking for an explanation for that ensemble. But that search would be triggered by the *match* of multiple apparent jumbles— not by any property or pattern inherent in the jumbles themselves.

9. This particular proposal has its difficulties, of course—as would virtually every other proposal. But explaining the grid "naturally" would require desparate measures.

10. Of course, if the relevant causes tracked back to primordial structures, that *would* tell us something about the agent involved.

11. To see that more unambiguously, imagine that we have a complete causal explanation back to the Big Bang of the present moon crater jumble, an objective measure of inherent complexity of the jumble array, and that we know the probability of precisely that jumble being produced. Now, without changing any of that, imagine that we discover that the present jumble in actual fact spells out "John 3:16" in Martian script. With no changes in causal

history, degree, or type of inherent complexity, the special mind correlativity now visible gives the case a vastly different complexion. On the other hand, suppose that human written language had developed in totally different directions, so that the inscription "John 3:16" carried no meaning whatever. In that case, nature's generating of that pattern in moon craters would have generated no surprise at all (or at least much less). Obviously, the unexpected match between our inscripted language and nature's production is a key element of the situation. This is related to the concept of *specification* in William Dembski's *The Design Inference.* It seems to me, however, that Dembski never gets beyond a purely formal indication of specification, which leaves the term without any of the content necessary to support actual design conclusions.

12. This particular phrase is Copernicus's. This may have been part of what Darwin was expressing in the M Notebook: "Some forms seem *instinctively* beautiful / as round ones . . . and even on paper two waving perfectly parallel lines. Again there is beauty in rhythm and symmetry, of form " (in Barrett, *Metaphysics,* pp. 12–13) [underlining is Darwin's, italics mine]

13. "Who's Out There?" by Jeff Greenwald, p. 66 contained the following:

> In 1820, German mathematician Carl Friedrich Gauss wanted to announce our presence to extraterrestrial passersby by clearing a huge right triangle in the Siberian forest. His plan was to plant wheat in the triangle, then border each side with a square filled with pine trees. Aliens cruising by would glimpse this sylvan representation of $a^2 + b^2 = c^2$ and know the planet's inhabitants had mastered the Pythagorean theorem. Other visionaries favored more flamboyant displays. In 1840 the Viennese astronomer Joseph von Littrow proposed digging a patchwork of enormous ditches in the Sahara—and setting them aflame with kerosene. Nearly 30 years later the French inventor Charles Gros unveiled a plan to reflect sunlight toward Mars using seven carefully placed mirrors. In theory, amazed Martians would behold the shape of the Big Dipper; a wink of intelligence from nearby earth.

Notice that the first plan involves a display exhibiting cognitive content, the second involves deliberate production of obvious counterflow and artifactuality, and the third involves deliberate production of a specific isomorphism.

14. Some have taken such adjustments to constitute basically the whole of design. For instance, J. S. Mill says: "For what is meant by design? Contrivance; the adaptation of means to an end" (*Nature, the Utility of Religion, and Theism* p. 176).

15. Indeed, the moon might not have been there.

16. Some aspects of that role will be discussed in a later chapter.

17. Recall the remark of Pauli (cited earlier) concerning a deeply felt, deeply held image finding a home in nature. Incidently, if scientific truth is mere social construct, it is not clear why some constructs should trigger such experiences and some not.

18. That perception of beauty might have some relevance to the scientific study of nature would not be surprising were Sir Thomas Brown correct that "Nature is the art of God."

19. We may have to move Oklo temporally for this and the next scenario, but nothing hangs on that.

20. At least, not without special intervention.

21. Again, the significance of the fact that we likely have no clue whatever as to the relevant probabilites should not be overlooked.

22. William Alston, "God's action in the world," p. 198.

23. Kant was even willing to claim in effect that this was the only inherent value there was.

24. Woodfield, in *Teleology*, says:

> The essence of teleology lies in welding a causal element and an evaluative element to yield an explanatory device. The causal clause identifies an actual or envisaged effect of a certain event, the evaluative clause says that this effect is good from some point of view, and the whole says that the combination of these elements provides *raison d'etre* of the event. (p. 206)

And C. A. Hooker, in *A Realistic Theory of Science* says that "the distinctive feature of an artifact is that it necessarily combines fact and value in an intimate way" (p. 214).

25. Value and probability can interact in interesting ways. As just noted, that some value is brought to realization against all odds raises a reasonable suspicion that intent may have been involved. On the other hand, that instances of value are realized with a high probability and frequency might also be grounds for suspecting that the system was set up in part exactly for the production of that value. After all, a machine simply is a system for rendering some result (output) *highly* probable, and the better the machine the higher the probability. So if, for instance, life is genuinely valuable, then it would not be surprising to find the cosmos structured in such a way as to render its emergence quite probable, if not inevitable.

26. I do not mean to suggest that secondary marks are necessary conditions either for design or for the recognizing of design. But just as certain geometric properties are usual indications of artifactuality, secondary marks are frequent indications of design. But that need not be invariable. For instance, I suspect that most of us would take the Martian titanium cube as a product of design, but it is almost totally lacking in complexity, and may not have been fashioned as a means to anything.

27. Nearly every actual event is wildly improbable, and nearly every causal path is wildly precarious. One might even argue that improbability is normal, and that high probability is what requires special explanation. In fact, many explanations that appeal to natural law are doing precisely that—explaining by identifying factors that place the phenomena in question in the category of probable things.

28. Keep in mind that phenomena involving no conterflow and produced wholly by nature are the present objects of discussion.

29. Intuitively, the tighter and more precarious a path is, the more reasonable it is to

take the path as a manifestation of care. But the issue is tricky. The path to *any* precise result is tight. However, some results have special properties that are easily degraded (e.g., the grid pattern vs. the jumble). Nearly any contingency being different in the causal path degrades the grid, but that is not true of the general category of jumbles. There is, of course, one obvious operative factor. We recognize and categorize arrays in selective ways. There is a huge range of possibilities we would indiscriminately classify as jumbles, the defining characteristics of a jumble being rather loose. The situation is very different with the grid—departures need not go very far before we cease to see it as, or classify it as, a grid. So precariousness is partly a consequence of the looseness of *our* natural categorization schemes. But that is no objection— it is merely another way of saying that the grid is mind correlative in a way that the jumble is not.

30. It is, of course, possible that such intent was part of a larger package and that the path is as it is because of constraints resulting from other simultaneous intentions. In this connection see Boyle's *Disquisition*, p. 220.

31. Some claim that value is an implicit assumption in any teleological argument (Alston, "Teleological Argument" p. 84.). However, where the case depends upon mind affinity, that need not be straightforwardly true. For instance, we can recognize design in the deep mind-correlative grid pattern of trees planted by the CCC. However, no special value was attached to that pattern, or even to the planting of the trees. The value was in the providing of unemployed workers with a paid task. Without knowing anything concerning value here, the designedness (and not merely the artifactuality) of the planting patterns can still be easily recognized.

32. To get an intuitive feel for the connection, consider the following. A nuclear explosive depends upon the operation of probabilistic quantum laws, and although the probabilities are arbitrarily small, and although it has never happened and would not be expected to happen in the entire history of the universe, it is *possible* for the quantum events upon which detonation depends to go simultaneously the "wrong" way, resulting in failure to detonate even with no system failures. Now, suppose that terrorists had planted a nuclear device beneath Mother Theresa's hospice, and that for the reason just cited it failed to detonate. What is one of the *first* possible explanations for that that occurs to one?

33. Mind affinity must be in some sense within the scope of possible agent determination in order to be evidence. In Sagan's *Contact*, the digits of pi in one stretch are all ones and zeros, arranged so that if laid out on a proper grid the ones form a circle. Were determination of the value of pi to that extent within the capabilities of a possible agent, then that pattern would indeed elicit rational suspicion of designedness. However, if the value of pi were necessarily as it is, then it could provide evidence only for an agent capable of determining necessities (as Descartes believed God could). If pi were essentially as it is, although not a necessary existant, a being creating a cosmos even if not able to determine that value of pi with its embedded mind correlativeness, might still choose to include pi in that cosmos, intending that the contingent

inclusion of something essentially mind correlative provide some evidence of designedness in the makeup of the cosmos.

34. Even Darwin worried about such phenomena, and some of the most insistant demands for explanation come from some opponents of design—e.g., Dawkins, *Blind Watchmaker,* pp. 5–6.

35. Kauffman states this quite clearly in, e.g., *Origins of Order,* p. 285. As hinted earlier, the implications of lowering the improbability might be surprising, given that machines are devices for rending probable the otherwise improbable. And again, Herschel advanced as evidence for design the fact that atoms of a particular sort are all identical, and that this identity gave them "the essential character . . . of a manufactured article" (quoted in Whewell, *Astronomy,* p. 302).

36. Contrary to Dawkins, that nature may be structured in such a way as to scale the odds does not in the *slightest* imply that it was not designed to do so. To argue that way is akin to finding on Mars a plant that produces vodka, and arguing that the fact that it does implies that it was not genetically engineered to do that. The fact that it has that result might not imply that it was intended to produce vodka, but that is a logically very distinct matter.

37. The most obvious such is, of course, Dawkins. The subtitle of his *Blind Watchmaker* is *Why the evidence of evolution reveals a universe without design.*

38. In many popular design arguments, complexity, improbability, and other secondary marks are cited in effect as evidence of counterflow, the intuition being that past some point, high degrees of either complexity or improbability are not produceable by nature. Even were such claims correct, the fact that some secondary marks would establish counterflow does not contradict the claim that secondary marks in the absence of counterflow have little evidential force for designedness.

39. For example, Chalmers, *Power,* vol. 1, pp. 13, 15–16, 34, 39; Whewell, *Astronomy,* 142ff, 381. See also Boyle, *Disquisition,* pp. 94–95.

40. Sometimes combined endorsements were explicit. Whewell, for instance, cites as evidence of design "the character of well devised means to a worthy end" (*Astronomy,* p. 74). The "well devised" refers to what I'm calling mind correlativity, the "worthy end" to value. In Paley's *Natural Theology,* we find the following: "He knows enough for his argument; he knows the utility of the end; he knows the subservience and adaptation of the means to the end. These points being known, his ignorance on other points . . . affect not the certainty of his reasoning" (p. 6). Here again we have value (utility of the end) and mind correlativity (adaptation of means to ends).

41. This is implicit even in recent design cases. For instance, Michael Behe, in *Darwin's Black Box* employs "irreducible complexity" as the basis for a design case, irreducible complexity being defined in terms of the development of and requirements for functionality. This basic intuition has a long history. According to Timothy Lenoir in *The Strategy of Life,* "Aristotle points to the fact of harmoniously interconnected sequences of patterned events as the distinguishing characteristics of beings endowed with life" (p. 6).

42. All those have been cited as bases for design arguments, the last in Behe's *Darwin's Black Box*.

43. In fact, something in this region is what Herbert Simon *defines* as artificial in his *Sciences of the Artificial*.

44. This is particularly stressed in Chalmers and Whewell. Referring to Newton, Robert Hurlbutt says " 'Design' in the context of this argument meant the orderly, harmonious arrangements of elements in systems or a system" (*Hume, Newton and the Design Argument*, p. 8).

45. Paley's watch is a paradigm case of multiple factors having to work together in precise way.

46. Something *like* a hypothetico-deductive case is possible here—this is the sort of mechanism an intending agent might very well use, and it is the sort of mechanism we find in actual operation. Although H-D is obviously not the whole confirmation story, such cases are evidentially relevant.

47. Scientists are generally reluctant to abandon an explanatory system before having an alternative to put in its place. Historically, that has sometimes translated into a reluctance to fully acknowledge problems with a reigning system when there is no viable alternative anywhere on the horizon. That generates a bit of pressure, and when an alternative appears that pressure can be almost explosively released in the form of insistant citations of obvious seriousness of exactly the previously denied problems. (In that connection, complexity theorists are among the happiest to acknowledge the probability problems associated with standard scenarios for the origin of life.) If, for whatever reason, design explanations of the emergence of life become popular, it will be discovered that everyone all along knew that the probabilities against any scenario of chance emergence were prohibitive, and demonstrations of that fact will become standard textbook fare.

Chapter 7. Beyond the Empirical

1. Such suspicions turn up in surprising places. For instance, Bacon in *Novum Organum*, Book 2, aph. 29 says: "Now these things are to be chiefly suspected, which depend in any way on religion" (Spedding, et al. *Works*, p. 238).

2. See Lakatos "Falsification," p. 89.

3. But there were many others. Both the Aristotelian inductive faculty and the Platonic dialectic were procedures for generating theories, where the method of generation (source) constituted the rational justification (warrant) for those theories.

4. Any set of data, no matter how large, can in principle be given an unlimited variety of alternative theoretical interpretations. And given that any substantive theory extends beyond the data to a virtually unlimited degree (e.g., spatially, temporally, dimensionally, and counterfactually), there is no empirical cure for the condition.

5. For instance, inductivists typically held that nearly all truth could be generated mechanically from pure empirical data. Many positivists, recognizing that attempt as impossible, chose to stick rigidly to the empirical, accepting the consequent inability of science to deal with, e.g., hidden theoretical causes. Hypothetico-deductivists, recognizing that any interestingly rich science was inevitably theoretical, rehabilitated theory by readmitting nonempirical inputs (such as human creativity) into the context of discovery, but tried to quarantine those inputs from the rest of science by imposing rigorous empirical constrains upon the context of justification. Falsificationists, recognizing some nasty problems with empirical-based hypothetico-deductive concepts of justification, chose to maintain some sort of empirical purity by denying to the entire realm of the theoretical any notion of confirmation, accepting as (temporarily) scientifically upright only theories that withstood stringent attempts at empirical refutation. Then, of course, came the postempiricists, who tended in many cases to welcome back not only the theoretical but anything else the theoretical wished to bring along.

6. As one example of how such allegations sometimes go, some Marxists have argued that Newtonian physics was essentially capitalism as science.

7. For instance, essentially every known theory faces problematic data. Scientists thus have to choose which data to accept, reject, take seriously or ignore, have to choose whether or when to abandon affected theories, etc.

8. For example, Nancy Cartwright, *Laws*, 3.

9. Perhaps no one puts more stress on beauty than Dirac (although Einstein might have been close). In fact, Dirac says that "A theory with mathematical beauty is more likely to be correct than an ugly one that fits some experimental data" (Hovis and Kragh, "Dirac," p. 104). For suspicion, see Crick, *Mad Pursuit*, pp. 138–39.

10. Knorr-Cetina, *Manufacturing*, p. 4. Positions like this have been strongly advocated by Polanyi (e.g., *Tacit Dimension*).

11. For example, the necessity of excluding the immediately experienced phenomenology of "secondary" qualities.

12. Of course, instrumentation can also produce spurious observational artifacts, but that isn't the issue here.

13. Kuhn, of course, fits into this category, as do many others. In a related context, Rorty claims that "we can explain the observation mode—that is, the beliefs acquired without inference [such as "there goes a neutrino"]—by *both* the moralist and the scientist by reference simply to their respective psychologies and sensibilities" [his emphasis] (*Objectivity*, p. 56).

14. One person taking a position like this is Feyerabend, *Against Method*, pp. 73, 78.

15. Of interest here is Putnam, *Realism*, p. 77.

16. Helen Longino (*Science*) takes a very similar line, and Polanyi (*Science, Faith and Society*) at least gives aid and comfort to that type of position.

17. Edward Teller characterizes understanding itself as "something personal and peculiar" (*Pursuit of Simplicity*, p. 92).

18. In this connection also see Putnam, *Realism,* p. 74, and Plantinga, *Warrant and Proper Function,* ch. 6 and "Reason," p. 52. Of interest also is Hume, *Enquiry,* section I part II.

19. There are those who deny that we ever even reach that point in some disciplines. von Neumann once said that "in mathematics you don't understand things, you just get used to them." See also Feynman, *Character of Physical Law,* concerning quantum mechanics.

20. That capacity might be some judgment concerening coherence. Or it might be an unshakable sense that the foundational logic operations that *seem* absolutely right to us, really *are* absolutely right—that our irresistable intuition that

if A implies B, then A implies B.

simply *has* to be right, and that our inescapable and involuntary cognitive endorsement of it, our inability to even imagine how denials of that intuition could even be coherent, testify to its absolute legitimacy. Or it might be something else entirely.

Whatever starting point we pick will have a similar status—complete and unavoidable dependence ultimately upon some faculty or set of faculties, some intuition(s), that we human beings have. That will hold true of any epistemological project—scientific understanding included. In fact, it will hold true even for skeptical denials of the legitimacy of any epistemo-logical project. Skeptics who claims for example that humans can have no genuine objective external *knowledge* because humans are locked inside the circle of their own ideas, or because genuine rigorous proofs of empirical matters are in principle impossible, or for whatever reason, are taking as an utter given some function or intuition of their own cognition upon which that skeptical position rests (e.g., that we *are* locked inside the circle of our own ideas, or that some undeniable truths in our cognition undeniably and reliably imply that we are, and that being so locked inescapably entails the impossibility of external knowledge, and so forth). They are merely beginning with some different (perhaps eccentric) intuitional standpoint—not from no intuitional standpoint at all. And the frequent skeptic attempt to escape all that by claiming that we cannot know anything *including* even that we don't know anything, is based merely on a leap of hope that making the principle recursive will save the principle from ultimate self-referential incoherence. But it doesn't work that way.

21. There are other related and essential judgments that are also not formally reduceable—e.g., *relevance.*

22. This is close to Duhem, *Aim,* p. 7.

23. Some of the bodies are not buried very deeply. For instance, deductive-nomological explanations generate expectations, but do not necessarily either remove mystery or allow seeing.

24. According to some, the relation is stronger than just mediation. According to Weinberg, beauty is part of what it is to *be* an explanation. See Weinberg, *Dreams,* p. 149. See also pp. 90, 131, 165.

25. Putnam, *Realism,* e.g., p. 85; Polanyi, *Science, Faith and Society,* p. 9. See also MacIntyre, *Principles.*

26. See Franklin, *Fifth Force*, p. 25. The matter of data significance, classification, acceptance and rejection also involve human decisions of various sorts. See also *Fifth Force*, e.g., p. 128, and Chalmers, *Fabrication*, ch. 5.

27. This leads Knoor-Cetina to claim that data may be not only theory laden, but decision laden as well. *Manufacturing*, p. 5ff.

28. Many of these stories are well known. For others, see e.g., Forman, and Jacob, *Scientific Revolution*, ch. 3.

29. Quoted in Polanyi, *Science, Faith and Society*, p. 88.

30. Although many advocates of what Clark Glymour calls the "new fuzziness" in philosophy of science may take things far too far, they do ask some crucial questions. For instance, Rorty: "Why should we think that the tools which make possible the attainment of these particular human purposes [scientific prediction and control] are less 'merely' human than those which make possible the attainment of beauty or justice? What is the relation between facilitating prediction and control and being 'non-perspectival' or 'mind-independent'?" (*Objectivity*, p. 58).

31. *A Treatise of Human Nature*, introduction, p. xv.

32. See again Putnam, *Realism*, p. 40.

33. See Feyerabend, *Against Method*, p. 285.

Chapter 8. The Legitimacy Criterion

1. *NAS, On Being a Scientist*, 2d ed., pp. 6–8. In fact, the section on values is perhaps stronger in the second edition than it was in the first edition (1989).

2. Scott, "Pandas."

3. In fact, even separating the two components might be problematic. There are historical and contemporary philosophical arguments that what we call "natural laws" might themselves simply be patterns of consistent divine action and governance within the material realm. Should that be true, separation of natural from supernatural in a way that would preserve the legitimacy of prohibitions on the supernatural within science would be far from easy.

4. With reference to the current creation-evolution dispute, stipulating that science consider only natural theories, while simultaneously teaching students that the results of any such scientific investigation are true (and the mere fact of teaching them tacitly implies that to most reasonable students), is to implicitly presuppose philosophical naturalism. That is an implicit ramification even if the specific theories in question are in fact true. This is I think, the point that Philip Johnson has been attempting to make in recent years. See, e.g., *Darwin on Trial*, and *Reason in the Balance*.

5. There is a theologically based variant here too. If instances of relevant supernatural activity are rare, produced effects—especially if not identifiable or attributable—would likely get set aside from scientific consideration as either anomalous or not adequately confirmed. Scientists routinely have to make choices concerning the legitimacy and importance of data, and since virtually every theory is associated with some anomalous data scientists must occasionally simply rule specific data out of consideration.

6. Or at the very least, nature speaks in no nonempirical voice about which we can have any warranted confidence that we can get the message right.

7. I suspect that the reason most scientists dislike social constructivism, historicism, and the like is that such views undercut accountability.

8. See especially here Nancy Cartwright, *Laws.* Chalmers, *Fabrication,* p. 66 goes so far as to suggest that there may be no observable regularities in the world of ordinary experience. That is perhaps part of the motivation behind Per Bak's remark that "A general theory of complex systems must necessarily be *abstract.* . . . We must learn to free ourselves from seeing things as they are!" (*How Nature Works,* p. 10).

9. As Peter Galison says in *How Experiments End:*

Despite such efforts, the experimentalist can never, even in principle, exhaustively demonstrate that no disturbing effects are present. The world is far too complex to be parceled into a finite list of all possible backgrounds.

Consequently, "[E]xperimentalists must decide, implicitly or explicitly, that the conclusions stand *ceteris paribus*" (p. 3). How are such decisions arrived at? Experiments are brought to an end by "the building up of persuasive arguments . . . in the absence of the logician's certainty" (p. 277). Obviously, the decisions that the accumulated arguments are persuasive *enough* are mediated by a wide variety of nonempirical factors.

10. Polanyi goes part way to this position in *Science, Faith and Society,* p. 95:

We must remember that our reliance on reproduceability suffers from a fundamental weakness. It is always conceivable that reproduceability depends on the presence of an unknown and uncontrollable factor which comes and goes in periods of months or years and may vary from one place to another.

11. Chalmers mentions "inadequate precautions against possible sources of interference" (*Fabrication,* p. 65) as an important source of experimental error. The basic objection to the supernatural in science is that there might be no precautions even in principle even possibly adequate. That is presumably the thrust of Scott's earlier cited remark about the impossibility of keeping the supernatural in or out of test tubes.

12. Were there such sprites, the nonuniformity of empirical results might be a key clue to their existence, although it would still remain—and remain difficult—to sort out which were "natural" cases and which were sprite cases.

13. It may be that other sorts of justifications can be given (philosophical, for instance), but to the extent that such justifications are essential, that merely reinforces the ineliminability of the nonempirical in science.

Chapter 9. Cases for Impermissibility

1. It might also be thought that the hazards of approaching nature armed with rigid definitions was pretty clearly demonstrated by some of the outcomes of Medieval science. And

according to Fred Hoyle, "the range of concepts permitted in so-called serious discussion has become decidedly subjective according to what seems 'plausible,' where the criterion of plausibility is rather arbitrary" (*Intelligent Universe*, p. 144).

2. There have, of course, been scientists who believe that scientific methods can be applied to questions in the spiritual realm. See, e.g., Maynard Metcalf in Francis Mason (ed.) *The Great Design*, pp. 210–11.

3. Indeed, part of the supposed problem is that claims that certain empirical events resulted from (indirect) divine activity are typically seen as *scientifically irrefutable* rather than impossible.

4. p. 125.

5. We have little or no clue as to how the specific phenomenology of, the conscious experience of, or the conviction of greenness is generated by our faculties, but that really makes no difference to its legitimacy. If it is claimed that we actually do have some such clue, that does not change the situation. The perceptual judgment that something was green was clearly scientifically legitimate for, e.g., Aristotle, and it is obvious that *he* had no clue as to the mechanism. In any case, understanding the mechanism cannot be a requirement for legitimacy, since discovering any such mechanism would obviously involve observation, and, being prior to discovery, it would otherwise be illegitimate.

6. Larry Wright, *Teleological Explanations*, p. 45. The claim that purpose is not empirical can be found at least as far back as Bacon (*De Augmentis Scientiarum*, Book III, ch. 5). In the context of artifactuality, actual function can be a good indicator of purpose, although some might question that (e.g., possibly Woodfield, *Teleology*, p. 289).

7. Popper was, of course, the primary figure. For brief summary discussion see my *Science and Its Limits* chapter 2.

8. Lakatos speaks of a "protective belt" of ancillary theories surrounding core theories. One function of principles in this protective belt is to take spears aimed at the deeper, protected theories.

9. Along this line, John Stuart Mill, in his 1874 *Nature and Utility of Religion*, claimed that the design case was "an argument of a really scientific character, which does not shrink from scientific tests, but claims to be judged by the established canons of Induction" (pp. 177–78 in Burrill, *Cosmological Arguments*, pp. 177–84).

10. Scott, "Darwin Prosecuted," p. 43. It is odd that science should be negotiating deals with *itself.* One would think that an objective, empirical science would be trying to negotiate with *nature.*

11. The story is told by John Fentress in Moorehead and Kaplan, *Mathematical Challenges*, p. 71.

12. Moorehead and Kaplan, *Mathematical Challenges*, p. 98

13. Wykstra, *Interdependence* is useful here.

14. See my *Science and Its Limits*, p. 105.

15. There are some who apparently believe that something like uniformity is an empirically testable principle. For instance, E. O. Wilson, speaking of "a belief in the unity of the

sciences—a conviction, far deeper than a mere working proposition, that the world is orderly and can be explained by a small number of natural laws," says:

> The idea of the unity of science . . . has been tested in acid baths of experiment and logic and enjoyed repeated vindication. It has suffered no decisive defeats. At least not yet, even though at its center, by the very nature of the scientific method, it must be thought always vulnerable. (*Consilience,* p. 4–5).

Since this "unity" principle is clearly metaphysical, Wilson perhaps accepts the view that the empirical can have metaphysical implications. (In fact, *Consilience* can be read as an extended plea for "the unification metaphysics.") But one wonders exactly what the significance of the alleged "repeated vindication" through human conducted tests of "experiment and logic" might be, in light of Wilson's later remarks that the evidence suggests that "rational calculation is based on surges of competing emotions, whose interplay is resolved by an interaction of heredity and environmental factors" (p. 223).

16. It might be argued that even were science to establish the scientific impossibility of a natural origin of life, and even if the only other rational alternative were a supernatural origin, that the logically inescapable conclusion—that life in fact had a supernatural origin—was not legitimately scientific and thus could not be accepted *in science.* At that point, the artificiality of the relevant definitions becomes fairly evident.

17. Closer to the present, gapless approaches can be seen in several of the essays by scientists collected in Mason (ed.) *The Great Design.*

18. Popper says "Every 'good' scientific theory is a prohibition: it forbids certain things to happen. The more a theory forbids, the better it is" (*Conjectures and Refutations,* p. 36).

19. Critics of gap arguments often proceed as though merely identifying something as involving a gap constitutes refutation. And the emotion attending this issue is rather surprising. Paul Davies, for instance, in an interview on "Science Friday" on NPR expressed his sentiments as follows:

> My own personal opinion is that the notion of God as a cosmic magician meddling with matter, moving atoms around and rearranging them is offensive not only on scientific grounds but on theological grounds as well. I'm sympathetic to the idea that overall the universe has ingenious and felicitous laws that bring life and indeed intelligence into being, and sentient beings like ourselves who can reflect on the significance of it all. But I *loathe* the idea of a God who interrupts nature, who intervenes at certain stages and manipulates things. That's no explanation at all, of course. That doesn't explain anything. Because you could point to any natural phenomenon and just say, 'Well, God did it. God meddled and did that.' It would be a very poor sort of god who created a universe that wasn't right and then tinkered with it at later stages. [emphasis mine]

20. Notice that *if* science has managed to close many such gaps historically, then it follows immediately that gap theories have falsifiable empirical content.

21. If life could not arise naturally under any circumstances, alien activity would provide no ultimate explanation, since their existence as life forms would itself constitute a gap.

22. Mistakes sometimes run the other way as well. In his 1688 *Disquisition*, Boyle refers to "those Civiliz'd *Chineses*. . . that took the first Watch the Jesuit brought thither, for a Living Creature" (p. 230) [emphasis in original].

23. That the standard objection centers on transcendence is claimed by, e.g., Worthing, *God, Creation, and Contemporary Physics*, p. 146, and Ferguson, *Fire in the Equations*, p. 74.

24. As briefly noted earlier, failure to recognize this fact was one of the more serious failings of positivism.

25. See my "Nomo(theo)logical Necessity."

26. Statements of this intuition are fairly common. See, e.g., Edey and Johanson, *Blueprints: Solving the Mystery of Evolution*, p. 291. Of relevance also is Lewontin in the introduction to Godfrey *Scientists Confront Creationism*. Of course, not all objections to admission of miracles to science grow out of hostility either to miracles or to religion more generally. Steven Shapin, in *The Scientific Revolution*, quotes Boyle as follows:

> None is more willing [than myself] to acknowledge and venerate Divine Omnipotence, [but] our controversy is not what God can do, but what can be done by natural agents, not elevated above the sphere of nature. . . . And in the judgement of true philosophers, I suppose [the mechanical] hypothesis would need no other advantage . . . than that in ours things are explicated by the ordinary course of nature, whereas in the other recourse must be had to miracles. (p. 105)

27. Most will admit the *possibility* of a supernatural being existing, and it seems implausible that a supernatural being capable of doing the miraculous would be incapable of giving us the resources for rational recognition of at least some miracles.

28. See again my "Nomo(theo)logical Necessity." The fact that there is no empirically definable difference between the two indicates that the choice of natural law over supernaturally maintained uniformity is not empirically driven, but has other sources.

29. If one were permitted to postulate one-time explanatory miracles at will, the only support for which was the mere contingent fact that the phenomenon being thus explained had occurred or had no known alternative natural explanation, then science would indeed face serious problems. But *any* "explanation" of this sort is scientifically suspect—whether involving miracles or not. In any case, notice that those conditions are in violation of precisely the ceteris paribus condition. If however (a) it were known that there was no natural explantion (including human or alien), or (b) if the phenomenon exhibited properties, such as conceptual content, that were clear evidence of design and agent involvement, or (c) if we had other rational grounds for believing a miracle had occurred, then the situation would be very different, and postulating of supernatural activity—even miraculous activity—would pose no blanket threat to science at all.

So like anything else that violates ceteris paribus conditions, miracles of a sort that violate those conditions cannot be handled within science. But given that there is no reason whatever to think that that exhausts the category of miracle, no global prohibition follows.

30. It should be noted, of course, that design cases that do not involve gaps do not even in principle offer explanatory shortcuts, since even in those cases there will still be a full causal explanation of the production of the characteristics constituting the evidence of design.

31. Robert Boyle, *A Disquisition*, p. 237. There were other, even earlier warnings. Bacon, in *De Dignitate et Augmentis Scientiarum*, said:

> For the handling of final causes in physics has driven away and overthrown the diligent inquiry of physical causes, and made men to stay upon these specious and shadowy causes without actively pressing the inquiry of those which are really and truly physical, to the great arrest and prejudice of science. (p. 436 Jones, *Francis Bacon*)

This passage was later quoted by Whewell (*Astronomy*, p. 352), who himself remarked that "final causes . . . ought to be, not the mothers but the daughters of our natural sciences" (p. 356).

32. Newton's linking theorizing to theological concerns is well known—e.g., his acceptance of the nutshell theory, comets as supernaturally directed solar system adjustments, his view of matter's inactivity, etc. For Boyle's views see, e.g., *Disquisition*.

33. It is worth noting that parallel charges have *also* been leveled against Darwinian evolution—even by some biologists. See D'Arcy Thompson, *On Growth and Form*, p. 5.

34. Frequently cited attempts—e.g., White's *A History of the Warfare of Science and Theology in Christendom* and Draper's *History of the Conflict between Religion and Science* —are both over a century old, outdated, historically inaccurate, and substantially polemically driven. That is recognized by virtually every present professional historian of science.

35. See Ruth Barton, *The X Club*.

36. Desmond *The Politics of Evolution*. See, e.g., pp. 111–12, 379–80, 178ff., 204 note 36, 227. Indeed, according to Desmond, politics even set part of the agenda for pre-Darwinian theories of anatomy and zoology.

And ironically, Steve Fuller suggests that "most of Darwin's evidence for natural selection had been gathered by naturalists trying to second-guess the creator's design strategy" (*Are Science and Religion Compatible?* p 12).

And although referring to a Kantian, non-anthropomorphic concept of teleology, Timothy Lenoir claims that in early-nineteenth-century Germany, "a very coherent body of theory based on a teleological approach was worked out, and it did provide a constantly fertile source for the advance of biological science on a number of different research fronts." (*The Strategy of Life*, p. 2). It would be interesting to know what proportion of the scientific community actually rejected design arguments, on whatever the ground turned out to be—i.e., whether or not the bulk of rank-and-file scientists historically actually did buy the prohibition and when. Perhaps they did—but it would be nice to have hard, numeric data.

37. Nagel, *The Last Word*, p. 131.

38. Dawkins, *Blind Watchmaker*, p. 6.

39. Kuhn's classical statement is *The Structure of Scientific Revolutions*, and Laudan's case can be found in "A Confutation of Convergent Realism."

40. In fact, the present discussion of anthropic principles and fine-tuning arguments within the physics/cosmology community might constitute an example of present relevance.

Chapter 10. Legitimacy

1. Maxwell's aether machinery, and Ptolemaic equants and eccentrics are well-known historical examples. Instrumentalisms can also consist entirely of cookbook procedures—e.g., calculation methods of Babylonian astronomy.

2. The situation might parallel that of a person playing a chess computer—a situation in which, according to Dennett, one's best strategy is to play *as if* the computer is a rational person (*Brainstorms*, p. 5).

3. Instrumentalisms are often a bit unstable. Realism seems to be the human intuitive default position, and until talked out of it that's how we tend to take our theories. When some theory keeps getting things right, we tend to find ourselves coming to think of it as true, regardless of warnings to the contrary. Thus, instrumentalisms have a way of transforming into realisms, in which case things introduced as instrumental end up as substantive parts of theory. In any case, even were *design* realistically interpreted not permissible within science, that would not affect legitimacy of employing *design* instrumentally.

4. Recall Waddington's response to Fentriss, discussed in the previous chapter.

5. See Williams's biography of Faraday in *Dictionary of Scientific Biography*.

6. Torrance, *Christian Frame of Mind*, pp. 150–51. Related claims have been made for Herschel, Newton, and others, some of which were briefly discussed earlier.

7. Prohibitionists who base their case upon claims that historical track records support such prohibitions are accepting exactly this confirmation principle.

8. Kant was of the opinion that scientific investigation was only possible when nature was thought of as if its laws were designed.

9. Dawkins, *Blind Watchmaker*, p. 21.

10. Woolf, *Some Strangeness in the Proportion*, p. 476.

11. These two categories are not, of course, completely separable.

12. Quoted in Dugas, *History of Mechanics*, p. 269.

13. According to Brian Arthur, "Nonscientists tend to think that science works by deduction. . . . But actually science works mainly by metaphor" (Quoted in Waldrop, *Complexity*, p. 327). And Arthur is not even referring to upper-level matters, which are much looser than some that are lower down the hierarchy.

14. Design is not only intuitively relevant here, but recall that on Lewis's technical account of causal dependence, similar subjunctives *define* causal dependence.

15. We may not recognize relevant empirical matters *as* consequences of design, but

that is a different matter, and one not significantly different from the fact that other ordinary, recognizably empirical matters are also often unrecognized as consequences of the deeper matters they in fact grow out of. The fact that for most of human history the nuclear source of sunshine was unrecognized does not in the slightest alter the fact that both the existence of sunshine and many of its characteristics are purely empirical, observational matters.

16. The *strength* of the cases for design would vary widely given the exact details of the data involved. Strength would also vary widely between cases where we did and did not know of the existence and character of the supernatural. How appropriate it might be to introduce the concept of design in some specific case could depend in part upon what we antecedently, independently know concerning the supernatural. In this context, then, the quality of our religious knowledge could have a bearing upon what rational support was given to a specific design conclusion by specific empirical data.

The impact of data upon questions of existence is also very different from its impact upon explanatory proposals once given the relevant existence. Thus, even if it could be shown that the *existence* of a supernatural agent could not be established upon empirical grounds, that would still leave open the possibility that genuine knowledge of the supernatural on other grounds could affect the legitimacy of reference to supernatural *activity* in scientific explanatory contexts.

Support for design conclusions need not be constructed from bits of data in isolation. It is generally recognized that Darwin's case for evolution was a cumulative case, involving interrelated congruencies (Whewell's "concilience of inductions"). But natural theologians had already been deliberately employing that type of case a quarter century prior to the *Origin*. For instance, Peter Roget, in the fifth *Bridgewater Treatise*, says, "the argument, as it is justly remarked, is cumulative; that obtained from one source being strengthened by that derived from another; and all tending to the same conclusion" (*Animal and Vegetable Physiology*, vol. 1, p. 33).

17. Le Gros Clark comments that "however far back the direct interference or action of the Designer is removed, that interference or action is not got rid of, but only put back to an earlier stage, where the necessity for it exists as much as ever" (*Paley's Natural Theology*, pp. 5–6).

18. The pattern carriers need not exemplify specific patterns they carry, any more than a carrier of a gene for blue eyes must have blue eyes. But pattern carriers will themselves exhibit designed*ness*.

19. Recognition of that designedness might depend upon prior experience, but so does recognition of an electron in a cloud chamber.

20. If we knew that biological organisms were results of agency, given their complexity, integrated functionality, etc., we could hardly avoid the conclusion that their makeup was deliberately planned. It is an indication of the importance of the idea of *development* that even those who do not believe present living organisms to be designed would be hard pressed to avoid design conclusions were it established that exactly the present living organisms had come into being *instantaneously*. That fact is, I think, further indirect evidence for *PDR*.

21. Cases in the literature frequently turn theological at this point—arguing that a supernatural agent would have done a much better job, would not have allowed so much natural suffering, etc. In various contexts, the riskiness of such speculations have been pointed out by everyone from Bellermine to Boyle. See the earlier quotation from D'Alembert.

22. In any case, there is no a priori reason to think that design should operate at the level of mutation, or even at the level of evolutionary paths. It might, for instance, not go below the level of just the production of life or of personhood.

23. As another example, Michael Behe, author of *Darwin's Black Box*, accepts the idea that low levels of what he terms "irreducible complexity" can sometimes arise via unpatterned, purely chance means. For instance, on his definition a lever is irreducibly complex, but a lever could result from a tree branch falling over a downed tree trunk (his example).

24. The situation may be complicated by one implication of *PDR*. It may be recalled that although according to *PDR* the evidential status of bridge properties transfers from the artifactual to the natural case, the evidential force of specific properties may be lower in the natural than in the artifactual case. Wherever the line in (a) is fixed, properties which in artifact cases might have such force as to intuitively suggest that they would be above the cutoff, might, in the natural case, fall below it.

25. If established, gaps would support cases for *agent activity*, but as argued early on, the move to *design* requires further steps involving mind correlativity. Beyond that, the only relevant effect of gaps here would be to shorten the chain of pattern carriers involved between agent activity and phenomena in question.

26. It is interesting that even philosophical naturalists assume that the thoroughly artificial activity of scientific experimentation can reveal natural truths. I do not think there is anything problematic in that assumption, but it is perhaps indicative of the depth of mind correlativity that the grain of artificially structured investigation seems to remain congruent with nature no matter how deep investigation goes. That that is true was not always obvious, and in fact was the locus of some disputes historically. See, e.g., Hooykaas, *Religion and the Rise of Modern Science*, chapters 3 and 4.

27. Strong or participatory anthropic principles can be seen as conceding the necessity of appeal to agent involvement, and as constituting attempts to appropriate results of (quantum mechanical) agent-linked payoffs without accepting supernatural agency.

28. If such a procedure did show that compared theories were on a par, it would follow that all theories were on a par, since exactly parallel questions can be asked concerning the foundations of any theory.

29. They may even be more inclined to admit the unanswerability of questions foundational to their views than are various naturalists.

Chapter 11. Are There Any Payoffs?

1. There is nothing whatever to be gained by claiming that uniformity is merely a philosophical principle. Its presupposition in scientific contexts is legitimate, whatever one calls

it, and were design to function in a similar way and at a similar level, semantically classifying design as nonscientific would have no significant implications for either its legitimacy or for its potential scientific indispensibility. On a related point, Dyson says, "I propose that we allow the argument from design the same status as the Anthropic Principle, expelled from science but tolerated in meta-science" (*Infinite in All Directions,* p. 297). We might accept Dyson's stipulation here, but if design was a real part of the real explanation for some phenomena in nature, if empirical investigation turned up facts which supported—or even entailed—supernatural agent activity or design, then the rational insignificance of the stipulated boundary would become apparent.

2. More currently, Midgeley suggests that "it is doubtful, in fact, whether our imagination can work without [teleological thinking]" (*Science as Salvation,* p. 3).

3. As Chalmers remarks in his 1834 *Bridgewater Treatise,* "The proper office of experience . . . is not to tell or to reassure us of the constancy of Nature; but to tell, what the terms of her unalterable progression actually are" (*Power,* vol. 2, p. 139).

4. The history of geology offers a particularly nice example of a related stance with respect to a distinct but correlative principle—uniformitarianism. Lyell's uniformitarianism involved a gradualist and overall steady-state picture of geology. When it became clear that geologic history had not been uniform in that sense, the picture was replaced by a uniformity of *geologic processes* (substantive uniformitarianism), underlying the variable contingencies that had undercut the earlier proposed steady state. Upon empirical failure of that second sort of uniformitarianism, geology moved to the present mere uniformity of *law* (methodological uniformitarianism) which is perfectly comfortable with previously proscribed global catastrophes, variations in process, variation in process rates, and so forth.

That sort of transition parallels that previously discussed of supernatural design in response to Darwin. Adaptation of organisms to ecological niches was initially linked to direct designedness. Once Darwinian evolution was perceived as undercutting that position, some advocates moved to a deeper level of design—design in the laws underpinning that adaptation-producing evolution (although some had for other reasons already made that move prior to Darwin). Some have gone further, arguing that nomic structures alone are unequal to the adaptive task, and have taken an additional step of locating design in the primordial initial conditions of the cosmos. Some of the protective moves here associated with supernatural design exactly parallel those taken with respect to uniformitarianism.

5. See Irving Langmuir, "Pathological Science," pp. 36–48.

6. Some of those characteristics are also shared by what Watkins calls "haunted universe" principles.

7. Were it not for a confidence in uniformity of some sort one might well not go into the lab to begin with, but that is a different matter.

8. Such payoff questions get even more complicated when one moves from the issue of appropriate principles to that of appropriate tools, although similar implications arise. For instance, R. Levins, in Moorehead and Kaplan *Mathematical Challenges* says:

The model of a laboratory experiment, the critical experiment of physics, is not an adequate one for . . . macro type theories . . . any more than, for instance, the hypothesis that the differential operator is a useful description of nature is a falsifiable one. You get differential equations that work and also lousy ones which don't tell you anything, but which do not cause us to reject the calculus. (p. 69)

9. For an especially nice discussion of this issue by a physicist, see Wilkinson, *Quarks and Captain Ahab*. See also Polanyi, *Science, Faith and Society,* pp. 9ff., 95–96.

10. John Hedley Brooke, *Science and Religion*. See especially chapters 1 and 6.

11. Goodfield has described "the very notion of a permanently insolvable problem [as] *anathema*" [my emphasis] (Goodfield, "Revolutions" p. 111). In short, the operative presumption is that there is nothing that is ultimately beyond comprehension.

12. Machine metaphors are well known, but nature as art has been suggested by sources as diverse as Sir Thomas Brown (17th c.) and Dorothy Sayers.

13. Adaptation was a primary theme of pre-Darwinian design arguments, and is a running topic in the *Bridgewater Treatises*. It was frequently cited as evidence of design. But to take it as evidence of design requires construing it as a consequence of designedness.

14. Obviously, any concept that is instrumentally useful must have empirical content in some sense, as noted earlier.

15. Some of the issues here with respect to perception, etc., are familiar, and Darwin himself commented on others—see, e.g., his July 3, 1881, letter to William Graham, in Francis Darwin, ed., *The Life and Letters of Charles Darwin,* I:285. Also of relevance is Thomas Nagel's position that evolution, if taken seriously, provides no warrant for our abstract theorizing capacities, and indeed renders them "highly suspect" (*The View from Nowhere*, pp. 78–79). On deeper matters, Antony Flew remarks, "The first thing to get clear is that we have no natural right to explanation; much less a similar right to explanation of the sort and in the terms which we may wish" (*God and Philosophy,* p. 99).

16. Davies, *Are We Alone?* p. 138.

17. In addition to Brooke, Reijer Hooykaas, M. B. Foster, Eugene Klaaren, and Colin Russell are worth consulting.

18. Quoted in Wilkinson, *Quarks and Captain Ahab*, p. 8.

19. At the core of the theorem was the fact that any theory can be associated with a set of empirical data consisting of all and only empirical contents of the theory. What is lost, of course, is any sense of explanation. Exactly the same loss is experienced in the present case. It will be held by some that neither philosophically essential underpinnings of science nor the rational justifications for those underpinnings is part of science proper. That claim, of course, turns upon definitions of *science,* and I see no reason to take the presupposed definition as normative. But even were we to accept the assumed definition, there is certainly something to be said for having some clue as to why science's foundations might be rationally defensible.

20. Davies, *Are We Alone?* p. 121. Boyle, oddly enough, once gave a related argument concerning atoms:

> For he, that shall attentively consider, what the atomists themselves may be compelled to allow, concerning the eternity of matter, the origin of local motion . . . the infinity or boundlessness of space, the divisibleness or non-divisibility of each corporeal substance into infinite material parts, may clearly perceive, that the atomist, by denying that there is a God, cannot free his understanding from such puzzling difficulties, as he pretends to be the reason of his denial; for instead of one God, he must confess an infinite number of atoms to be eternal, self-existent, immortal, self-moving. (from *The Excellency of Theology, Compared with Natural Philosophy*, pp. 140–41)

21. Harrison, *Masks of the Universe*, p. 252. The designer that Harrison may have in mind is not necessarily supernatural. Harrison suggests that it may be possible for technologically advanced aliens to trigger the formation of quantum bubbles that would expand into universes.

22. As above, e.g., the intelligibility of nature, the appropriateness of our conceptual resources for understanding nature, the relevance of our perceptual faculties for investigating nature, the uniformity of nature, the fundamental importance of the empirical to science, important conceptual and heuristic resources, etc.

23. The suspicion is nicely captured by Brooke's assertion that "the questions that flowed from viewing nature as a product of design simply became too blunt to yield precise information at the rock face of research" (*Science and Religion*, p. 219).

24. At one point it was thought that von Neumann had demonstrated the irreducibly random character of quantum results, thereby ruling out deeper (hidden) variables. It is now generally held that his argument did not demonstrate that after all. Of course, quantum matters may still be irreducibly random. But even so, that does not *preclude* supernatural design—see my "Design, Chance, and Theistic Evolution."

25. I take this to be Descartes's basic conception—see, e.g., his *Principles of Philosophy*, part IV, para. 187, in Cottingham, et al., *The Philosophical Writings of Descartes*, vol. 1, p. 279. Defenses of views of this type were sometimes in part theological—see Brooke, *Science and Religion*, chapter 4.

26. Weingberg is of interest in this context (see, e.g., *Dreams*, chapter 3, "Two cheers for Reductionism"). Weinberg refers to reductionism "as a statement of the order of nature, which I think is simply true" (p. 54). The status reductionism has for Weinberg may be suggested by the following in a footnote (p. 54):

> For instance, even though physicists cannot actually explain the properties of very complicated molecules like DNA in terms of the quantum mechanics of electrons, nuclei, and electric forces, and even though chemistry survives to deal with such problems with its own language and concepts, still there are no autonomous principles

of chemistry that are simply independent truths, not resting on deeper principles of physics.

That might sound as though Weinberg is speaking of theoretical and not ontological reduction, but that is apparently not the case. He prefaces the above by saying, "Each of these three categories [of reductionism earlier suggested by Ernst Mayr] is defined by what scientists actually do or have done or could do; I am talking about nature itself."

27. Prigogine and Stengers, *Order out of Chaos*, p. 7.

28. Various tangled motivations operate in this neighborhood. For instance, a recent issue of *Science* contained the following: "Many scientists opposed [Lemaitre's 'primordial atom' theory] in part because it seemed overly reminiscent of the Genesis story of a discrete moment of creation" (Easterbrook, "God and Science: A Warming Trend?")

29. As Wilkinson notes, "We have . . . no *a priori* right whatever to suppose that our native concepts will be of the slightest use for describing the behavior of the natural world on . . . vastly different scales" (*Quarks and Captain Ahab*, p. 15–16).

30. There may have been such incidents historically, although some cases are not so clear as the standard mythology suggests. In fact, it is generally recognized that in some instances such theological doctrines as divine voluntarism—that God freely chose what and how to create—underlay insistence that investigation of nature be thoroughly empirical. See, e.g., Brooke, *Science and Religion*, p. 26.

31. Recall, for example, the earlier meteor-crater diagram of a mathematical theorem, with each individual meteor having an unbroken natural causal history tracking back to the Big Bang.

32. The proper mode of investigating something depends in part on characteristics of the object investigated. We typically cannot specify in advance what various aspects of nature are like. We thus often cannot specify or decree in advance what the proper mode of investigation will be either. In fact, the history of science is in part a history of discovering how to investigate different aspects of nature.

33. We can also sometimes determine purpose even when the phenomenon is nonfunctional, and we can also sometimes determine that something has a purpose even when unable to determine what that purpose might be.

34. Doctrinaire philosophical naturalists might be an exception, but their concerns would have roots beyond science.

BIBLIOGRAPHY

Alston, William. 1967. "Teleological Argument for the Existence of God." In Paul Edwards, ed. *The Encyclopedia of Philosophy.* New York: Macmillan, pp. 84–88.

———. 1989. "God's Action in the World." In William Alston, *Divine Nature and Human Language.* Ithaca: Cornell University Press, pp. 197–222.

Asimov, Isaac. 1979. *Extraterrestrial Civilizations.* New York: Fawcett.

Babbage. Charles. 1838. *The Ninth Bridgewater Treatise: A Fragment.* London: J. Murray.

Bacon, Francis. 1899. *Advancement of Learning and Novum Organum.* New York: Colonial Press.

———. 1901. *Novum Organum.* Ed. Joseph Devey. New York: P. F. Collier.

Bak, Per. 1996. *How Nature Works: The Science of Self-Organized Criticality.* New York: Springer-Verlag.

Barrett, Paul. 1974, 1980. *Metaphysics, Materialism and the Evolution of Mind: Early Writings* of Charles Darwin. Chicago: University of Chicago Press.

Barrow, John D. 1995. *The Artful Universe.* Oxford: Clarendon Press.

Barton, Ruth. 1976. *The X Club: Science, Religion, and Social Change in Victorian England.* Ann Arbor: University Microfilms.

Beck, Lewis White. "Extraterrestrial Intelligent Life." In Regis *Extraterrestrials,* pp. 3–18.

Behe, Michael J. 1996. *Darwin's Black Box.* New York: Free Press.

Bell, Charles. 1837. *The Hand: Its Mechanism and Vital Endowments as Evincing Design.* London: William Pickering.

Bonner, John Tyler. 1988. *The Evolution of Complexity by Means of Natural Selection.* Princeton: Princeton University Press.

Boyle, Robert. 1688. *A Disquisition about the Final Causes of Natural Things: Wherein It Is Inquir'd Whether, And (if at all) with What Cautions, a Naturalist Should Admit Them?* London: H. C. for John Taylor.

———. 1965. *A Free Inquiry into the Vulgarly Receiv'd Notions of Nature.* Reprinted in Hall, *Robert Boyle.*

———. 1674. *The Excellency of Theology, Compared with Natural Philosophy.* London: H. Herringman.

Brams, Steven. 1983. *Superior Beings: If They Exist How Would We Know?* New York: Springer-Verlag.

Broad, C. D. 1947. *The Mind and It's Place in Nature.* London: Kegan Paul, Trench, Trubner.

Brooke, John Hedley. 1991. *Science and Religion.* Cambridge: Cambridge University Press.

Buell, Jon, and Virginia Hearn. 1994. *Darwinism: Science or Philosophy?* Richardson, Tex.: Foundation for Thought and Ethics.

Burrill, Donald, ed. 1967. *The Cosmological Arguments.* Garden City: Doubleday.

Butler, Samuel. 1911. *Evolution, Old and New; or, the Theories of Buffon, Dr. Erasmus Darwin, and Lamark, as Compared with that of Charles C. Darwin,* 3d. ed. London: A. C. Field.

Cairnes-Smith, A.G. 1985, 1993. *Seven Clues to the Origin of Life.* Cambridge: Cambridge University Press.

Cartwright, Nancy. 1983. *How the Laws of Physics Lie.* Oxford: Clarendon Press.

Chalmers, Alan. 1990. *Science and Its Fabrication.* Minneapolis: University of Minnesota.

Chalmers, Thomas. 1834. *On the Power, Wisdom and Goodness of God as Manifested in the Adaptation of External Nature to the Moral and Intellectual Constitution of Man.* London: William Pickering.

Clark, Le Gros. nd. *Paley's Natural Theology.* London: Society for Promoting Christian Knowledge.

Cottingham, John, Robert Stoothoff, and Dugald Murdoch, eds. 1985. *The Philosophical Writings of Descartes,* vol. 1. Cambridge: Cambridge University Press.

Crick, Francis. 1988. *What Mad Pursuit.* New York: Basic.

Darwin, Charles. 1974. *Metaphysics, Materialism, and the Evolution of Mind: Early Writings of Charles Darwin.* Transcribed and annotated by Paul H. Barrett. Chicago: University of Chicago Press.

———. 1987. *Charles Darwin's Notebooks18: 36–44.* Ithaca: Cornell University Press.

Darwin, Francis. 1897. *The Life and Letters of Charles Darwin.* New York: D. Appleton.

Davies, Paul. 1995. *Are We Alone?* New York: Basic.

Dawkins, Richard. 1987. *The Blind Watchmaker.* New York: Norton.

Dembski, William A. 1998. *Mere Creation: Science, Faith, and Intelligent Design.* Downers Grove: InterVarsity.

———. 1998. *The Design Inference: Eliminating Chance through Small Probabilities.* New York: Cambridge.

———. 1998. "On the Very Possibility of Intelligent Design." In Moreland, *Creation Hypothesis,* pp. 113–38.

Dennett, Daniel. 1978. *Brainstorms: Philosophical Essays on Mind and Psychology.* Montgomery, Ver.: Bradford.

Descartes, Rene. 1983. *Principles of Philosophy.* Trans. Valentine R. Miller and Reese P. Miller. Boston: Reidel.

Desmond, Adrian J. 1989. *The Politics of Evolution: Morphology, Medicine, and Reform in Radical London.* Chicago: University of Chicago Press.

Dewey, Chester. 1839. "On the Polished Limestone of Rochester." *The American Journal of Science and Arts* 37 (October): 240–42.

Draper, John W. 1897. *History of the Conflict between Religion and Science.* New York: D. Appleton.

Dugas, Rene. 1955. *A History of Mechanics.* Trans. J. R. Maddox. London: Routledge and Kegan Paul.

Duhem, Pierre. 1954. *The Aim and Structure of Physical Theory.* Princeton: Princeton University Press.

Dyson, Freeman. 1988. *Infinite in All Directions.* London and New York: Penguin.

Easterbrook, Gregg. 1997. "God and Science: A Warming Trend?" *Science* 227 (15 August): 890–93.

Edey, Maitland A., and Donald C. Johanson. 1989. *Blueprints: Solving the Mystery of Evolution.* Boston: Little, Brown.

Eldredge, Niles. 1981. *The Monkey Business.* New York: Washington Square.

Esbjornson, Robert, ed. 1984. *Manipulation of Life.* San Francisco: Harper and Row.

Fergusen, Kitty. 1994. *The Fire in the Equations.* Grand Rapids: Eerdmans.

Feyerabend, Paul. 1988. *Against Method.* London: Verso.

Feynman, Richard. 1975. *The Character of Physical Law.* Cambridge: MIT Press.

Flew, Anthony. 1966. *God and Philosophy.* New York: Dell.

Forman, Paul. 1971. "Weimar Culture, Causality and Quantum Theory, 1918–1927."*Historical Studies in the Physical Sciences* 3:1–115.

Franklin, Allan. 1983. *The Rise and Fall of the Fifth Force.* New York: American Institute Physics.

Fuller, Steve. 1998. *Are Science and Religion Compatible?* Science and the Public Series.United Kingdom: Open University.

Futuyma, Douglas. 1983. *Science on Trial.* New York: Pantheon.

Galison, Peter. 1987. *How Experiments End.* Chicago: Chicago.

Ghyka, Matila. 1977 (1946). *The Geometry of Art and Life.* New York: Dover.

Goldsmith, Donald. 1985. *The Evolving Universe,* 2d ed. Menlo Park: Benjamin/Cummings.

Goodfield, June. 1981. *An Imagined World.* New York: Harper and Row.

———. 1984. "Without Love, Oath and Revolutions." In Esbojornson, *Manipulation of Life,* pp. 93–117.

Gooding, David. 1980. "Metaphysics versus Measurement: The Conversion and Conservation of Force in Faraday's Physics." *Annals of Science* 37:1–29.

Greenwald, Jeff. 1999. "Who's Out There?" *Discover* 20:4 (April): 64–70.

Hall, Marie Boas. 1965. *Robert Boyle on Natural Philosophy.* Bloomington: Indiana.

Hamming, R. W. 1980. "The Unreasonable Effectiveness of Mathematics." *The American Mathematical Monthly* 87:2 (February).

Haraway, Donna. 1989. *Primate Visions.* New York: Routledge.

Harrison, Edward R. 1985. *Masks of the Universe.* New York: Macmillan.

Hildebrandt, Stefan, and Anthony Tomba. 1996. *The Parsimonious Universe: Shape and Form in the Natural World.* New York: Springer-Verlag.

Hooker, C. A. 1987. *A Realistic Theory of Science.* Albany: State University of New York Press.

Hooykaas, Reijer. 1993 (1972). *Religion and the Rise of Modern Science.* Vancouver, B.C.: Regent College.

Horgan, John. 1995. "From Complexity to Perplexity." *Scientific American* 272, 6: 104–109.

Hovis, R. Corby, and Helge Kragh. 1993. "P. A. M. Dirac and the Beauty of Physics." *Scientific American* 268, 5: 104–109.

Hoyle, Fred. 1983. *The Intelligent Universe.* New York: Holt, Rinehart, and Winston.

Hoyle, Fred, and Chandra Wickramasinghe. 1981. *Evolution from Space.* New York: Simon and Schuster.

Hume, David. 1975. *Enquiries Concerning Human Understanding and Concerning the Principles of Morals.* P. H. Nidditch, ed. New York: Oxford University Press.

———. 1978. *Treatise of Human Nature,* 2d ed. Ed. L. A. Selby-Bigge. Oxford:Oxford University Press.

Hurlbutt, Robert H. 1985. *Hume, Newton and the Design Argument,* revised edition. Lincoln: University of Nebraska Press.

Jacob, Margaret. 1988. *The Cultural Meaning of the Scientific Revolution.* New York: A. A. Knopf.

Jeans, Sir James. 1932. *The Mysterious Universe.* New York: Macmillan.

Johnson, Philip. 1993. *Darwin on Trial.* Downers Grove: InterVarsity.

———. 1995. *Reason in the Balance.* Downers Grove: InterVarsity.

Jones, Richard Foster, ed. 1937. *Francis Bacon: Essays, Advancement of Learning, New Atlantis, and Other Pieces.* New York: Odyssey.

Kant, Immanuel. 1965. *Critique of Pure Reason.* Trans. Norman Kemp Smith. New York: St. Martins.

Kauffman, Stuart A. 1993. *The Origins of Order: Self-Organization and Selection in Evolution.* New York: Oxford.

Keller, Evelyn Fox. 1985. *Reflections on Gender and Science.* New Haven: Yale University Press.

Kingsley, Charles. 1863, 1890. *The Water Babies.* London: Macmillan.

Kitcher, Philip. 1982. *Abusing Science.* Cambridge: MIT Press.

Klaaren, Eugene. 1977. *Religious Origins of Modern Science.* Grand Rapids: Eerdmans.

Knorr-Cetina, Karin. 1981. *The Manufacture of Knowledge.* New York: Pergamon Press.

Kosso, Peter. 1998. *Appearance and Reality.* Oxford: Oxford University Press.

Kuhn, Thomas. 1970. *The Structure of Scientific Revolutions,* 2d ed. Chicago: University of Chicago Press.

Lakatos, Imre. 1970, 1979. "Falsification and the Methodology of Scientific ResearchPrograms." *Criticism and the Growth of Knowledge.* Ed. Imre Lakatos and Alan Musgrave. Aberdeen: Cambridge University Press, 91–196.

Langmuir, Irving. 1989. "Pathological Science." Transcribed by Robert Hall in *Physics Today* 42, 10: 36–48.

Laszlo, Ervin. 1972. *The Systems View of the World.* Oxford: Blackwell.

Laudan, Larry. 1978. *Progress and Its Problems.* Berkeley: University of California Press.

———. 1981. "A Confutation of Convergent Realism." *Philosophy of Science* 48: 19–49.

Lenoir, Timothy. 1982. *The Strategy of Life: Teleology, and Mechanics of the Nineteenth Century German Biology.* Dordrecht: Reidel.

Lewis. C. S. 1967. *Christian Reflections.* Grand Rapids: Eerdmans.

Lewis, David. 1973. "Causation." *Journal of Philosophy* 70:556–67.

Lewontin, Richard C. 1993. Introduction to *Scientists Confront Creationism.* Ed. Laurie Godfrey. New York: W. W. Norton, p. xxiii.

Longino, Helen. 1990. *Science and Social Knowledge.* Princeton: Princeton University Press.

MacIntyre, Alasdair. 1990. *First Principles, Final Ends, and Contemporary Philosophical Issues.* Milwaukee: Marquette University Press.

Margenau, Henry, and Roy Varghese, eds. 1992. *Cosmos, Bios, Theos.* LaSalle: Open Court.

Mason, Francis, ed. 1934, 1972. *The Great Design.* Freeport: Books for Libraries.

Midgeley, Mary. 1992. *Science as Salvation.* London: Routledge.

Mill, John Stuart. 1874. *Nature, the Utility of Religion, and Theism.* London: Longmans, Green, Reader, and Dyer.

Moorehead, Paul, and Martin Kaplan. 1967. *Mathematical Challenges to the Neo-Darwinian Interpretation of Evolution.* Philadelphia: Wistar.

Moreland, J. P. 1994. *The Creation Hypothesis.* Downers Grove: InterVarsity.

Nagel, Thomas. 1986. *The View from Nowhere.* Oxford: Oxford University Press.

———. 1996. *The Last Word.* Oxford: Oxford University Press.

NASA. *SETI.* NAS 1.83 114/990.

National Academy of Sciences. 1995. *On Being a Scientist,* 2d ed. Washington, D.C.: National Academy Press.

Newton, Isaac. 1704. *Opticks.* London.

Nozick, Robert. 1981. *Philosophical Explanations.* Cambridge: Harvard University Press.

Pagels, Heinz. 1982. *The Cosmic Code.* New York: Bantam.

Paley, William. 1963. *Natural Theology.* Ed. Frederick Ferre. Indianapolis: Bobbs-Merrill.

Parker, Gary. 1994. *Creation: Facts of Life.* Colorado Springs: Master.

Peat, F. David. 1988. *Superstrings and the Search for the Theory of Everything.* Chicago: Contemporary.

Plantinga, Alvin. 1974. *The Nature of Necessity.* Oxford: Clarendon Press.

———. 1983. "Reason and Belief in God." In Plantinga and Wolterstorff, eds., *Faith and Rationality,* pp. 16–93.

———. 1993. *Warrant and Proper Function.* Oxford: Oxford University Press.

Plantinga, Alvin, and Nicholas Wolterstorff, eds. *Faith and Rationality.* Notre Dame: University of Notre Dame Press.

Polanyi, Michael. 1946. *Science, Faith and Society.* Chicago: University of Chicago Press.

———. 1967. *The Tacit Dimension.* London: Routledge and Kegan Paul.

Polkinghorne, John C. 1984. *The Quantam World.* London: Longman.

Popper, Karl R. 1963. *Conjectures and Refutations: The Growth of Scientific Knowledge.* London: Routledge and Kegan Paul.

Prigogine, Ilya, and Isabelle Stengers. 1984. *Order out of Chaos.* London: Heinemann.

Putnam, Hilary. 1987. *The Many Faces of Realism.* LaSalle: Open Court.

Quine, W. V. O. 1953, 1961. *From a Logical Point of View.* New York: Harper and Row.

Ratzsch, Del. 1986. *Philosophy of Science.* Downers Grove: InterVarsity.

———. 1987. "Nomo(theo)logical Necessity." *Faith and Philosophy* 4, 4: 383–402.

———. 1996. *Battle of Beginnings.* Downers Grove: InterVarsity.

———. 1998. "Design, Chance, and Theistic Evolution." In *Mere Creation.* ed. William Dembski, pp. 289–312.

———. 2000. *Science and Its Limits.* Downers Grove: InterVarsity.

Regis, Edward Jr., ed. 1985 *Extraterrestrials: Science and Alien Intelligence.* Cambridge: Cambridge University Press.

ReMine, Walter. 1993. *The Biotic Message.* Saint Paul: Saint Paul Science.

Roget, Peter. 1834. *Animal and Vegetable Physiology Considered with Reference to Natural Theology,* vol. 1. London: William Pickering.

Rorty, Richard. 1991. *Objectivity, Relativism, and Truth.* Cambridge: Cambridge University Press.

Ruse, Michael. 1982. *Darwinism Defended.* Reading, Mass.: Addison-Wesley.

Russell, Colin. 1985. *Cross-Currents: Interactions between Science and Faith.* Grand Rapids, Mich.: Eerdmans.

Sagan, Carl. 1974. *Broca's Brain.* New York: Random House.

———. ed. 1973. *Communication with Extraterrestrial Intelligence.* Cambridge: MIT Press.

Scott, Eugenie. 1990. "Of Pandas and People." *NCSE Reports* 10, 1: 16–18.

———. 1993. "Darwin Prosecuted." *Creation/Evolution* 13, 2 (Winter).

Shapin, Steven. 1996. *The Scientific Revolution.* Chicago: University of Chicago Press.

Simon, Herbert A. 1981. *The Sciences of the Artificial,* 2d ed. Cambridge: MIT Press.

Smith, John Maynard. 1995. "Genes, Memes, and Minds." *NY Review* 62, 18 (16 November).

Sorrell, Tom. 1991, 1994. *Scientism: Philosophy and the Infatuation with Science.* London: Routledge.

Spedding, James, Robert Ellis, and Douglas Heath, eds. 1878. *Works of Francis Bacon,* vol. 1. New York: Hurd and Houghton.

Stenger, Victor J. 1988. *Not by Design.* Buffalo: Prometheus.

Stevens, Peter S. 1974. *Patterns in Nature.* Boston: Little, Brown.

Teller, Edward. 1981. *The Pursuit of Simplicity.* Malibu: Pepperdine University Press.

Templeton, John, ed. 1994. *Evidence and Purpose.* New York: Continuum.

Thomson, D'Arcy. 1961. *On Growth and Form.* John Tyler Bonner, ed. Cambridge: Cambridge University Press.

Torrance, Thomas F. 1985. *The Christian Frame of Mind.* Edinburgh: Handsel Press.

Trigger, Bruce. 1989. *A History of Archeological Thought.* Cambridge: Cambridge University Press.

Tyson, Neil de Grasse. 1997. "Romancing the Equation." *Natural History* 106, 10 (November) 80–82.

van Inwagen, Peter. 1994. "Doubts about Darwinism." In Buell and Hearn, *Darwinism: Science or Philosophy?* pp. 177–91.

Waldrop, Mitchell. 1992. *Complexity.* New York: Simon and Schuster.

Watkins, J. W. N. 1958. "Confirmable and Influential Metaphysics." *Mind* 344–65.

Weinberg, Steven. 1992. *Dreams of a Final Theory.* New York: Pantheon.

Weiner, Jonathan. 1994. *The Beak of the Finch: A Story of Evolution in Our Own Time.* New York: Knopf.

Weyl, Hermann. 1952. *Symmetry.* Princeton: Princeton University Press.

Whewell, William. 1834. *Astronomy and General Physics Considered with Reference to Natural Theology.* London: William Pickering.

White, Andrew D. 1896. *A History of the Warfare of Science and Theology in Christendom.* New York: D. Appleton.

Wigner, Eugene. 1960. "The Unreasonable Effectiveness of Mathematics in the Natural Sciences." *Communications of Pure and Applied Mathematics* 13: 1–14.

Wilcox, David. 1994. "How Blind a Watchmaker?" *Evidence of Purpose.* Ed. John Templeton.New York: Continuum, pp. 168–81.

Wilczek, Frank, and Betsy Devine. 1988. *Longing for the Harmonies: Themes and Variations from Modern Physics.* New York: Vintage.

Wilkinson, Sir Denys Haigh. 1997. *The Quarks and Captain Ahab; or, the Universe as Artifact.* Stanford: Stanford University Press.

Williams, L. Pearce. 1970–1980. "Faraday." In *Dictionary of Scientific Biography.* New York: Scribner, pp. 527–40.

Wilson, E. O. 1998, *Consilience.* New York: Vintage.

Woodfield, Andrew. 1976. *Teleology.* Cambridge: Cambridge University Press.

Woolf, Harry, ed. 1980. *Some Strangeness in the Proportion: A Centennial Symposium to Celebrate the Achievements of Albert Einstein.* Reading: Addison-Wesley.

Worthing, Mark William. 1996. *God, Creation, and Contemporary Physics.* Minneapolis: Fortress Press.

Wright, Larry. 1976. *Teleological Explanations.* Berkeley: California.

Wykstra, Stephen. 1978. *The Interdependence of History of Philosophy of Science: Toward a Metatheory of Scientific Rationality.* Ph.D. dissertation, University of Pittsburgh.

Zee, A. 1986. *A Fearful Symmetry.* New York: Macmillan.

INDEX

Printed in the United States
54042LVS00004B/13-30